Sports Journalism

Sports Journalism

AN INTRODUCTION TO REPORTING AND WRITING

Kathryn T. Stofer
James R. Schaffer
Brian A. Rosenthal

ROWMAN & LITTLEFIELD PUBLISHERS, INC.
Lanham • Boulder • New York • Toronto • Plymouth, UK

Published by Rowman & Littlefield Publishers, Inc.
A wholly owned subsidiary of The Rowman & Littlefield Publishing Group, Inc.
4501 Forbes Boulevard, Suite 200, Lanham, Maryland 20706
www.rowmanlittlefield.com

Estover Road, Plymouth PL6 7PY, United Kingdom

British Library Cataloguing in Publication Information Available

Library of Congress Cataloging-in-Publication Data

Stofer, Kathryn T.
   Sports journalism: an introduction to reporting and writing / Kathryn T.
Stofer, James R. Schaffer, and Brian A. Rosenthal.
      p. cm.
   Includes bibliographical references and index.
   ISBN 978-0-7425-6173-1 (cloth : alk. paper) —
   ISBN 978-0-7425-6174-8 (pbk. : alk. paper) —
   ISBN 978-1-4422-0083-8 (electronic)
   1. Sports journalism. I. Schaffer, James R., 1949– II. Rosenthal, Brian A.
III. Title.
PN4784.S6S88 2010
070.4'49796—dc22   2009020212

Printed in the United States of America

DEDICATIONS

To my sports fans and journalists of the future: Cassidy, Hayden, Katie and Trista. —KS

To Suzanne, Sarah, and Stephen, the athletes in my life; and Mary Lynn, their coach. —JS

To the memory of my grandparents, Erwin Rosenthal, Donald and Martha Sherman, and my aunt, Lois Eona. —BR

Contents

Acknowledgments   ix
Preface   xi

Chapter 1   **Living the Life**   **1**
             Routine? What Routine?   3
             Take Down or Reversal?   6

Chapter 2   **Covering the Game**   **7**
             A New Kind of Sports Reporter   8
             Advance Stories   11
             Game Summary   16
             Post-Game Analysis   23

Chapter 3   **Finding the Sources**   **29**
             Beat Reporting   30
             Developing Sources   31
             Building Relationships with Sources   49

Chapter 4   **Asking the Questions**   **53**
             Interviewing Skills   54
             Asking the Right Questions   58
             Interview Settings   62
             Using Quotations   65
             Style, Placing Attribution   69

Chapter 5	**Working with the Media**	**81**
	Sports Information Directors	82
	Credential Requests	88
	News Releases	88
Chapter 6	**Choosing the Words**	**105**
	Journalistic Writing Style	106
	Proofreading	128
Chapter 7	**Writing the Story**	**133**
	Sports News Values	134
	Feature Stories	141
	Leads	145
	Nut Graf	154
	Story Structure	157
	Columns	163
Chapter 8	**Following the Style**	**171**
	AP Style	171
	Headlines	174
	Captions	186
	Libel and Other Legalities	189
Chapter 9	**Making the Numbers Count**	**201**
	Understanding the Game	202
	Interpreting the Game	210
	Feeding the Fans	212
	Dollars and Cents	212
	Arbitration Suits	213
	For the Record	213
Chapter 10	**Highlighting the Greats**	**217**
	Participatory Journalism	218
	Giants of the Past	219
	A More Muscular Prose	222
	Modern Masters	224
Appendix A	AP Sports Guidelines and Style	237
Appendix B	Society of Professional Journalists' Code of Ethics	261
Appendix C	Glossary of News and Sports Terms	265
Index		277
About the Authors		287

Acknowledgments

SPECIAL THANKS to our families, friends and colleagues for their faith, patience, encouragement and belief, and many times their willingness to handle extra responsibilities while we wrote this book. It truly takes a team to win the game!

■ ■ ■

Kathryn T. Stofer appreciates and thanks those who helped make this book a reality, especially Brian for accepting the challenge and Jim for keeping all of us sane and focused through the process. To the consultants and copy editors who helped strengthen the text in so many ways: John Wood, Jeanne Tool, Tammie Wall, Sharon Brooks, John Brooks, Roger Doerr, Karen Doerr, Kendra Bargen, and, for his special graphic contributions, Isaiah May.

■ ■ ■

James R. Schaffer would like to thank Joe Gisondi for reading the manuscript and helping us better understand blogging; Ryly Jane Hambleton for her many insights into reporting and tireless dedication to her craft; and Karl Skinner for his encyclopedic knowledge of small college sports.

■ ■ ■

Brian A. Rosenthal extends his grateful thanks to Kathy Stofer for allowing her former pupil the opportunity to share what he's learned from the professor, and for her friendship and support; to James Schaffer, whose periodic visits over coffee kept a new author from turning gray before 40; to his former and current Lincoln Journal Star sports editors, John Mabry and Todd Henrichs, for their patience and understanding; to close friends and colleagues Steven M. Sipple and Mike Babcock for their knowledge, wisdom and humor, especially during the stressful and trying times of a sports writer's career; to Ted Harbin and David Plati for their professional insight and help in chapter five; and to his parents for their continuing love and support.

Preface

WRITING AND talking about sports rank right up there with baseball, Mom and apple pie. That makes sports journalism an excellent career choice for those who love the excitement of the game, the rush of being in the press box or on the sidelines at game time, and the interaction with players, coaches and fans.

Sports reporters are journalists who write about sports. They're expected to understand and speak the idiom but write so those who don't can still feel they're in the midst of the action. Fans and editors expect them to know the rules of the game and the rules of journalism and be able to meld the two into colorful, action-packed game stories, picturesque profiles, informative features and thoughtful analysis in any medium.

Enter "Sports Journalism: An Introduction to Reporting and Writing." After teaching a course in sports reporting and writing for three years while searching for a textbook that met our requirements, the authors discovered we were not alone in wishing for a tool that would provide a basic introduction to a sports reporting career and to the writing skills a novice sports reporter or media relations person needs. So we pulled together the curriculum developed for the three-credit hour course, added examples, suggested activities and discussion topics for further review and created a book of easy-to-access information. The text is made timely for each class by supplementing it with current examples, trips to sports events and visits with guest speakers.

The authors intend the introductory chapters of "Sports Journalism" to acquaint students with issues and challenges in sports media today including

- transitions in technology
- the expectation that all journalists have multimedia skills
- the participation of citizen journalists and bloggers who contribute photos and information via media Web sites
- an industry-wide scale back in publications, staff and advertising dollars
- a shrinking news hole created by an industry in transition and a fluctuating economy
- the need to balance coverage of women's sports and the revenue and non-revenue collegiate sports with that of professional teams and local school and club sports
- the erratic hours and deadline-dictated lifestyle of the sports journalist.

The writing skills chapters in "Sports Journalism" elaborate on news values and the conventions of the journalistic genre as they apply to sports writing while providing simple guidelines for novice sports writers.

The core of the book focuses on

- writing in the journalistic genre from news values to nut grafs, inverted pyramids to Model Ts, simple sentences to headlines
- using basic writing tools such as S-V-O, active voice and attribution
- building relationships with sources, colleagues and media contacts
- interviewing
- using numbers and statistics
- practicing AP style
- learning legal terms

- promoting the ethical standards set forth by the American Sports News Editors and the Society of Professional Journalists.

Checklists and illustrations assist writers with such tasks as

- story organization
- news release format
- media guide content.

Plus there are

- anecdotes about athletes and sports media writers
- glimpses of historical moments in sports journalism such as Grantland Rice's immortalization of the Four Horsemen of Notre Dame.

Upon Further Review at the end of each chapter

- provides exercises for practicing concepts and skills introduced in the chapter
- stimulates discussion of classic and contemporary issues in sports
- suggests activities to accompany chapter content.

The end matter adds a practical, professional perspective via

- the AP Sports Guidelines and Style
- the Society of Professional Journalists' Code of Ethics
- a glossary.

Assignments that supplement sports reporting and writing classes vary from season to season and school to school, but they usually include

- writing game stories, features and columns
- interviewing athletes, coaches and players

- participating in news conferences
- exploring print, broadcast and online coverage options
- filing stories on deadline.

Today's sports writer does much more than write about sports. The job description now includes words like blogger, videographer, commentator, talk show anchor and Webmaster.

Filled with examples from newspapers, Web sites, sports books and the authors themselves, "Sports Journalism" is an easy-to-read textbook that can also serve as a handbook to help beginners get started in sports media and media relations careers.

The authors bring a synergistic combination of experience and skills to "Sports Journalism." Among them, they have more than 20 years of professional sports and media writing experience, 48 years of college teaching experience, 12 published textbooks, and four graduate degrees in writing and mass communication.

In today's rapidly changing multimedia environment, the authors recognize that parts of this book are already technologically dated. We also recognize that the fundamentals of writing well and acting honorably and ethically will remain at the heart of the profession, no matter what the medium. For that reason, "Sports Journalism" is dedicated to encouraging those values in journalists who choose to spend their time with the people who play the games.

CHAPTER 1

Living the Life

MY NAME IS Brian Rosenthal, and when people find out I'm a sports writer, they usually begin the conversation with the same question.

"So, do you get into all the games for free?"

I always smile and nod. Yes, sports writers get into games for free. As a matter of fact, I say, we not only have free admission (and many times, free food), we're getting paid to sit in some of the best seats.

The response usually goes something like, "Man, that's cool. You get paid to go to games? Must be rough."

If only they knew.

Being a sports writer can, in fact, be rough.

Long hours. Odd hours. Weekend and holiday hours. Hours waiting in an airport parking lot, hoping to eye that potential coaching candidate being whisked away in a Cadillac SUV with tinted windows. Hours counting the few trees along desolate highways in western Kansas.

Hours getting sunburned at state track meets. Hours in line at airline ticket counters. Hours in the middle of the night when you awake in a cold sweat, wondering if you remembered to put the score of the game in the story you'd written a couple of hours earlier. Hours that eat up your week but never seem to be reflected in your biweekly paycheck.

Photo 1.1
Sometimes being a sports writer means finding yourself in odd situations, like chasing a coach who's trying to escape the media in his vehicle.
© REPRINTED WITH PERMISSION FROM THE LINCOLN JOURNAL STAR.

Hours sharing with friends your most memorable encounters with famous athletes and coaches. Hours laughing about embarrassing moments. Hours in packed stadiums on crisp fall Saturdays. Hours in warm-weather climates in the dead of winter.

Hours remembering you're glad you're a sports writer, after all.

Know Your Territory

Preparation is the key to sports writing.

For instance, when in El Paso, Texas for the Sun Bowl basketball tournament, I spent some free time in Juarez.

Lee Barfknecht of the Omaha World-Herald and I walked through the streets of Juarez and reached the city square.

A man, speaking through a bullhorn, had a large crowd of more than 5,000 people pretty excited. It turned out he was elected mayor, but he wasn't from the ruling party and he was not going to be seated.

I knew a little Spanish, and Barfknecht asked me what was going on. I said the man was upset. The crowd was agitated and we needed to leave soon, as we were surrounded by policia, some government troops and German shepherds.

We slowly stepped backward, left the city, walked across the bridge to El Paso and stepped into a bar.

A riot had broken out. Water cannons. The dogs going after protesters. Some shootings.

Nebraska played well in the tournament.

—Ken Hambleton, Lincoln Journal Star

Routine? What Routine?

Another common question about my job: "What is your schedule?"

My answer: "What day is it?"

There are no 8-to-5 jobs in sports reporting. That's great during slow times when it might be easy to sneak away on a sunny spring day. It's not so great during state tournaments and coaching searches. And just when you think you're enjoying a Sunday off, a phone call with a tip about a football recruit giving an oral commitment can throw your day out of whack in an instant.

Sports reporting is also becoming more of an "on-call" job with newspapers focusing and relying on fresh Web content. The Internet never sleeps. Sometimes, neither do sports writers.

Take this day, for instance.

On a cold November morning, the University of Nebraska is expected to fire football coach Bill Callahan. Also that day some 60 miles away, Nebraska's basketball team is preparing to play in-state rival Creighton.

Being involved with both events as a sports writer for the Lincoln Journal Star, my day goes like this:

- 6:20 a.m. University athletic department sends out an e-mail, calling for a 9:30 a.m. news conference.
- 6:30 a.m. I arrive on the north side of Memorial Stadium, sitting in my car (heater running) with my coffee cup in my lap and a donut in hand. I notice at least a dozen other reporters. The stakeout begins.
- 6:40 a.m. I step outside my car and make some footprints in the light dusting of snow. Make some small talk with other reporters. We decide it's not likely Callahan or any of his staff members will show their faces here with this much media present.
- 7 a.m. My newspaper colleagues, staked out elsewhere, inform me via cell phone of the "secret entrance" from which Callahan is expected to emerge following his meeting with interim athletic director Tom Osborne.
- 7:20 a.m. Callahan arrives in his Lexus. A security guard opens the gate.
- 7:25 a.m. Osborne arrives in his Chevy Tahoe. He enters the gate.
- 7:35 a.m. The meeting between Osborne and Callahan is over. Callahan leaves and waves to reporters from the windows of his Lexus.
- 7:40–9 a.m. Some furious phone calling, text messaging, and typing, all to get as many updates as possible on the newspaper's Web site.
- 9:30 a.m. Attend news conference at Memorial Stadium, where Osborne announces he's fired Callahan.
- 10 a.m. Gather a few post-news conference quotations from players to assist the main beat writer and columnist in coverage.
- 10:30 a.m. Time to drive to Omaha for the Nebraska-Creighton basketball game.
- 11:40 a.m. Arrive at Qwest Center Omaha in plenty of time for the 1 p.m. tip-off. Traffic wasn't so bad, what with everyone at home watching the football news conference live on television.

- 1 p.m. Basketball game begins. Creighton takes a commanding first-half lead. I notice Osborne, hours after firing Callahan, is in attendance in a suite. Makes for a good note.
- 5:30 p.m. File story on Nebraska's loss to Creighton.
- 5:45 p.m. Drive through McDonald's. Order the #4.
- 7 p.m. Arrive back in Lincoln at the office. Get up to speed on the latest with football, which is now a coaching search. I make some phone calls to players and offer assistance in other ways.
- 11 p.m. Head home and sprawl out on the sofa.

That's far from a routine day. But in sports reporting, nothing is routine.

A Man's Best Friend?

I was at the 1994 Orange Bowl, which started about 8 p.m. and had a halftime that lasted hours, it seemed.

Anyway, Nebraska and Florida State changed the lead four times in the final two minutes or so. I had four 10-inch leads written so I could pop in the score and hit send to beat the deadline for the early edition.

The game ended, our columnist, Mike Babcock, sent my lead, and I headed to the locker rooms for quotes. I sprinted across the field. I didn't notice that police, with police dogs, were surrounding the field.

About halfway to the Husker locker room, a large German shepherd lunged and growled at me. I did a sideways broad jump. Looked back and saw a couple of cops laughing.

I had to keep going. Got my quotes for a better lead story and a sidebar. And after a stop in the Florida State locker room, noticed a bowl of candy in the hallway.

I grabbed a handful, started toward the field to go back to the press box, and threw a handful of candy at the dogs. They went for the candy, and I got to the elevator without the scare.

—Ken Hambleton, Lincoln Journal Star

For every 16-hour day, there might be a day spent "working" from home. For every recruiting story or coaching search, there's an interview with the next great pro. For every bitterly cold spring junior varsity soccer match, there's a courtside seat at the NCAA Tournament. For every paycheck that you hope lasts until the next, there's a free trip to Los Angeles, Seattle or San Antonio.

And yes, admission is free.

Take Down or Reversal?

Sports writers will find themselves in situations where they need to think quickly and be creative.

For example, I've covered the Kansas state high school wrestling tournament at beautiful Kansas Coliseum in Wichita. The sports writer's challenge, at that time, was one that should not have been a challenge at all: simply gathering results of each match.

The problem was that the Kansas State High School Activities Association, which put an area high school's athletic department in charge of hosting and coordinating the event, was charging media members for typed results of matches. I wasn't the only one who found that practice bizarre, ill-conceived, inconvenient and downright stupid. Who in the world charges sports writers for statistics?

A group of sports writers tried combating the situation by putting one newspaper in charge of obtaining a copy of the official results. The group hauled in a photocopier, had some young volunteers make as many copies as needed, and either handed them out to sports writers or filed them in folders for later use.

It was a fine system . . . until the photocopier croaked (on championship Saturday, no less). Deadlines were fast approaching. Sports writers, having to succumb to the KSHSAA and its member schools' rule for paying for results, were digging through pockets for loose change.

That is, except for one sports writer. He went to the head table, where high school volunteers working for the KSHSAA were forming a line and stapling together final packets of results. Looking young enough to pass for a high school student, he got in line, began piecing together his own packet and went about his business. Nobody seemed to be the wiser.

—Brian Rosenthal, Lincoln Journal Star

CHAPTER 2

Covering the Game

I always turn to the sports section first. The sports section records people's accomplishments. The front page has nothing but man's failures.

—Chief Justice Earl Warren[1]

ON CRISP FALL Saturdays in Princeton, New Jersey, ten-year-old John McPhee would run onto the field with the Tiger football team and stand on the sidelines with them. McPhee's job was to station himself behind the goalpost after each score and catch the extra point. That seemingly insignificant job, however, led to a life-changing insight:

One miserable November afternoon, soaked in a freezing rain, I turned around and looked up at the press box. I saw people up there with typewriters, sitting dry under a roof in what I knew to be heated space. In that precise moment, I decided to become a writer.[2]

You may not have had a flash of inspiration quite like that, but if you're smart enough to come in out of the rain, you're ready to be a sports writer.

A New Kind of Sports Reporter

Who's the most famous sports writer in America? For many people, it might just be Ray Barone, a fictional character who appeared in the popular TV sitcom, "Everybody Loves Raymond."

The show was loosely based on the life of comedian Ray Romano, an avid Mets fan and intrepid golfer. Ray Barone, his fictional alter ego, writes for Newsday and spends as much free time as possible on the golf course.

Although Barone is a writer, the fact that he is a television character offers a good clue as to what the next generation of sports writers face. Most will need to be mojos, "mobile journalists," who can compose blogs, shoot video and continue to handle all the traditional responsibilities of print journalists.

Recently, for example, at one midsize newspaper, reporters were asked to learn two years' worth of video training in seven days. As one of those reporters, Ken Hambleton, put it, "Sending a crusty, ink-stained wretch of a sports writer into the world of videos, podcasting and blogs is like putting a powerboat in the creek. We learned the zoom out, zoom in, pan, the rule of thirds, the computer crashes for no reason at all, white balance, shutter and iris settings."[3]

All this in an effort to bring the newspaper's sports pages into the 21st century.

The New American Sports Fan

Fans have obsessed over their favorite teams, no doubt, for as long as there have been fans, but the Internet has helped create a new generation of committed sports fans. Take Will McDonald, for example.

McDonald, a University of Iowa doctoral student, painstakingly records an account of each game played by his favorite team—the Kansas City Royals—on his blog. The blog has become a popular hangout where Royals fans follow the action and swap opinions.

Many post comments such as:

"$3 million a year doesn't get you much these days"

"Never before seen batting order, the 67th of the season"

"Ha Ha Ha!!! I love it! Right off Pujols' dome."[4]

This interest, one shared by thousands of fans across the country, has blurred the line between sports fans and professional journalists. So much so, in fact, that the NCAA escorted a person out of the press box for blogging a live College World Series baseball game. Chris Thorman, who runs the Kansas City Chiefs' blog at www.arrowheadpride.com, said: "It's totally changing the landscape for sports fans. What separates the mainstream media from the typical blogger is the access. The Kansas City Star's beat writer will have more access, will have nuanced conversations with players, and see things we can't."[5]

Today, major sports teams rarely give credentials to bloggers. But that could change. "I think the time is coming when bloggers will be credentialed and at games," said Will Leith, founder of deadspin.com.[6] In what may be a precedent-setting move, the New York Islanders are planning a bloggers' box for an upcoming season—a press-like area set aside just for them.

In fact, nearly all print journalists are facing the same paradigm shift. According to David Dunkley Gyimah, a pioneering video journalist in the U.K., they must learn to understand "visual narrative" and allow it to drive storytelling.

As Gyimah puts it, "Vloggers [video bloggers] will undoubtedly rule the net. Their short, sometimes idiosyncratic productions are well suited for a medium where time is compressed and users' attention spans shortened."[7]

And that's not all. Increasingly, sports writers are finding it necessary to cover a whole range of stories far outside the normal bounds of playing fields and arenas. They must become pharmacists,

Photo 2.1
A press conference.
©REPRINTED WITH PERMISSION FROM THE LINCOLN JOURNAL STAR.

for example, to understand the bewildering array of legal and illegal performance-enhancement drugs, such as steroids. They must add the police beat to their repertoire as an unfortunate number of college and pro athletes run astray of the law.

They must also be prepared to follow their sport into whatever bizarre territory it takes them. On one windy morning, for example, a college rowing team needed rescue after wind-whipped waves started to swamp the boat. The reporter soon found himself at the edge of a lake examining what was left of a racing shell.[8] Joanne Gerstner, a sports reporter for the Detroit News, noted, "Sports writing is really about medicine, business, sociology, psychology. It's a lot more than a home run or a slam dunk. I have to be able to decipher contracts. I have to be able to describe a knee injury."[9]

But just because sports writing has evolved to include new, electronic-based media and a wider field of play does not mean that the essential standards have changed. The age-old principles of good journalism—accuracy and objectivity—still hold.

Irrational Pastimes

Most people acknowledge that America is a nation of sports nuts. Sports, too, get nuttier and nuttier. From motorcycle racing on ice to rattlesnake rodeos, each weekend fans turn out for another dubious sport. Battle of the Monster Trucks, anyone? John Cherwa, associate sports editor at the Los Angeles Times, explains:

> "Trash sports, that's our official name for them. Because they're not traditional and, in many cases, they're not real. Supposedly, in Atlanta, they have a thing called cat chasing. They throw a cat out of an airplane and then different parachutists try to chase and catch the cat. I don't know if it's true, but I've heard of it." [10]

Not all these activities actually involve sweating. "Poker players used to be guys avoiding their wives," comments author Michael Lewis. "Now, apparently, they are professional athletes."

And yet sports are one thing that gets Americans fired up. Sure, some Americans like C-SPAN, but their numbers are overwhelmed by ESPN addicts. Occasionally, political leaders can inspire, but none cause grown men to paint their faces, tattoo their chests and howl like werewolves. As Lewis writes, "For every little boy or girl who wants to grow up to be a member of Congress there are, oh, about one million who intend to become major league baseball players or professional basketball players or ice skaters or gymnasts." [11]

For this chapter, we'll turn our focus on the main event: the sports contest itself. We'll skip monster trucks, by the way, and concentrate on more familiar sports. For all the hoopla, color and spectacle, the sports writer's first obligation is to get out to the ballpark, to report, in other words, on the game.

Advance Stories

The three major game-related sports stories include the advance, the recap (or gamer), and the post-game analysis. Sometimes these stories may be composed days apart, but in the harried life of an electronic sports journalist, they may all be due within a 24-hour cycle. A preview of an upcoming game that compares teams and players, discusses team records and gives lineups is known as an advance. The advance story requires diligence but the deadline pressure is light.

Athletes will tell you that games are won or lost in practice. Sports writers will tell you the same thing about stories—the key work is doing research before a game. The reporter tries to find out all she can about the teams, the coaches, and the issues he'll be covering. Sports writer Steve Sipple comments, "Background is the one time when I don't have to worry about asking the right question. It's the one time when I'm able to relax and have fun while I familiarize myself with an athlete or an issue."[12]

Prepare, Prepare, Prepare

How can you best prepare to write an advance? First, read all the relevant information you can from professional magazines such as Sports Illustrated to local sources like your rival school's paper. In so doing you will pick up on how others cover sports and discover possible angles you can use. What happened in last year's game? What's the history between the two schools?

Second, get to know the team's vital statistics. This knowledge will not only give you insights into how the game might play out (i.e., one team often gets out to a fast start), but also give you something to talk about during interviews.

Finally, get to know the people you'll be covering. Go to practices and remain afterward to speak with players, coaches and trainers. Try to establish a good working relationship with them. These people should feel comfortable coming to you with their story ideas. In turn, they should be confident that you will represent their comments fairly and accurately.

It's crucial that you prepare well for interviews with sports figures. Athletes and coaches are often too ready, willing and able to respond to questions with pat answers. How often have you heard a coach say, "It was a really big win for us" or "We are

Softball Isn't Baseball with Curls

Softball is not just baseball played with a bigger ball. Tennis isn't outdoor ping-pong. Cross country is the only sport where the spectators run around the course to watch the race. Volleyball and beach volleyball? Two different sports. Sometimes knowing the subtle differences between sports is crucial to covering them effectively.

Take softball. Obviously, the ball is much larger and, as a result, the field dimensions are significantly different. The outfield fences are not as deep since a larger ball does not carry as far, and the bases are 60 feet apart, 30 feet closer than for a baseball field.

The game is also played much more quickly than a typical three-hour major league game. Softball games go seven innings, two fewer than professional baseball, and the game moves at a faster pace. Pitchers do not spend much time worrying about runners who cannot leave a base until the ball leaves their hand. So they just concentrate on batters.

> "We don't always rely on the three-run homer like many baseball teams," says Kelley Green, softball coach at Lock Haven College. "You will have more sacrifice bunts in softball than baseball to move runners into scoring position."

Pitching is also vastly different. In baseball, teams require a rotation of four to five pitchers, who need much more time for recovery. Baseball pitchers rarely go beyond 100 pitches in a single game. In softball, pitchers often pitch on consecutive days, if needed. The underhanded motion does not put as much strain on the shoulders and arms, but the windmill delivery results in pitches that are just as fast.

As with anything, you need to fully understand a sport before you can properly cover it. You can learn much by reading the NCAA's rule book. You can watch some practices and speak to coaches and players for background information. Obviously, the more you cover games, the more you will learn. (Most of these suggestions are gleaned from Joe Gisondi's blog, onsportz.blogspot.com.)

playing the games one at a time"? This information is of little use to you or your readers. You must be prepared to ask as many specific questions as necessary until you get the information you need to write a genuine story, one with something new or insightful. Look for trends. If you're observant, before long you will spot changes, changes you can develop into thoughtful, well-informed questions.

Pre-Game Tips

Mark Derowitsch, a sports writer for the Lincoln Journal Star, once quipped, "You could train a chimpanzee to write an advance." Indeed, professional sports writers sometimes seem to be monkeying around because their previews of upcoming games are painfully predictable. The lazy sports writer merely notes the time and place of the game, mixes in a few statistics, and adds a quotation from each coach. This formula produces the same stale story week in and week out.

In this respect, sports writing is similar to news writing. "You're looking for information," explains Michael Wilbon, sports columnist for the Washington Post and cohost of "Pardon the Interruption," a sports talk show on ESPN. "You're looking for documents. You're looking for anecdotes. You're looking for good quotes. You're looking for something the competitor doesn't have."[13]

Your advances, however, shouldn't serve as sedatives for your readers. In fact, they should have exactly the opposite effect. Think about the anticipation your classmates share for the contest ahead. Typically, the next game is the most talked-about topic on campus—among the players, the general student body and even the faculty.

How can you add flavor to your advances? Find an angle that your readers might not know about. For instance, New York Times columnist Selena Roberts devoted an entire column to the pressure women tennis stars feel to conform to certain ideas about body types: "Serena Williams, the snippy bloggers have remarked, has been carrying too much junk in the trunk after a winter weight gain."[14]

Each advance you write should include something fresh, something new. Put simply, try to spice up or featurize your advances to keep them from sounding the same. Interviews, historical features or short human interest stories can help create a far more interesting sports page. Of course, don't forget to include the basic information about the game.

The following should be included in each advance you write:

- The significance of the matchup. Will this game decide who goes to the playoffs? Will one team finally win its first game of the year? What are some recent trends?
- Both teams' records, background of the rivalry and last year's score.
- Key players, key statistics, injuries and starting lineups.
- Styles of play.

Don't overlook advances on other sports. The tennis, golf and wrestling teams might not attract the crowds that the football and basketball teams do, but they are putting forth as much effort—and often have as much at stake—as the teams that are more visible. They can also attract large crowds; at Iowa and Oklahoma, wrestling teams fill large arenas for dual meets.

Make sure that the sports activities of both males and females are reported. More women sports writers are entering the field, including Robin Roberts and Sage Steele of *Good Morning America* and ESPN; their voices will help change the sports landscape. The popularity of the U.S. women's soccer team, for example, is a good sign of just how much readers care, so be sure to cover these events just as diligently as men's sports.

Game Summary

As a sports writer, you often have the best seat in the house. You might be on press row (usually at courtside), in the press box (high above the crowd) or on the sidelines. Your job depends on your ability to see all of the action with minimal distractions. Your goal is to write the second of the major game-related stories: a game summary or recap of what happened. Part of that job will take you deep inside the game.

Lee Barfknect, a football and basketball beat writer for the Omaha World-Herald, describes his duties this way:

> "My job is to take fans where they normally can't go—the sidelines, the field, and the locker rooms. And I have the opportunity to interview the athletes and coaches they don't get a chance to talk to. You have to know how to use the amount of access that you're given."

With access, though, comes responsibility. Fans depend on you to provide insight into the bad news (the cause of the crucial fumble or why the star volleyball player was benched), as well as the good news (a wind-aided home run, perhaps). Most likely, if you're curious about something, your readers will be, too. Almost anything that grabs fans' attention at a game deserves at least a brief description or explanation in your game story.

The key plays may call for more elaboration, too. How, then, should you decide which plays are crucial? The first step is taking detailed game notes that highlight the momentum swings and the key performances. It may seem a bit old-fashioned to "keep the book," but keeping careful notes forces the reporter to pay close attention to the action. For example, look for moments when a team goes on a 10-2 run or when a tennis player wins 12 straight points. Then, see how this fits in the context of the entire game. Prepare to ask pointed questions about those particular moments.

When the game ends, a writer on deadline needs to get good quotations quickly. To get these quotes, the writer must ask tough questions—after all, who wants to talk about a loss? In fact, a coach or player may not like many of the questions that he gets, but don't be afraid to do your job. Sometimes you won't get an answer. Sometimes you'll get an angry response. Generally, though, if a question is legitimate, coaches and players will be willing to cooperate.

A Front-Row Seat, but Keep Your Yap Shut

A press pass gets you into the inner sanctum, the holy of holies—the press box. Usually situated high above the stadium, the press box affords the best seat in the house and munchies galore. Sounds like a fan's dream, right? Wrong. "Sports writers don't root for teams; they root for stories—the more unusual, compelling and head-scratching the better," explains Omaha World-Herald writer Lee Barfknecht.

Sports writers can certainly be emotional in the press box, but it's not the place for shouts of glee or heart-rending moans. Working in this venue leaves reporters with only one option: be professional. Cheering for one team or another is a sure way to find yourself getting tossed out of the press box, probably on the widest part of your anatomy. If you cheer, your copy might also be one-dimensional. So, remember: the press box is only for the cheering-impaired.

Objectivity?

But a sports writer doesn't have to be completely neutral either. Don't readers expect the local writers to be (secretly, perhaps) rooting for the home team?

Was it the same game? Depends on where you're standing. Sports reporters try to be objective, but they also stress what the players on their team did or didn't do. Writers should avoid taking a hometown angle, unless they're writing a column, and even then they should try to be as even-handed as possible.

Whose Sideline Are You On?

Consider a high school football game where an intense crowd and an over-enthusiastic band may have changed the game's outcome. In the closing moments, Fremont High faced a third down and one on their opponent's 7-yard line. The quarterback had to ask the officials to quiet the crowd twice, but when the ball was put in play, one of the Fremont players jumped before the snap, causing a procedure penalty and eventually dooming the drive.

In the Fremont paper, the writer said players had to face "tough odds" on their opponent's home field and left the game with a "sour taste." The Fremont coach was quoted as saying, "Whether it was the noise that caused us to jump, I don't know. It would have been nice if the kids had been able to hear the signals."

On the other hand, the home team's paper credited the win to a "raucous crowd" that "rattled Fremont's effort to overcome a one-point deficit." "The crowd was really enthusiastic," gushed the home team's coach.[15]

Sports Jargon

Good sports writing depends on the same writing and reporting techniques as any other area of the news. But, in addition to following basic style rules, sports writers must also deal with the unique terminology of each sport.

If you've ever been thrown a curve, driven up the wall or played the field, you can chalk it up to the world of sports.

In baseball, for example, the writer will be expected to use terms such as bullpen, ground-rule double, pitchout, pickle, rundown and sacrifice. In volleyball, fans will expect to see terms such as dink, kill and overhand pass.

Metaphors

"Sports metaphors are everywhere; they permeate all walks of life," says Robert Palmatier, co-author of a dictionary of 1,700 sports metaphors.[16]

"They've always been used because sports are common to all cultures," says Harold Ray, sports historian. "They just make communication easier."[17]

On the other hand, beginning sports writers too often rely on jargon and clichés. Jargon is highly specialized language developed for a special use. If you use *cagers* instead of *basketball players* or *grid mentor* instead of *football coach*, you are using jargon. Your story may be unclear to some of your readers and seem silly to others.

Clichés are trite, overused words or expressions. When you use expressions such as *split the uprights* or describe a close game as a *barn-burner*, *squeaker* or *nail-biter*, you are merely echoing other worn-out writing. Avoiding clichés will help your stories be fresh and lively.

Post-Game Heroics

Dick Enberg, a sports commentator for NBC, once said that "the beauty of all sports is how grown adults can act like little kids." Indeed, sports can bring out the same emotions in 30-year-old professional baseball players as they do in eight-year-old Little Leaguers. Sports writing is about reporting those emotions.

Whether it's a blowout or a close game, every sports event produces at least one prevailing emotion. Capture that emotion in your story. Support it with descriptions and quotations. Make that emotion the theme of your entire story. You'll rarely find a sporting event that doesn't produce some sort of drama you can write about.

How do you evoke that emotion on paper? How do you make the action come alive? In addressing that issue, Daryl Moen, a journalism professor at the University of Missouri, often tells his students the story of a blind newspaper publisher. The publisher would ask reporters to come into his office and tell him about their stories. Often, they would just tell him the facts—the who, what, where, when, how and why of the story. Patiently, the publisher would ask about the emotions that were evident on the faces of the people. He'd leave each reporter with one piece of advice: "Make me see. Make me see your story."[18]

Don't just make your readers see, however. Make them hear the crack of the bat, the rip of the basketball net and the roar of the crowd. Make them smell the locker room after two-a-day practices. Make them feel the volleyball slam against the hardwood floor. Make them taste the bitterness of defeat. In other words, use all your senses—sight, sound, touch, smell and even taste.

Catching a Break

Covering the Nebraska State Games has proven to be one of the most interesting things I've done.

I covered the arm wrestling competition the summer of 2003.

Two well-muscled guys, both rookies, were first up.

After grunting, straining and pushing for more than three minutes, one guy's arm broke. Snapped. The loud crack. The blood. The bone sticking through the skin.

The injured guy was too shocked to move. The other competitor got sick. Many in the room ran in panic.

I remembered my first aid training and helped the guy until the paramedics arrived. I got a pretty good interview, too. The injured guy said he'd try again next year—left-handed.

—Ken Hambleton, Lincoln Journal Star

For example, Linda Robertson of the Miami Herald wanted to give some scale to the size of pro football players: "Like American houses, Hummers, and hamburgers, football players are a reflection of the bigness of our society."

Paul Solotaroff, writing for Men's Journal, described the incredible saga of star wrestler Kyle Maynard, who has only stumps for arms and legs:

> "If you think a limbless teen can't outpoint his foes, you've never seen Maynard scamper side to side, darting for a hold. Wrestlers may start matches on their feet, but bouts are won and lost on all fours, and Maynard is already down there, waiting."[19]

But don't overdo it. Make sure you support your descriptions. For example, writing that the volleyball players were "down in the dumps" isn't really honest. Unless you're a volleyball player, you don't know how they feel. Instead, ask the players about their disappointment. Describe their distraught faces and the tears streaming down their cheeks. And then capture the emotion with revealing quotes.

One way to tap all your senses is to draw on specific details to evoke a scene. Take, for example, Rick Reilly's description of how close one golf ball came to dropping into the creek:

> "One less drop of rain. One more run of the mower. A cup less of fertilizer last fall. One more breath from a nearby butterfly. A blade of grass with weak knees. An eyelash less luck. Any of these things could have cost Fred Couples the Masters. But somehow, some way, Couples' golf ball hugged the steep slope at August National's 12th hole, clung to it the way a sock clings to a towel fresh out of a hot dryer. The ball steadfastly refused to fall into the water."[20]

If Reilly can make a golf shot, of all things, come alive, just think how dramatic you can make your stories. Effective sports writers use crisp, lively words—especially verbs—to describe the action. Consider this example from Selena Roberts on the presence of several women drivers in the Indy 500:

> "Three women earned a place on the starting grid of 33 drivers, a first for a race that cut its teeth in 1911. At 25, Danica Patrick is the commercialized one; at 35, Milka Duno is the mysterious one; and at 26, Sarah Fisher is the experienced one. Never have so many jumpsuits been fitted with curves for ladies who dig the turns."[21]

Covering Professional Events

Imagine you're a college reporter who has covered a few events on campus. Usually, you wear jeans and a t-shirt, blending in with the other college students on campus. Suddenly, you receive an unusual assignment: Cover the U.S. Open. You're scared to death. How do you act? What do you wear? As one college sports reporter put it, "I guess my biggest fear is when I go to pick up my media credentials, they'll figure out I'm not a pro yet."

In the case of the country's largest golf event, a writer would probably head for the USGA's Media Center, an aircraft-carrier-size collection of tents. One tent contains the cable-connected desks of 350 journalists who never need to leave the premises to cover the tournament. In fact, they'll probably see more of it if they don't.

That's because their desks face a scoreboard 100 feet wide that presents the hole-by-hole progress of each player. On either side of the scoreboard are two 36-square-foot TV screens where the writers can follow the action, as presented by NBC and ESPN.

Does all this work make you hungry? No problem. In one of the tents you'll find a dining area with a dozen TV screens so you won't miss a minute of the action.

After players finish their rounds, some agree to do a short press conference called a "flash interview," which takes place just outside the locker room. If a golfer has an unusually notable round, he might be invited to a more formal news conference in the Media Center.

But what if you miss a key interview because you're finishing your peanut butter, pickle and olive sandwich? No worries. A stenographer takes notes at each interview and with breathtaking speed, transcripts of the interviews will have been typed, stapled and placed in wall racks where you can pick them up.[22]

Observe the other professional journalists as they work. In most situations, you'll find journalists swarming around the players after their rounds. Feel free to do the same. You are allowed to record comments made to other journalists, but don't interrupt if a reporter and player are clearly off to the side in a more private setting. You can stand nearby and wait your turn to jump in with some questions. You should try to seek out angles no one else has found. Before the round begins, select two or three golfers to follow— at least for a few holes—so you can get details that won't be visible to the writers in some tent all copying the same comments. Make sure you get out on the course to capture that first-hand flavor.

Post-Game Analysis

Once the dust has settled and the ink on the game recap has dried, the sports writer has a chance to, as Wordsworth might say, reflect in tranquility, or in other words, analyze what the heck just happened. An analysis is the third kind of standard game article and one that features opportunities for the most writerly kind of prose. Roger Angell, baseball correspondent for the New Yorker, usually files stories months, if not years, after the events they describe took place. He's going for something besides who won and lost:

> When I began writing sports pieces, it was clear to me that the doings of big-league baseball—the daily happenings on the field, the managerial strategies, the celebration of heroes, the medical and financial bulletins, the clubhouse gossip— were so enormously reported that I

> would have to find some other aspect of
> the game to study. I decided to sit in the
> stands—for a while at least—and watch
> the baseball from there. I wanted to con-
> centrate not just on the events down on
> the field but on their reception; I wanted
> to pick up the feel of the game as it hap-
> pened to the people around me.[23]

One thing writers go for in analysis pieces is perspective. They seek to compare current performances with those of the past. So, Angell, for example, tries to measure one pitcher's great year against others: "Many observers believe that Bob Gibson's 1.12 earned-run average in 1968 is one of the Everests of the game."[24] Comparing a pitcher's achievement to climbing Mt. Everest gives vivid testimony to the scale of his accomplishment.

A sports analyst writes for true aficionados, fans who don't need to have every reference explained. Here's Angell on one of baseball's famous moments: "My father told me about *the* famous last game of the 1912 World Series, in Boston, and seeing Fred Snodgrass drop *that* fly ball in the tenth inning, when the Red Sox scored twice and beat the Giants."[25]

The game, *that* fly ball. Presumably, the true fan can supply the missing information. The members of baseball's family, Angell tells us, are "devoutly attached to its ancestors and its family records."

Sports writers love adjectives, and an analysis piece is just the right place to use them. Many coin inventive hyphenated modifiers such as *pennant-winning*, *ear-wrenching*, and *one-base-at-a-time attack*. Writers can also indulge their taste for humorous exaggeration. The artificial turf of a football field might have the "consistency of an immense doormat" while a normally gruff manager might turn from a "grizzly bear to Gepetto."

They open the spigot on the full range of punctuation from dashes to italics and parentheses, not to mention the occasional sentence fragment. Sentence structures become exceedingly flexible and free-swinging. Take the following passage, for example, from a description of a Detroit Lions exhibition football game by George Plimpton. Plimpton was allowed to play quarterback for five snaps, and he steadily moved the team backward toward its own end zone. On his final play, he pitched the ball to a halfback who was tackled on the one-yard line. After the final play, as Plimpton trudges wearily toward the bench, he notices that the fans start to applaud. At first he can't believe the people in the stands are clapping for him and then he begins to understand:

> I thought about the applause afterward. Some of it was, perhaps, in appreciation of the lunacy of my participation and for the fortitude it took to do it; but most of it, even if subconscious, I decided was in relief that I had done as badly as I had: it verified the assumption that the average fan would have about an amateur blundering into the brutal world of professional football. He would get slaughtered. If by some chance I had uncorked a touchdown pass, there would have been wild acknowledgment—because I heard the groans go up at each successive disaster—but afterward the spectators would have felt uncomfortable. Their concept of things would have been upset. The outsider did not belong, and there was comfort in that being proved.[26]

Plimpton's description probes deeply into the psychology of the game—the certainty fans have, for instance, that what they see players do is impossibly hard. His sentences resemble those of a philosophy professor, except for a delightful metaphor, one where he imagines a popular mayor waving to the crowd from a convertible. Analyzing a game, season or player gives the writer a chance for sheer exuberance. Why not, for example, stretch a metaphor throughout an entire paragraph as Roger Angell does here:

> Steve Garvey always seems to be *standing at attention* in the batter's box. As he waits for the pitch, *his back is straight* and his bat shows *not a tremor* of anxiety or anticipation. His feet are apart, of course, but *perfectly parallel* with the back line of the box. When he swings, his head snaps down, as if he were *checking the shine on his tunic buttons*. What he is doing, of course, is watching the ball—really watching the ball. He swings *exactly the same way* at every pitch: *perfect swings*. Last year, he batted .304, which is *exactly* his lifetime average in eleven seasons with the Dodgers. Garvey is *a soldier of hitting*.[27] [author's italics]

Long before the reader reaches the punch line, he knows he is being carefully set up. The physical description of Garvey, as if he were in a military inspection, the repetition of *perfectly* and *exactly*, and the listing of his hitting statistics all suggest a machine-like consistency. Garvey isn't a player; he is a soldier.

Other metaphors are useful when describing the techniques of each game—throwing, catching and hitting, for example—skills that are simple to the point of banality and yet breathtakingly complex (physicists have yet to fully explain how a curveball works). A split-finger fastball, for example, could be described as "baseball's Rubik's Cube"; fielders must deal with "bazooka shots that are lined past them or at them" or cope with a sneaky bunt, "baseball's shiv in the ribs."

Settling back with one of these analyses, the reader feels the arm of a favorite uncle wrap itself around his or her shoulder and senses the joy of yet another trip out to the old ballpark.

Upon Further Review

1. What new challenges do sports journalists face today?
2. Describe the key elements in preparing to write a story about a game.
3. Can a sports writer take sides? Why or why not? What difference does it make if the writer is doing a story or column?

Notes

1. This quote appears in Sports Illustrated, July 22, 1968.

2. The story of John McPhee's appearance at a Princeton football game is recounted in his article, "Rip Van Golfer," which appeared in the New Yorker on Aug. 6, 2007.

3. Ken Hambleton writes a sports column for the Lincoln Journal Star called "Dear Mr. Sportsknowitall."

4. Will McDonald, "Royals review," www.royalsreview.com.

5. Chris Thorman, www.arrowheadpride.com.

6. Will Leith, www.deadspin.com.

7. David Dunkley Gyimah created viewmagazine.tv to illustrate how one person could create online broadcasts. This quote appears in "insideSolojos: Videojournalism" on his Web site, www.mrdot.co.uk/videojournalism_today.html.

8. The college rowing team's mishap was recounted by Algis J. Laukaitis in the Lincoln Journal Star, April 16, 2007.

9. This quote appears in "Getting into the game," by Ed Finkel, Medill, Summer 2004.

10. Cherwa is quoted in Funny Times, an American humor newspaper, www.funnytimes.com.

11. The quotes from Lewis appear in his introduction to "The Best American Sports Writing 2006" (Boston: Houghton Mifflin, 2006).

12. Steve Sipple is a sports writer for the Lincoln Journal Star.

13. Michael Wilbon is quoted in "Getting into the game," by Ed Finkel, Medill, Summer 2004.

14. This quote from Roberts' column appeared in the Sept. 1, 2006, issue of the New York Times.

15. These two stories appeared on Oct. 11, 1981, in the Lincoln Journal Star and the Fremont Tribune.

16. Robert Palmatier's book on sports jargon is "Sports Talk: A Dictionary of Sports Metaphors" (New York: Greenwood Press, 1989).

17. Harold Ray is the co-author (with Robert Palmatier) of the "Dictionary of Sports Idioms" (Lincolnwood, Ill: National Textbook Company, 1993).

18. Daryl Moen says that "the goal of all writers is to make readers see and smell and feel and taste and hear." He offers more writing tips on his Web site at web.missouri.edu/~moend/writing/index.htm.

19. Solotaroff's story on Kyle Maynard can be found in "The Best American Sports Writing 2006" (Boston: Houghton Mifflin, 2006), pp. 1–14.

20. Reilly's article on the Masters, "Bank shot," appeared in the April 20, 1992, issue of Sports Illustrated.

21. Roberts' article, "Sports of the times; Creeping equality, a bit of fraternity and a slick of asterisks at Indy," appeared in the May 27, 2007, issue of the New York Times.

22. This account can be found on Joe Gisondi's blog, onsportz.blogspot .com, an excellent place to find information on how to cover virtually every sport. Gisondi has more than 20 years of experience as a sports reporter and now teaches journalism at Eastern Illinois University.

23. Angell's description can be found in the foreword to his first collection of baseball pieces, "The Summer Game" (Lincoln: University of Nebraska Press, 2004).

24. The account of Bob Gibson's exploits appears in "Distance," New Yorker, Sept. 22, 1980.

25. This quote appears in "The Summer Game," p. 293.

26. This description comes from George Plimpton's book "Paper Lion" (New York: Harper & Row, 1966).

27. Angell's account of Steve Garvey appears in the May 4, 1981, issue of the New Yorker.

CHAPTER 3

Finding the Sources

E VER HEAR OF a youth basketball coach who conducts the season's first practice—or maybe two or three practices—without even tossing a basketball onto the court?

The idea is to show the players how the game of basketball involves more than dribbling and shooting. It's about running, hustling, setting screens, playing hard-nosed defense, doing the grunt work.

Fans may not notice or appreciate those things on game day. Still, that extra work is vital to the overall success of the team. Without it, the final product—the game—will not be top quality, and fans will wonder what is wrong.

The same concept applies for sports reporters. There is more to the job than writing stories and producing highlight packages, much like there is more to basketball than shooting and dribbling. Audiences expect a high-quality product but don't really care or understand the legwork involved.

Sports reporters have ample legwork to do before even opening a laptop or picking up a camera—developing and working with sources, staying informed, keeping abreast of developing situations and creating story ideas. That is best accomplished by first establishing beats.

Beat Reporting

A beat reporter is a reporter who covers the same team or the same sport on a regular basis. Beat reporters are more common at newspapers, which usually have larger sports staffs than electronic media outlets and can afford to divide sports and teams into individual beats.

Having the same sports writer responsible for covering one team makes sense from an organizational standpoint for the newspaper. There is less confusion within the sports department over who is covering what. Also, having a beat reporter makes it simpler and faster for the team or school when contacting an outlet's sports department with information or news. Readers are better able to relate to coverage when the same person is providing stories.

Some beat reporters follow the same team for years. Other times, newspapers will shift duties and reassign beats, mainly to keep reporters from getting too comfortable, and to give readers a fresher, different viewpoint from another beat reporter.

Sometimes a beat reporter covers more than one team or one sport. A high school beat reporter may cover dozens of area high schools. A college beat reporter might follow only one school but be responsible for covering several sports with that school. A beat reporter for the Big Ten Conference will cover multiple schools and multiple sports.

Beat reporters are sometimes responsible for a variety of sports beats. The same person covering the local Division I-A football team might also be responsible for local horse racing coverage in the summertime. A women's college basketball beat reporter could double as the men's gymnastics beat reporter, even though the seasons overlap. It can be a delicate balancing act.

Conversely, a beat might be too large for one person to handle. Some newspapers will put two or three reporters on the same beat. Communication becomes critical among beat writers.

Responsibilities of a Beat Reporter

A beat reporter has access to a team that fans do not. Part of the reporter's responsibility is to take fans where they cannot go by providing as many details and as much information as possible. Who is injured? Which players are surprising coaches with strong practice play? Which assistant coaches are on the road recruiting? Is the head coach considering another job?

Obviously, these questions are not easily answered if beat reporters believe writing features and traveling to games on the company's dime are their only duties. Those are just the highlights.

Thorough beat reporters have the daily pulse of the team they cover. If somebody asks you where the head coach is making a public appearance Thursday night, or for which postseason awards the star quarterback is a candidate, you should have a knowledgeable answer.

A primary goal of a beat reporter is to be the first to provide news to the audience. Beating competing media outlets to a breaking news story is known as getting a scoop. Another goal for beat reporters, then, is to not get scooped. In this case, a tie isn't a win, but it is certainly better than a loss.

A beat reporter's busiest time is in-season. Football beat reporters are busy from August through November. Basketball beat reporters live in gymnasiums from November to March. High school beat writers follow whichever sport is in season (or sometimes three sports) for a school year, then begin the cycle again come fall.

But the off-season is when some beats, especially those involving college teams, have the most legwork. Coaching changes, roster moves. Recruiting, recruiting and more recruiting. Some beats, because of avid fan bases, are year-round. North Carolina basketball and Alabama football are examples. And with limited access and resources in the off-season, finding stories and keeping tabs on the goings-on within a team can become more challenging for a beat reporter.

That is when developing and maintaining sources becomes especially important.

Developing Sources

Cultivating a broad range of sources can take weeks or months for a new beat reporter. The process really never ends. Beat reporters are constantly updating their e-mail contact list, adding numbers to their cell phone address books and filing business cards. It is virtually impossible for beat reporters to thoroughly cover the same team on a regular basis without the help of sources.

Primary Sources

Primary sources are most important. These are people who have information or opinions that are vital to the outcome of your story. Coaches, players, athletic directors or management are all considered primary sources for any beat reporter. Game stories will almost always contain information gleaned from interviews with coaches and players.

> Charles Richardson had hoped to emerge from a pile of humanity in time to shake the hands of his opponents.
>
> He was too late. By the time Richardson's Nebraska teammates had finished dog-piling their team captain and hero, stunned Texas Tech players had quickly trotted off the court.
>
> "I ain't ever been in that situation before," said Richardson, whose three-pointer at the buzzer lifted Nebraska to a dramatic 61-59 victory over Texas Tech on Tuesday night at United Spirit Arena.
>
> Should Richardson find himself in a similar situation, he hopes he and his teammates can hold their composure a little better.
>
> "We needed to show more class," Richardson said of Nebraska's dizzying celebration on the south end of the court. "I know how it feels to lose like that. I know we were all excited, but I was trying to get the guys up off me." [1]

Richardson, the player who made the game-winning shot, is the obvious primary source.

A story about a player being suspended from the team will have essential information from the coach—why the player is being punished, how long the player will be suspended and terms of the suspension. Coaches make those decisions; therefore, they are the primary sources in such circumstances.

When players break records, reach milestones or are honored with prestigious awards, they become primary sources. Fans want to know their thoughts and reaction, no matter how predictable the response may be. Can you imagine a story on the Heisman Trophy winner without any words from the winner himself?

Most stories are best presented with multiple primary sources. A story about a coach's future employment with a team, or possible loss of employment, needs information from more than just the coach. In fact, the coach, while still considered a primary source in the situation, may be reluctant to divulge details.

Reporters need to contact athletic directors or management to ask questions about possible contract negotiations. A "no comment" response is possible but sometimes just as telling.

The coach's agent also becomes another primary source. Agents many times serve as a spokesperson in lieu of the coach, and might provide clearer details.

In feature, investigative or other sports news stories not necessarily related to a beat, primary sources will vary, depending on the topic.

Local businesspersons and investors become primary sources for a story about a city trying to attract an independent baseball team. A story about the possibility of adding an early signing period for college football recruiting could best be told with insight from self-proclaimed recruiting experts. An off-the-wall feature story on sports Internet message board junkies cannot be told without talking to the junkies themselves.

In these cases, the primary sources are not necessarily people reporters work with on a regular basis, or with whom they have a strong relationship. But they are essential to that particular story.

Secondary Sources

Think of secondary sources as condiments to a hamburger. You could probably survive without them, but they certainly add much-needed flavor and zing.

Secondary sources are just that: secondary. They are not essential to the outcome of a story but add information that makes a story more complete.

That story about the Heisman Trophy winner? Members of his family might be able to share an entertaining anecdote or two to spice up your story. His teammates could probably attest to his work ethic or competitiveness. Reaction from fans on the street can give your audience another viewpoint.

Secondary sources are most common, and perhaps most important, for longer, in-depth feature stories.

Secondary sources also ensure your audience that you are not being lazy and producing one-source stories—stories that are told using only one primary source. Unless it is a breaking news story, or deadline story, you should tell your story using more than one source.

A short feature story on the 12-year-old baseball player with one arm could easily be told after you talk to just the player himself. But why stop there? Secondary sources—his teammates, opposing players, parents, spectators—will give your story much more depth . . . and save you a scowl from your editor.

Material Sources

Not all sources are people. Material sources, or non-people sources, are physical items such as record books, media guides or perhaps even other stories that can provide information for a reporter.

A sports reporter filing a report after a game must have the leading scorers, and preferably other statistical information that would appear on a post-game box score or statistical sheet. A writer working on a biographical story on the new assistant volleyball coach will likely turn to the school's media guide.

A feature story on the five women's volleyball players living together in the same house will probably have several quotations from the players themselves. Perhaps the reporter wants to include some historical perspective and research other instances of teammates housing together. A material source might be the archives—a Web site search, or perhaps a look into a newspaper's library.

Be careful, though. Just because material is archived does not mean it is 100 percent correct. Archived material—past stories, clips—should be verified for accuracy.

Behind-the-Scenes Sources

Not all sources will appear as a prevalent part of your story. In fact, some sources may not appear in your story at all.

Behind-the-scenes sources are people who provide pertinent information or ideas for stories but are not necessarily used as a primary, or even secondary, source in your actual story. For beat reporters, developing behind-the-scenes sources is a key part of keeping up with the goings-on within a program.

How many times do you hear a student manager, team trainer or player's roommate quoted in a story? It does not happen often. But those people can still be useful to sports reporters. In many instances, they are more involved with the team than you are and probably have access to some information you do not.

Behind-the-scenes sources go beyond managers and trainers. Boosters and friends of the program, former players, athletic department personnel—anyone who is around the team with access you might not have—can help. Behind-the-scenes sources need to be knowledgeable, trustworthy and dependable.

Many times, information from behind-the-scenes sources will be shared on the condition of anonymity. In other words, a source may say something like, "Here's what's going on, but you didn't hear it from me." Your source is speaking off the record. Any information gathered off the record cannot be used in your story.

Reasons for speaking off the record are numerous and, most times, understandable. In the case of behind-the-scenes sources, they are usually trying to protect their own status or employment. Reporters oblige by not sharing their identity with anyone, except editors.

What good is off-the-record information if you cannot use it? That is where good sports journalists implement their reporting skills.

Let's say you are a beat writer for a college football team. Daily practices are closed to the media, but you are invited to conduct interviews after practice. With 100-plus players dispersing at once, it is possible you did not notice the first-string cornerback was absent.

That is when a good relationship with a team manager becomes helpful. He might alert you, off-record, that Joe Smith was injured in practice. Now privy to the information, you ask the coach, who must address the situation on the record. Information gathered on the record can be used in a story, and the source can and will be identified.

The coach becomes the primary source in a story or notebook item about Smith needing an MRI on his injured knee. But information from a behind-the-scenes source, the manager, helped produce the story, even though he is not mentioned. This is also known as a news tip.

Momma Knows Best

In the wild season of 1994, Nebraska's football team lost quarterback Tommie Frazier early on to blood clots. Not long after, his backup Brook Berringer suffered a collapsed lung during the first half against Wyoming.

He recovered enough to finish the game but was taken to the hospital.

I followed up with a visit to the hospital after I filed my game stories.

Walking into the emergency room, I saw Frazier, there for blood testing. I asked what he saw. "I saw Brook come through here on a stretcher. I don't know what's going on."

Nobody was giving out information. I stepped outside to think about what to do. I asked a woman what she was doing there. She said her son was in the hospital for a collapsed lung. Mrs. Jan Berringer shared her fears and her hopes with me for the next hour.

—Ken Hambleton, Lincoln Journal Star

Sometimes, behind-the-scenes sources can tip reporters on feature stories. Perhaps, in a conversation with a source close to the program, you learn that an incoming freshman basketball player had a brother die of a heart ailment during a pickup basketball game. Or that the senior All-American gymnast broke her back when she was 12 and was told she would never walk again. Those are details that might not appear in a media guide, or be told unsolicited by the athlete. You learned of the information only with help from a behind-the-scenes source. Again, it is not likely that source will be quoted or mentioned in your story. That does not make the source any less important.

Not all information from behind-the-scenes sources will result in an immediate story. General conversations with these people may simply keep you abreast of what is going on, or what might happen. As a responsible beat writer, you are better informed, even though you might not find it necessary to report every minor detail.

Many beat reporters are responsible for blogging or answering online questions from fans and readers. That is when staying informed on many topics, with the help of behind-the-scenes sources, becomes particularly helpful.

Anonymous Sources

In the case of the injured cornerback, it's pretty simple. You are tipped about the injury, off the record, from your behind-the-scenes source. You gather information, on the record, from your primary source, the coach, and produce your story.

Easy, right?

Not all situations are so tidy. Usually, the bigger or more scandalous the story, the harder it is to prod your primary sources to talk on the record when broached with the subject.

What then?

That is when your behind-the-scenes sources might become even more essential under the cloak of anonymity. Anonymous sources are unnamed sources that become your primary sources, mostly in breaking sports stories.

Stories with anonymous sources should be avoided, if at all possible, and used only in extreme situations. Audiences are normally very hesitant to believe stories with unnamed sources, or do not want to believe the information presented.

Editors and producers are equally hesitant. Many news organizations require that more than one anonymous source be used in such stories, and those sources must be independent of each other.

The decision on whether to run a story with unnamed sources is not taken lightly. Writers and editors meet and discuss variables of the situation.

- What is the news value?
- Who are the sources?
- Can they be verified?
- How dependable are they?
- Is there absolutely nobody who will speak on record?

The risk of running stories with unnamed sources is understandable. What if the sources are wrong? Even the most trustworthy and knowledgeable people are capable of mistakes. Remember, a reporter's credibility is at stake and could be forever damaged.

Then again, what if you have a major scoop? Breaking a story about steroids use or an impending big coaching change might boost a young reporter's career and give a news organization some notoriety.

Even when stories with anonymous sources turn out to be correct, they still might not be popular in the public's eye.

In November 2003, the Lincoln Journal Star cited three anonymous sources saying Nebraska's head football coach, Frank Solich, would be asked to leave at season's end. The story was splashed across the front news page of the Sunday paper, a week before Nebraska's final regular season game.

> Athletic Director Steve Pederson wants Frank Solich out as Nebraska's head football coach, according to three sources close to the situation.

Pederson will try to persuade the sixth-year head coach to formally announce his retirement following NU's Nov. 28 game at Colorado, offering him a job in the Athletic Department and a lucrative buyout package, said the sources, who agreed to talk on the condition they not be identified.

"He wants Frank gone. He's made up his mind," said a longtime, out-of-state booster with close ties to the department.

The sources said Nebraska's first-year athletic director reached his decision eight days ago, after watching fans stream for the exits early in the fourth quarter of Nebraska's 38-9 loss to Kansas State, its worst home defeat in 45 years. The blowout, NU's second on national television this month, appeared to bore ABC sportscasters before the network cut to a more competitive game. It also came on the heels of Pederson's Nov. 6 news conference announcing a $40 million fund-raiser for new athletic facilities.

"Texas and Kansas State weren't competitive games. They were the straws that broke the camel's back," said a Texas booster also with strong ties to the program. After the K-State game, the source said, Pederson walked to the skyboxes to reassure boosters that "we're going to do something, don't get upset."

Pederson denies he's spoken to anyone about a plan to force Solich's

> retirement, and some of the program's biggest boosters deny they've ever heard that plan. Former Coach Tom Osborne said he hasn't spoken to Pederson about such a plan.
>
> "I am on the record as saying I have not discussed this matter publicly or privately," Pederson said at the Devaney Center Saturday night, where he was attending the NU men's basketball season opener. The athletic director declined to comment further. Solich also declined to comment. [2]

The backlash included the Journal Star building being egged. Hate e-mails. Critical letters to the editor.

Among the complaints and concerns were that unnamed sources should not be quoted, for they may have hidden agendas. The newspaper was irresponsible in its reporting and showing a lack of respect for Solich. The newspaper was engaging in sensationalism and simply trying to sell more papers. Using anonymous sources is unethical.

But the story turned out to be true. One week later, the large headline across the Sunday front page read: "Solich fired."

> Nebraska football coach Frank Solich was fired by Husker athletic director Steve Pederson Saturday night in a meeting at South Stadium.
>
> Pederson called Solich into the athletic director's office at 7:30 p.m. and told him of the decision, according to Solich's daughter, Cindy Dalton.
>
> "Pederson told Dad that he really hadn't made up his mind until five minutes before Dad walked through the door," Dalton said. "Dad said he

couldn't believe that Pederson had the nerve to say that to his face."

Solich, 59, was fired one day after leading Nebraska to a 31-22 win over rival Colorado in Boulder. That gave the No. 25-ranked Huskers a regular-season record of 9-3 overall and 5-3 in the league.

Last Sunday, the Journal Star, citing three anonymous sources, reported Pederson would try to persuade Solich to announce his retirement after the Colorado game. [3]

Of course, the opposite happens, too. Stories using anonymous sources may be incorrect. The reasons could be multiple—bad information, last-second changes or developments—but your audience does not care. Your story was inaccurate, and your credibility will be damaged. To what degree might depend on your experience as a beat reporter, or your affiliation.

In December 2007, ESPN had breaking news that Louisiana State University football coach Les Miles was leaving to become the head coach at his alma mater, Michigan. The sources were not cited.

Miles, however, never left LSU. In fact, he held a news conference hours before LSU played Tennessee in the Southeastern Conference Championship game to deny reports he was leaving LSU. He didn't field questions. LSU won the game, and the following month won the Bowl Championship Series national championship. West Virginia coach Rich Rodriguez was eventually hired at Michigan. ESPN's report had been wrong. [4]

Some fans and audience members perhaps brushed off the erroneous Miles report, and likely never stopped watching the popular sports network just because of that one piece of wrong information. Fans might not as easily excuse a young beat reporter at a smaller newspaper for making a similar error.

Sometimes, a potential source will contact a beat reporter with information that could lead to a breaking sports story, or perhaps a scoop. That is another example of a news tip. Reporters should make every effort to confirm and identify the source, who might anonymously call or e-mail. Regardless of whether reporters can identify the source, they must verify the information through one of their regular primary sources, secondary sources or, in some cases, behind-the-scenes sources—anyone who can verify whether the newfound information is true.

When Rodriguez left West Virginia for Michigan, coaching candidates began surfacing for his replacement. One such candidate, the Lawrence (Kan.) Journal-World reported on its Web site, was Kansas coach Mark Mangino. The newspaper reported that Mangino's agent had released a statement saying Mangino was in "serious negotiations" with West Virginia. [5]

The source was not anonymous. But it also was not real. A man claiming to be Mangino's agent had released a similar statement to several media outlets and also made phone calls to reporters, trying to convince them of this "news." The elaborate hoax tricked the Journal-World, which did not verify whether the man was actually Mangino's agent or check the origin of the released statement.

The newspaper ran a correction and apologized for misleading readers—an embarrassing, yet lesson-providing mistake that could have been prevented by making a couple of phone calls to verify the source, rather than rushing for a possible scoop. [6]

Citizen Journalists as Sources

Some sports reporters might deny they ever visit fan message boards—those Web sites where fans of whatever college or professional team can express their thoughts and opinions (24 hours a day, seven days a week), converse with other fans, or fans of the opponent, and do it all under the nice, tidy anonymity of a goofy screen name like "Bobcatbob327" or "Iluvthedawgs!"

Even high schools are not immune to the crazed fan who praises, criticizes or spreads false information under an anonymous name.

It is today's version of coffee shop talk or barber shop gab. It is the place where rumors begin, then grow, then somehow gain credibility with some fans, or perhaps innocent bystanders who know no better, simply because they are on a Web site. The problem, of course, is that nobody is held accountable, whether the information is accurate or simply a hoax. Hence many sports reporters will say they would rather deal with a migraine on deadline than associate themselves with message boards.

But those sports beat reporters who say they ignore message boards entirely are probably fibbing. And if they are really telling the truth, they should probably face reality and admit that, like it or not, anonymous message board posters—a form of citizen journalists—are part of their job.

Let's say Bobcatbob327, a regular on his favorite fan message board, posts something he has heard about his team—the Bobcats, of course—and the prized freshman quarterback who is deciding to transfer because he is unhappy with playing time. The rumor spreads quickly. You, the beat reporter, receive a phone call from your friend, who has read this hot item on a message board.

Can you afford to ignore this tip simply because it appeared somewhere anonymously? Probably not. Do you immediately write a story using the message board as a source? Definitely not. But as with any anonymous tip, you, the beat writer, begin digging, asking, checking and verifying.

Bobcatbob327 might be right, and even though some of his message board buddies will praise him for the scoop, other fans will wait until you, a responsible beat reporter who is held accountable, verifies and reports the news.

What if your late-night, last-minute digging is all for naught, and Bobcatbob327 turns out to be wrong? Ah, the headaches of being a beat reporter in the age of the Internet.

Shouldn't a good beat reporter get the information before it finds the fingertips of a rapidly typing anonymous message board regular? Ideally, yes. Getting scooped is never fun, especially when your competition is anonymous.

However, when that freshman quarterback makes a decision to transfer, then one minute later shares the news with his roommate—who, coincidentally, is Bobcatbob327—and the roommate instantly begins spreading the news via a message board, with or without the quarterback's knowledge or consent . . . well, the coach might not even know, so how would the beat reporter?

These are not necessarily everyday occurrences for beat reporters. But a thorough beat reporter will at least keep tabs on some message boards, whether for possible tips or just to gauge the pulse or feeling of the fan base. Some topical feature stories could result, too.

None of this, however, means beat reporters should depend solely on message boards or blogs for information.

Contacting Sources

So you have begun to cultivate some sources—primary, secondary and behind-the-scenes.

- How do you reach them?
- When do you talk to them?
- How often?

Much of that will likely depend on the reporter's beat, and the available access. A high school beat reporter overseeing an extensive coverage area might have dozens of coaches to contact on a weekly, biweekly or maybe monthly basis, depending on the number of schools and sports involved (and the number of reporters). It likely requires a couple of phone calls to the school—maybe to a secretary, maybe directly to the coach, maybe to an assistant. High schools, depending on their size and location, will vary on their policies (if any exist) for interviewing coaches. Coaches, in turn, might set ground rules for interviewing athletes.

A phone call to the coach's home or athlete's home might be more common on the high school level—again, depending on the school's size. The coach of a Dallas metro high school football team might keep an unlisted phone number. A reporter might find—and interview—the coach of a small-town Kansas girls' basketball team at the downtown bowling alley.

Contacting collegiate and professional coaches and athletes can be a little more involved. Beat reporters generally have a set standard time for interviewing coaches and players—before practice, after practice and after games, or during a specially arranged time.

Colleges and universities set guidelines, usually listed in their media guides, for non-beat reporters or visiting reporters to arrange interviews. The drill usually goes something like this:

- Contact the sports media relations department at least 24 hours in advance with the interview topic and request. Most reasonable requests, but not all, are granted.

Be aware: Coaches are known to suddenly, and without cause or reason, cut off media access to players. It might be for a day. It might be for a week. It's usually not a regular occurrence, but when it happens, beat reporters must quickly adjust.

Being a beat reporter can be a rewarding experience. In some rare instances, though, it can be a nightmare.

A Beat Reporter's Nightmare

Covering the NBA's New York Knicks used to be considered a prized beat. That changed considerably, as John Koblin wrote in the New York Observer.

Koblin described rocky relationships between reporters and coach Isaiah Thomas and detailed public relations personnel eavesdropping and noting reporters' interviews.

On Nov. 24, a little before noon, 16 bleary-eyed reporters shuffled into a tiny interview room a few feet away from the Madison Square Garden basketball floor. It had ivory cinder-block walls and dim fluorescent lighting that didn't recall a media workspace so much as it did a detention cell.

They were attempting to interview the Knicks' religiously evasive head coach, who informed them, after a contentious exchange, that they indeed had the right to criticize the team. Afterward, the reporters complained about what they viewed as a patronizing lecture. One called him a "psycho." It was, in all respects, a typically bitter start to a day in the life of a New York Knicks beat reporter.

Not that it was always like this. After all, covering the Knicks was once one of the most coveted beats in the country. "It's Madison Square Garden, it's New York City, it should be one of the top beats in New York," said Newsday beat reporter Alan Hahn.

Instead: "It's maddening. What it should be and what it is—it's a shame."

Frank Isola, the 12-year Knicks-beat veteran for the Daily News, said, "It used to be fun here. Now, there are some nights when you're trying to talk your boss out of sending you here and maybe lie and tell him you're sick or something."

"I'll admit," said Howard Beck, the New York Times Knicks reporter, "that the beat makes me miserable."

"Some of the things they practice here are completely against what you'd expect a normal team to do," said Newsday beat reporter Alan Hahn. "They come up with things all the time. There's zero access to players. They would rather you don't even write."

To their credit, the Knicks' press officials don't deny Garden chairman James Dolan's unusually hands-on role in managing their downtrodden core of reporters.

"I think it's fair to say that Jim [Dolan] is aware of, and a part of, the shaping of the media policy," said Barry Watkins, the senior vice president of communications for the Garden. "I believe our policies work for everybody across the board," Watkins said. "If some particular people don't like or don't feel good about it, I can't control what they think."

Garden policy has meant that before and after every game, there is a media relations official—a minder, really—with a BlackBerry in hand who furiously types away while listening to reporters' conversations. The notes that the official takes are then e-mailed up the chain of command.

When I spoke with Isola, the News reporter, on the Garden floor, he pointed to a media relations official watching us. "He's taking note that I'm talking to you," he said.

Before a game against the Jazz, six reporters were speaking with forward Malik Rose. Nick Brown, a public relations official for the Knicks, was recording the proceedings on his BlackBerry, in an e-mail prepared for the Knicks' head of P.R., Jonathan Supranowitz.

Sometimes Mr. Supranowitz does the monitoring himself.

"I take notes, absolutely," Supranowitz said. "A P.R. person must be present for every interview. That's a Garden policy."

(Even, apparently, for interviews with other P.R. people: Supranowitz typed into his BlackBerry while I was speaking with his boss, Mr. Watkins.)

Even if a reporter pitches a fluff piece on a player, it can't be done alone. "Once you give a one-on-one interview, they all want one-on-one interviews," said Mr. Watkins. "Instead of being available all at once, that player or coach has to do separate interviews every day, and that's just not something we can do. We want to make sure players and coaches and all executives can focus on the task on hand."

For working reporters at the Garden, typical meal options include a small plastic cup of coke and a sandwich with ham, processed turkey, Swiss cheese and hard white bread, all for $8. When they're at their floor seats watching the game, they're given small fuzzy-picture TVs to watch replays.

It's a strictly no-frills operation.

"I guess it doesn't matter what they do to us, the beat guys," Hahn said. "But you'd think they'd care a little more about presentation when other reporters come to town. They don't." [7]

© Reprinted with permission from the New York Observer.

Sometimes, individual athletes will make themselves off-limits from media. Some want to focus, some do not want the attention, and some just plain do not want to deal with reporters. The higher the level of sport, the more likely that is to happen.

Building Relationships with Sources

Relationships with Coaches

Beat writers should develop solid, working relationships with sources, particularly primary sources like coaches. You will be working with them on a regular basis, so establishing and maintaining a strong relationship is important.

How does that happen?

When you are new on a beat, make an appointment to introduce yourself. Tell the coach a little about yourself—where you are from, where you have worked. Talk about the working relationship you hope to establish. This does not need to be a long meeting; just long enough for the coach to know who you are and what you will be doing.

Chances are, the coach will lay some ground rules—when you may contact him, how you may contact him and what his policies are for interviewing athletes. Some coaches might give you a personal cell phone number, with instructions on when and when not to call it. Others might give a stern lecture if you ever A) find out his cell phone number, or B) have the audacity to call it.

The ideal relationship is one in which the coach and beat reporter have as many off-record conversations as they have on-record interviews. That's not very common. Many coaches, especially on the college and professional levels, are hesitant to share off-record information with reporters, for fear they will see it appear on-record anyway, or maybe find it on the blogs or message boards.

Other coaches may be more forthcoming and trustworthy. If a coach eventually does feel comfortable enough visiting off-record with you, then, by all means, do not burn him or her by leaking the information or, worse yet, reporting it. That is a good way to ruin a working relationship with a primary source.

Not every meeting with a coach needs to be an interview. Sometimes it's good to visit, off-record, about other subjects, other sports and other teams. It can be an icebreaker at the beginning of a working relationship and will allow you to see each other's nonworking side. Such conversations can help build a general rapport.

That, however, does not mean beat reporters should be "buddy-buddy" with coaches, or other primary sources, for that matter. In fact, getting too friendly is not a good idea. It could create an obvious conflict of interest.

What happens when a high school football coach—the same guy you've begun hanging out with at the local pub—gets into trouble with the law? Would you approach that story any differently than you would if the same thing happened to that other high school football coach across town . . . the one who has been sort of gruff to you in past interviews? Of course, it is easy to say you would be the consummate professional and be 100 percent impartial. Explain that to the fan who has seen you and the coach hanging out at the pub after games.

Public encounters with sources can and do happen. Just understand the fine line between what is appropriate and what is not, and the potential ramifications if you cross the line.

There will be—and should be—times when beat reporters and coaches will not agree. How a beat reporter deals with these instances depends on the situation and the coach. Most times, a short meeting clears the problem. With more severe issues, it might be necessary for third parties—sports editors, athletic directors—to become involved.

Whatever the problem, it is important to communicate and come to some sort of resolution. Having a beat reporter and a coach constantly at odds is not good for either party.

Relationships with Athletes

Relationships with athletes will differ depending on the level of sport you are covering. You are not likely to have as much day-to-day contact with high school athletes as you might with athletes on a college team. Part of that is because high school beat reporters are usually responsible for coverage of several high schools, making it more difficult to have regular personal contact with so many athletes.

Age also is a factor. High school athletes may not be as mature when it comes to interviews and dealing with reporters. Therefore, you are not as likely to develop a working relationship. The extent of your contact may be post-game or post-meet interviews.

There may be exceptions if you are covering a very high-profile high school athlete, or if your beat is college recruiting. Then your primary sources are 16-, 17- and 18-year-olds, and developing some sort of relationship, no matter the athlete's maturity level, is important.

For a college beat reporter, developing relationships with athletes becomes more important. Any one of them, at any time, may become a primary, secondary or behind-the-scenes source, and sometimes all three.

If you are new to the beat, introduce yourself to as many athletes as possible. Usually, reporters have access to athletes either before practices or after practices, depending on the team's or school's policies. If a team has open practice, attend as often as possible, and as long as possible. When you are visible to athletes, they will not only have an opportunity to get acquainted with you, but will also see and appreciate your interest and willingness to know what's going on. Yes, they will notice.

Be friendly and conversational in interviews. Strike up conversations or make idle small talk with players—the ones you normally interview, and even the ones you don't. Walk-ons enjoy some attention, too. Over time, players will know and, ideally, trust you. Those relationships might be helpful when you need some inside information.

Athletes are like coaches—some will relate with reporters better than others. That is expected. As with coaches, there will be times of friction with athletes. Especially on the college level, not everything you write will be glowing and positive. Nor should it be. Some athletes who are upset with a particular story, or the media in general, might begin declining interviews or brush off your attempts at small talk.

While it is usually not good to have an athlete avoid you, it's not as critical as having a coach cut you off. In most cases with disgruntled athletes, your best and probably only choice is to let them be. Most times, they will come around. If not, you have others to turn to for that sound bite or quotation.

And, as with coaches, never burn an athlete as a source, and don't get too friendly with the star point guard.

Upon Further Review

1. You've joined your school's newspaper staff and have been assigned to the women's basketball beat. It's August. What immediate steps would you take to prepare yourself for this beat? What else would be on your list of things to do before the season begins?
2. A trusted source informs you of possible NAIA or NCAA infractions on the men's soccer team. When you approach the coach with questions, he wants to know why you're asking and who told you the information. What do you do? How could you prepare yourself for this situation?

Notes

1. Brian Rosenthal, "Huskers beat Red Raiders at buzzer," Lincoln Journal Star, Feb. 7, 2007, p. 1D.

2. Matthew Hansen, "Solich could be forced out," Lincoln Journal Star, Nov. 23, 2003, p. 1A.

3. Steven M. Sipple, "Solich fired," Lincoln Journal Star, Nov. 30, 2003, p. 1A.

4. "Source: Miles will remain coach at LSU," ESPN.com news services, Dec. 1, 2007, http://sports.espn.go.com/ncf/news/story?id=3136391.

5. Ryan Wood, "Mangino in negotiations with West Virginia," LJWorld.com, Dec. 19, 2007.

6. Ryan Wood, "Mangino to West Virginia rumors a hoax," LJWorld.com, Dec. 19, 2007, www2.ljworld.com/news/2007/dec/19/mangino_negotiations_west_virginia/ (updated version).

7. John Koblin, "Life in Knicks Hell," New York Observer, Nov. 27, 2007.

CHAPTER 4

Asking the Questions

THE BIG GAME is finished. Confetti is flying everywhere. Bands are playing. Fans are screaming. Players are dousing the coach with whatever is in the big water jug on the sideline. Pure celebratory mayhem.

Meanwhile, on a makeshift platform stands one of the winning team's star players. He is wearing a championship hat and hoisting the championship trophy. A least a dozen microphones and tape recorders are dangling in front of his smiling mouth. Television cameras are zooming. The audience is waiting to hear from this happy champion.

Then, it happens. On cue, one of the dozen reporters will begin the brief post-game interview session with the time-honored question:

"How does it feel?"

You have heard that question before, right? Has a player ever responded by saying, "It feels horrible," or "You know, George, it really doesn't feel as exciting as I thought it would. I was expecting more"?

Of course not.

Is it irresponsible or unethical for sports reporters to ask an athlete how he feels after the championship game? Well, no. But are there more insightful questions that might elicit better, more telling, more colorful—and less predictable—answers for the audience?

Absolutely.

Getting good quotations is the result of good interviewing, one of the finer skills—and one of the most important ones—for good, thorough sports reporters.

Interviewing Skills

Interviews are essential to any sports story. Descriptive game stories need reaction from the coaches and participants. But interviews do more than provide emotion from sources. Sports reporters must remember to ask solid questions to obtain necessary, accurate information for all types of stories. A story on fund-raising for a stadium expansion project will require some basic information questions. How much money has been raised? Who has donated? What timelines are involved?

An investigative piece on possible NCAA recruiting violations will require some tough questions for the athletic director and coach, and maybe the recruited athletes. Those interviews will likely provide both reaction and information. Feature stories need several interviews for background information and for feeling.

Preparing for Interviews

There are several rudimentary principles for preparing for interviews. These include the following basics.

- When possible, arrange interviews at least 24 hours in advance.
- Inform the interviewee of your general topic.
- Write down at least five questions for personal reference.
- Research, research, research.
- Use a tape recorder, but take notes, too.

The No. 1 rule for sports reporters before conducting interviews?

Do your homework.

By being informed, you are saving time for not only yourself, but also your interview subject. If you have only 15 minutes to spend alone with the newly hired junior college baseball coach, do not spend the first 10 minutes asking basic background information that, in most cases, you could have researched before the interview.

Instead of asking "Where was your previous job?" you could ask, "When you coached at Northeastern, how did you manage the rotation two seasons ago when you lost your star pitcher? What did you learn from that experience?"

Not only are you asking a more insightful question, you are showing the coach you care enough and are responsible enough to have done some background work.

Most interviews are arranged in advance—ideally, at least 24 hours. (See chapter 3 on how to contact sources for interviews.) The people being interviewed will often ask about the topic, mostly to give them an opportunity to prepare, although in some cases the subject matter might determine whether that coach or athlete grants the interview request. A star athlete who has experienced personal struggles might be happy to talk about her quest for a school record but not be willing to share thoughts on a close friend's death or relative's illness. If your story is about athletes dealing with off-court issues while in pursuit of greatness, your interview request might be denied. But better to know a day ahead of time rather than wait until a specially arranged interview that produces nothing.

By arranging an interview ahead of time, sports reporters also give themselves time to prepare intelligent, insightful questions. Write out at least five specific questions. Take them to the interview for personal reference.

Also take your tape recorder, and ask your sources for permission to use it. It is common courtesy, and interviewees almost always oblige. They want you to get their words correct as much as you do. But also use a notepad. Batteries in recorders can die easily, or a recorder can be lost or broken not long after an interview. There is no right or wrong way of taking notes. Some reporters use shorthand. Others scribble. Some write down key words. As long as you are able to decipher what you have written, that is all that matters.

More experienced sports reporters might say they are able to think of questions in their sleep, especially for general, day-to-day interviews on a beat. True, not all experienced beat writers will have a list of questions on their notepads when doing a post-practice interview with a player. But there will probably be an occasional exclusive, sit-down interview with a hard-to-reach athletic director, or maybe a famous athlete visiting the area. Writing specific, prepared questions becomes more important in those situations. If legendary basketball coach Bobby Knight is visiting your campus tomorrow and says he will spend 10 minutes visiting with the school newspaper, how would you treat the interview?

Not all interviews will allow for heavy research time. Take post-game interviews, for example. Questions will be more impromptu. Still, it is important to be as well-informed as possible. That means paying attention to the event. When a middle-distance runner has just set a school and state record for the fastest 800-meter time—1:51.59—at a high school track meet, a question such as "Is that a personal best time for you?" is kind of embarrassing, especially when the record has been announced repeatedly over the public address system.

Impromptu questions also occur with breaking news stories. When a beat reporter learns a coach has suddenly resigned, he will immediately try contacting the coach for an interview, which won't leave much time for writing out questions. Reporters' instincts, however, should kick in, with the general who-what-where-when-why-how-questions.

Learning the Hard Way

Interview access for college athletes will vary depending on the school's policies. Some colleges and universities try to protect their student athletes from too much media hounding and allow for interviews maybe only once or twice a week. Other schools, particularly those which may want more media attention, will be more open.

David Plati, associate athletic director/sports information at the University of Colorado, takes another factor into account when considering the positive aspects of student-athletes doing interviews—the educational experience: "I know when an athlete does an interview, he's going to have a tougher interview later in life than somebody asking about his football accomplishments."

Coaches are experienced enough to know what to say and what not to say to the media. But even though many athletes are given a crash course on how to handle interviews, some 18-year-olds can be a little loose and outspoken in front of reporters.

That's when some media relations staffs coil into damage control mode. Plati, though, views those experiences as important lessons for college students:

"People get burned in interviews all the time. Whose fault is it most of the time? Most of the time, it's the interviewee. He said something he shouldn't have said. Don't pin it on the reporter who got the answer you shouldn't have said and ran with it. That's their job.

"You have to live through that experience of being burned, and you live through that by your mistakes."

Most often, those situations involve calling out an opponent and providing the proverbial bulletin-board material. "That's survivable, I think, in the big picture of things," Plati said.

Asking the Right Questions

Asking athletes how they feel after the big win is not on top of the list of quality questions. So what is a good question?

Any question that elicits a colorful response, an interesting anecdote or useful information is considered good. Of course, it's hard telling which exact question will produce those desired results. From a journalistic standpoint, a certain question might be considered bad, corny or poorly-worded, but if it somehow results in that perfect quotation or a lively sound bite, that question wasn't so bad after all, was it? Truth be told, even the "How do you feel?" question, as cliché and predictable as it seems, just might, once in a great while, produce something fun and surprising.

That doesn't mean good sports reporters should expect bad questions to generate great results. Most times, they don't.

As veteran freelance sports journalist Mike Babcock said, "There are no bad interviews, only bad questions." Here's a guideline for asking good questions:

Ask a Question

Sounds simple enough, right? Then do it. Do not make a statement.

Statements by sports reporters will most likely be filled with opinion. Reporters are not there to tell a coach what went wrong in a game. Also, statements are not questions, and therefore do not require a response.

> "Coach, your running game really stalled in the fourth quarter, and your offensive line looked tired."

How is a coach to respond? Sometimes, he might elaborate and bail out a reporter who did not really ask a question. Other times, a curmudgeon-like coach might respond with "That's a statement, ask me a question. Next question."

OK, so let's rephrase.

"Coach, why did your running game produce only four yards in the fourth quarter?"

The coach still might be a little grumpy, but at least he is forced to answer a question and not give you a blank stare.

Ask Open-Ended questions

Ask a yes-no question, and you might get a yes-no answer. That is OK if you are simply after pertinent information. "Did you fracture your leg?" and "Will your starting forward be eligible?" are questions that can be answered with one word but still provide needed information.

The situation is different when you are trying to generate longer responses for a useful quotation.

"Did your offense have a difficult time adjusting to their zone defense in the second half?"

Remember the curmudgeon coach? He is not in very good humor, so he likely will answer the question as briefly as possible: "Yes. Next question."

That didn't get you very far, did it?

A better approach would be to use an open-ended question, or a question that asks an opinion or interpretation from the source. The source is open to respond in any way.

"What difficulties did their zone defense give your offense in the second half?" or "How did their zone defense affect your offense in the second half?"

Closed-ended questions limit the source's response. It's like a question with a multiple-choice answer.

"Do you prefer coaches with loose coaching styles, or coaches who are strict?"

How is the player going to respond? Probably by saying "I like a strict coach," or "Give me a coach with a loose approach."

Again, the better approach is to change the question so it's open-ended.

"What coaching style do you prefer?"

This allows the athlete to respond in many ways, and might generate a better response.

Don't Ask Leading Questions

Whereas open-ended questions allow for sources to respond freely with their opinions, leading questions take the opposite approach. Leading questions are questions that try to lead the source to respond in a certain way. Much like statements, leading questions can be dripping with opinion. Sometimes, they are obvious clues a sports reporter has already drawn his own conclusion on a subject and is merely trying to gather quotations that will support his angle.

"Joe, you're probably happy to see a change in coaching staffs, aren't you?"

This question is leading Joe into responding about what the reporter perceives as positive aspects of a coaching change. That seems to be the reporter's angle. That doesn't mean Joe necessarily sees it the same way. Sure, Joe is free to dispute the question, but he might go along with the line of questioning and give the response the reporter wants.

Instead, the sports reporter should make the question open-ended.

"Joe, what are your thoughts on the change in coaching staffs?"

Now Joe is able to respond freely.

Ask Follow-Up Questions

Remember the five questions you wrote out in advance? Those do not have to be—and probably should not be—the only questions you ask. They are merely something to get the interview started.

Do not be afraid to stray from the path after even one question. That first question might elicit a response that requires another question, or a follow-up question. Follow-up questions might be needed to clarify a response. They might help encourage the source to expand on a thought or anecdote that you find interesting or helpful. They might seek further information.

> "You just said your foot has been bothering you. What's wrong with it? When did you hurt it?"

Sometimes a simple follow-up question can change the course of an entire interview, and perhaps your story. A follow-up question could also lead to a sidebar, separate story or an item in a notebook.

Pay Attention and Observe

Sometimes, sports reporters become so focused on asking the right questions and searching for good answers that they can miss the obvious.

Interviewers should always pay attention to nonverbal signs. A roll of the eyes might indicate disgust. A smile might be a sign of sarcasm. A player answering questions while staring at the ground throughout the post-game interview might be distraught. These are all signs of emotion that sports reporters could describe in order to give life to a story.

Observations should not be limited to the interviewee. Look around. The coach's desk might be cluttered with game film and scouting reports. That might help describe the coach's frenzied week in preparing for the big game. Fans might be gathering outside the locker room, waiting for the player you are interviewing to finish and sign autographs. That observation could come in handy in a feature story about that player's popularity.

Interview Settings

The types of questions sports reporters ask might depend on the interview setting. If it is just you and your source, you will probably ask questions in a more conversational setting. A large group of reporters might limit your number of follow-up questions. News conferences usually produce more general questions.

One-on-One Interviewing

Just you and your source. It is the best possible setup for a sports reporter, but one that requires the most work and research.

You are the only one asking questions, so you better have a good plan. The advantage is the exclusivity—no other reporters are present, so there is always a chance for a breaking news item or scoop, even if the interview was meant for a simple feature.

Small Group and Post-Game Interviews

Have you ever seen a television interview in which an athlete is standing in front of his locker with a bunch of tape recorders and microphones in his face? Post-game interviews can truly be a mad scramble, and a hectic time for sports reporters on deadline.

For newcomers, some post-game interviews involving a small to medium group of reporters can be intimidating. Squeeze your way into the huddle with your tape recorder or camera. Be assertive, but polite. Speak up with your questions. Do not dominate with too many questions, but do not let other reporters ask all the questions, either.

In some instances, you might be hopping from player to player, from huddle to huddle, trying to gather information from as many sources as possible. The experience can be stressful and, at the same time, exhilarating.

Role Reversal

Sports reporters will often find themselves on the other side of interviews.

Sports talk radio shows love to pick the brains of the local beat reporter the week before the big football game to get any inside information, insight and predictions. Sports reporters might ask each other questions about a hotshot recruit on a weekly vid-cast or podcast on a newspaper's Web site. Fans might even have an opportunity to ask questions of sports reporters on a live Internet chat, or through sports blogs.

Sometimes it's good practice to be on the receiving end of questions. And it's kind of fun to be the one saying "No comment."

Other times, a post-game interview might be a quiet one-on-one interview. Or, what begins as a one-on-one interview might suddenly grow into a group. Be prepared for either scenario.

Most colleges and high schools will conduct post-game interviews in a designated room or area and not allow reporters in locker rooms. (The policy differs in professional sports, where most locker rooms are open to reporters.) Reporters will corner athletes in a hallway by the locker room, outside the team bus or even underneath the stadium bleachers. The setup is not always ideal, especially when the marching band goes by or fans from the opposing team stop to yell obscenities. Be ready to deal with distractions.

News Conferences

The most formal of interviews, news conferences are designed for sources to share information simultaneously with a group of reporters. News conferences are more structured and organized than small group interviews.

The source, not the sports reporter, is in control of a news conference. Most news conferences begin with opening statements from the coach or athlete. Sports reporters will follow with questions. News conferences can last anywhere from five minutes to half an hour or longer, depending on the subject or circumstances. On some occasions, the source will simply appear long enough to make an announcement and not take any questions. The source, or a person representing the source, such as a sports information director, will usually decide when the news conference ends.

Some tips for dealing with news conferences:

- Arrive ahead of time. News conferences might start early, and it's awkward and a little embarrassing if you are scurrying around a room, finding a place for your tape recorder and searching for a place to sit when the coach is already talking. What's worse, you might miss the biggest news.

- Pay attention. Sometimes those weekly media luncheons with the football coach might be a little boring and make you a little sleepy (especially after eating the free pizza), but stay alert. Never ask a question that has already been asked.

- Watch what you ask. Remember, the answers to your questions are fair game for all members of the media. If you are working on an exclusive story, do not ask questions that might tip other reporters. If possible, save the in-depth questions for a one-on-one interview.

- Be considerate. Do not dominate the news conference by asking a string of questions. Keep the follow-up questions to a minimum. There might be more time to spend with the subject after a news conference, but don't depend on it.

Many times, post-game news conferences are broadcast live via closed-circuit television, with a feed going directly to the press box. This allows sports reporters on a very tight deadline to listen to the coach and players and gather a couple of quick quotations before filing the story. The drawback is those reporters are merely listening to questions and answers and not participating. But when a trip to the interview room and back might take too much time on deadline, listening to and watching a telecast is a good option.

Electronic Interviewing

Although not the preferred means to interview a coach or athlete, sometimes the only option for interviews is via electronic means. Telephone interviews are the most acceptable form of electronic interviews. Sports reporters can ask questions and generate responses but are not able to see nonverbal signs, which is a drawback.

News teleconferences are also common. They operate on the same principles as a news conference, only via telephone. Reporters dial a number, and when prompted, a moderator opens one reporter's line for a question. All reporters who are dialed into the conference can hear the questions and responses. Remember: Keep your speaker phone on mute when you are not asking a question.

Interviews via e-mail should be used as only a last resort. When a source has time to read through a written list of questions, the answers sound scripted and wordy. Also, follow-up questions might not be possible, and there are no nonverbal signs. Of bigger concern is the interview's authenticity. It is hard to be 100 percent certain your source is the one who provided the answers to your questions, and not an agent, coach, friend or sports information director. Inform your readers when you have conducted an interview via e-mail.

The Internet can also be a helpful tool with interviews. Those post-game news conferences with a live feed to the press box are many times broadcast live on the Internet. (They are also often archived.) A beat reporter covering a university's athletic department might cover the hiring of a former athletic director at a new university. When that new school is 2,000 miles away, and the press conference to announce the hiring is scheduled to begin in 90 minutes . . . well, even a company jet might not save the day. But watching the news conference via the Internet is an option. The reporter will not be able to ask questions but will at least be able to listen, gather quotations and write a story on what happened.

Sports reporters who maintain social networking sites, such as Facebook and MySpace, could also relay questions, or at least make contact with a hard-to-reach source, via those Web sites.

Using Quotations

Quotations add flavor, detail, emotion and information. Without them, sports stories would be nothing but a play-by-play account of a game. Features would be a long narrative. Breaking sports stories would be a string of facts and numbers.

Fans want reaction and insight. What did the coach think of his decision to go for the two-point conversion in overtime? Why did the wrestler suddenly change his strategy? How did the volleyball players react when learning their victory qualified their team for the state tournament?

Quotations allow sports reporters to tell a story through sources while remaining neutral. You are quoting sources with opinions or general thoughts that you, as a reporter, cannot express.

Types of Quotations

Direct Quotations

A direct quotation is an exact, word-for-word account of what a person says. It is enclosed in quotation marks and is attributed to the source. Direct quotations should be used to convey a person's emotion or opinion. The more colorful, the better.

> "The pitcher has got only a ball. I've got a bat. So the percentage of weapons is in my favor and I let the fellow with the ball do the fretting."
>
> —Hank Aaron

> "You can't sit on a lead and run a few plays into the line and just kill the clock. You've got to throw the ball over the goddamn plate and give the other man his chance. That's why baseball is the greatest game of them all."
>
> —Earl Weaver

> "If the NBA were on channel 5 and a bunch of frogs making love were on channel 4, I'd watch the frogs, even if they were coming in fuzzy."
>
> —Bobby Knight[1]

Of course, not every quotation will be as lively or entertaining as what comes out of Bobby Knight's mouth. Still, try to use quotations that reveal something interesting. Do not quote clichés. Sports reporters are discouraged from writing clichés, so why quote a coach or player using one?

> "We've got to take it one game at a time."
>
> "He really brings a lot to the table."
>
> "This was a total team effort."

Sigh. These quotations add nothing to your story and might bore your reader to sleep.

Quotations that include numbers and statistics are also unnecessary.

> "Clay scored 18 points, but 10 of those came in the fourth quarter and gave us a lift. He made all six of his free throws."

If you are covering that game, you should know how many points Clay scored, and when he scored them. Having the coach repeat that information to you in a post-game interview does not benefit you or add any spice to your story.

Numbers can appear in quotations, though. Sometimes a source talking about statistics can be colorful and insightful, like this one from Mickey Mantle:

> "During my 18 years I came to bat almost 10,000 times. I struck out about 1,700 times and walked maybe 1,800 times. You figure a ballplayer will average about 500 at bats a season. That means I played seven years without ever hitting the ball."[2]

Paraphrases

A paraphrase summarizes what a person says without changing meaning. Because it is not word-for-word, a paraphrase does not have quotation marks. Reporters might paraphrase to shorten a long quotation that can be summed up in a few words or to better explain a quotation that may otherwise be confusing.

Take the following direct quotation from Duke basketball coach Mike Krzyzewski.

> "I think the experience of having been in those situations in the conference, really in over half of our games, we have been losing or just about to lose. It is tough to simulate those types of situations and you have to experience them. So far this year we have experienced them in a positive way and again you're experiencing them today. Our team turned it into something positive, which is good toughness on our part."[3]

The general thought this coach is trying to convey can easily be relayed in a paraphrase.

Krzyzewski said his team has benefited from playing in many close conference games and has become tougher.

There. You have used 17 words to explain what Krzyzewski took 76 words to say. Now you have more room to detail the game-winning basket or squeeze in an interesting note.

Attribution

When reporters attribute, they are crediting a source for information. Direct quotations and paraphrases are always attributed. The preferred verb of attribution is "said."

> "If a tie is like kissing your sister, losing is like kissing your grandmother with her teeth out," George Brett said. [4]

Why stick with "said"? It is clear, concise and neutral. It does not imply. It does not offer opinion. It cannot be misinterpreted. It is safe and all-inclusive.

Inserting other attributive verbs in place of "said" can change meaning or imply a source's emotion that might not be accurate.

> "This is the worst game I've ever seen this team play," he *snapped*.

"We have got to be more aggressive in the second half," she *insisted*.

"Bygones are bygones. The hard part is over," he *exclaimed*.

"Exclaimed" insinuates he shouted. "Insisted" sounds like she was pretty tense. And did he really "snap?" Your definition of "snapping" might differ greatly from your readers' or your source's definition.

Some sports writers may feel compelled to substitute and switch attributive verbs so the story does not become boring. Don't. It is OK to use "said" repeatedly. Readers do not pay close attention to attributive verbs anyway. They simply want to know who is speaking.

Here are some commonly overused or misused verbs of attribution that writers should avoid:

asserted	remarked	declared
cautioned	explained	opined
quipped	charged	claimed
recalled	maintained	shouted
warned	noted	added
went on to say	continued	pointed out

Style, Placing Attribution

Here are some style rules for using direct quotations:

Use a comma inside quotation marks before the attribution, and use a period at the end of the attribution.

Correct:
> "Coach always says if you set a good screen, you're more than likely going to be the one getting the wide open shot," Perry said.

Incorrect: "Coach always says if you set a good
                    screen, you're more than likely going
                    to be the one getting the wide open
                    shot." Perry said.

Incorrect: "Coach always says if you set a good
                    screen, you're more than likely going
                    to be the one getting the wide open
                    shot", Perry said.

Use subject-verb order with attribution.

Correct: "That last play was just luck," Smith
                    said.

Incorrect: "That last play was just luck," said
                    Smith.

Use only one form of punctuation at the end of a direct quotation.

Correct: "How many times is this going to
                    keep happening to us?" he said.

Incorrect: "How many times is this going to
                    keep happening to us?," he said.

Use a period after the attribution, and conclude the quotation with a period inside the quotation marks. (For direct quotations that are

longer than once sentence, it is best to insert the attribution after the first sentence, then continue with the quotation.)

Correct: "Football is what I've got," Sam
              Keller said. "Football is what I love
              and what I'm good at. What you have
              and you love, you need to embrace.
              You realize what you love to do, and
              you get a fresh start at it."

Incorrect: "Football is what I've got," Sam
              Keller said, "Football is what I love
              and what I'm good at. What you have
              and you love, you need to embrace.
              You realize what you love to do, and
              you get a fresh start at it."

Incorrect: "Football is what I've got. Football is
              what I love and what I'm good at.
              What you have and you love, you
              need to embrace. You realize what you
              love to do, and you get a fresh start at
              it," Sam Keller said.

Use single quotation marks to separate quotations within quotations.

Correct: "He came to me and said, 'I don't
              know,' and he said he didn't feel good.
              So, I said he wasn't going to play."

Incorrect: "He came to me and said, "I don't
                  know," and he said he didn't feel
                  good. So, I said he wasn't going to
                  play."

Sometimes, direct quotations may be several sentences. Quotations may be divided into paragraphs, although if your quotation lasts longer than two paragraphs, it had better be a good one.

When a quotation covers more than one paragraph, do not use quotation marks at the end of paragraphs, until the quotation is complete.

Correct: "I thought it was an extremely
                  hard-fought game," Roy Williams
                  said. "Both teams really wanted to
                  play well, but their team played bet-
                  ter than we did. They were the most
                  disciplined team on the game
                  tonight.
                       "The team that did the most of
                  the little things won the game
                  tonight. Whether it is shooting the
                  ball in the hole or making free
                  throws in the second half or getting a
                  hand up on the outside shot—the
                  team that won the game was the
                  most disciplined.
                       "They did the best job doing what
                  their coaching staff wanted them to
                  do." [5]

Quotations should always be paragraphs to themselves.

Cleaning Quotes

Not every "uhm," or "yeah," or "ya know" needs to be included in a direct quotation. Sports reporters are allowed to omit the stumbles, so long as the meaning is not changed.

The Associated Press style book says "never alter quotations, even to correct minor grammatical errors or word usage."

> "We was happy to win the game," he said.

That might sound like fingernails on a chalkboard to some, but if that is what the player said, that is what should be written, according to the Associated Press. However, local style may override this rule.

Sometimes, direct quotations may include profane words. In such instances, writers should use the first initial of the profane word, followed by dashes.

> "Their season went to the s———. That one kid, he hasn't done s——. He's back, but he got his a— kicked," Sam Jones said.

Writers might want to shorten a direct quotation rather than use a paraphrase. It is OK to take out repetitive, unnecessary words—as long as the quotation's thought or meaning stays the same—by using an ellipsis to indicate omitted words.

Perhaps a writer wanted to directly quote Krzyzewski, but not all 76 words.

> "I think the experience of having been in those situations in the conference. . . . It is tough to simulate those types of situations, and you have to experience them," Krzyzewski said. "So far this year we have experienced them in a positive way, and again you're experiencing them today."[6]

Lost in Translation

I once had an assignment to interview a delegation of Chinese youth track officials who were coming to Lincoln to watch a Junior Olympic meet.

I called the university and asked if they had any interpreters. They said, "Sure," and the guy would meet me when I interviewed the Chinese.

He got there early and I thanked him for coming. He said he was happy to help me meet the Japanese team. I corrected him and said I was meeting with Chinese officials.

He said he didn't speak Chinese. The Chinese didn't speak English. He said he'd try.

I asked a question, such as, "How many youth track programs do you have in China?" He would muddle through something. My answer coming back was something along the lines of "Chinese have a great history of track and field."

I'd ask the next question, something along the lines of, "What is the experience of your delegation in running track programs for youth in China?"

The answer was "23,756."

Another question like, "Do you like the weather here?"

The answer, "Our youth programs are growing by leaps and bounds."

—Ken Hambleton, Lincoln Journal Star

Quote Sheets

Transcribing your interview—listening to your recorder and typing out every word your source spoke—can take time, sometimes twice as long as the interview itself. That is time well spent.

Having your own quote sheet, or a written transcription of direct quotations from a source or sources, is helpful when you are trying to determine which are the best direct quotations, which quotations you would rather paraphrase, and which quotes probably will not make your story.

While writers create their own quote sheets for personal use, sports media relations staffs also often release quote sheets after news conferences and events. These quote sheets can be helpful if you don't have time to transcribe a 45-minute news conference, are trying to search for that perfect quote on deadline or perhaps weren't able to attend the event. Usually, the questions (or question topics) and answers will both be on these quote sheets.

Quote sheets from other outlets are helpful and permissible but should be used with some caution. The person transcribing the interview might not be as thorough as you when it comes to a word-for-word account. Words may have been inadvertently omitted or changed, and not all quote sheets are a complete account of what was said. Be aware of spelling, and realize that quote sheets may not adhere to AP style and may contain run-on sentences.

Here is an example of a quote sheet from the post-game news conference of a Duke–North Carolina basketball game. Quotes are from both head coaches and one player. Notice how a roster would be helpful when coaches are on a first-name basis with their players.

What parts of this quote sheet contain good direct quotations? What parts may be better paraphrased?

Duke–North Carolina quote sheet

Duke Head Coach Mike Krzyzewski

Opening statement:

> Well it was a heck of a game. They are strong and Hansbrough is such a great player. I'm proud of our guys; we had such balanced scoring. A number of our guys made big plays and it is hard to single out just one guy. This is a game where there are so many points where the game can go the other way. It just seemed like when it was going to turn one of our guys made a play. I thought it was Lance's best game. He really played well and got into double figures. Kyle, obviously, got a double-double as well. I

thought DeMarcus' experience, in foul trouble the whole game and played most of the second half with four. To stay in the game we really needed his experience at the end. Obviously we are ecstatic about the win and we know we beat a heck of a team. We have to get rested and get ready for Saturday, that's the thing about the ACC you cannot celebrate too much.

On North Carolina cutting the lead to one point a couple of times:

I think the experience of having been in those situations in the conference, really in over half of our games we have been losing or just about to lose. It is tough to simulate those types of situations and you have to experience them. So far this year we have experienced them in a positive way and again you're experiencing them today. Our team turned it into something positive, which is good toughness on our part.

On how special this team can be:

Well they are pretty special right now for me. I mean they are 20-1 and 8-0. We know who we are; we are a very unconventional team. We are not a very strong physical team, but I think we are strong emotion wise and toughness; we are really a together group. You just have to hope that you don't get killed at some point in the game by somebody's strength. It is a tough team to impose your will, like a counter puncher you might win a round dancing around a little bit and then the threes we hit in the first half. You just find different ways to win and because we have versatile players they are able to do that thus far.

On perimeter defense:

Our perimeter defense was good. They missed some open looks and so did we, it was a real hard fought game. That is why I think the free throw shooting by both of the teams is a little bit below of what we both normally do, a lot of times you change your routine. Guys were backing off the line and stuff like that. That one exchange from about eleven minutes to nine, if one team scored on their drives or our threes, but neither one did. I thought that tired both teams out a little bit.

Greg Paulus (player)

On meeting challenges and this one being tough:

It was definitely up there. These guys are so good, and this place was rocking. It seemed like every time we tried to get a run, they just kept making a run at us and wouldn't go away, and they deserve a lot of credit for that.

On hitting three-pointers:

We definitely drove the ball, got a couple good penetrating kicks. I'm not sure what we shot, but it seemed like whenever we needed a three, we had guys that took big shots and knocked them down.

On getting to the basket:

We've got great wing players that can really put the ball on the floor and create the space for guys like myself, and just taking our shots when we get them.

On the win:

It's a good win for us. It's a big ACC win, and it's an even bigger win doing it on someone else's home court. It's a good sign for us, and hopefully we can keep it going. We don't want to stop there, we want to keep building on it and keep getting better.

North Carolina Head Coach Roy Williams

Opening statement:

I thought it was an extremely hard fought game. Both teams really wanted to play well, but their team played better than we did. They were the most disciplined team in the game tonight. The team that did the most of the little things won the game tonight. Whether it is shooting the ball in the hole or making free throws in the second half or getting a hand up on the outside shot—the team that won the game was the most disciplined. They did the best job doing what their coaching staff wanted them to do. I need to find someway, somehow, to get my team to the point where we do the little things that make the difference between winning or losing a basketball game. I do believe that Duke has all the ingredients. They have played sensational basketball all season. I think I read one of their comments at the end of the season was over last year with the four straight losses that they had great motivation all summer and the preseason. They have great chemistry. I am very impressed with their team. They were the most disciplined team. The team had the best coaching and they were the team that won the game. The good thing is, I told the team yesterday that if we won the game today that they weren't going to give us a trophy and stop the season and if they won the game they weren't going to give them the trophy and stop the season. We've got a lot of games left to play but we have got to play a lot better and find the little things—down the stretch, we get it to five and they miss two shots in a row and they get the rebound because we don't box out. One time we had two guys standing there and I think it was Gerald standing there, and he just laid it up. I have to do a better job getting my team to make plays and make all the little things happen for us.

On the decision on whether Ty Lawson would play:

It was an easy decision. I told him if we had doubts about it I wasn't going to play him. I asked and he said, "I don't know" and the decision was that I wasn't going to play him. So it was pretty easy. He came to me and said, "I don't know" and he said he didn't feel good. So, I said he wasn't going to play.

On Duke's shooting:

They got any shot they wanted. I don't know very many times tonight our defense dictated what shot they got. They had better spacing; they were more patient. I asked, and they thought I was kidding—it shows how poor of a coach I am, at one time out I told them I wanted a dunk or a 35 second shot clock violation. We didn't get either one of them.[7]

© Reprinted with permission from Duke University sports information

Upon Further Review

1. The university athletic director has called a news conference to begin in two hours. You only know the topic is "a change in direction for the baseball program." What steps should you take to prepare for this news conference?
2. Your editor returns your feature story on the freshman All-American gymnast and says it's filled with too many quotations. How do you determine which quotations to keep, and which to omit? What are other options?

Notes

1. These three quotes were found on the Web site quotemountain.com, www.quotemountain.com/quotes/sports_quotes/baseball_quotes/.

2. Quote found on the Web site quotemountain.com, www.quotemountain.com/quotes/sports_quotes/baseball_quotes/.

3. Quote from post-game news conference, Feb. 6, 2008, courtesy Duke University sports information.

4. Quote found on the Web site brainyquote.com, www.brainyquote.com/quotes/quotes/g/q131189.html.

5. Quote from post-game news conference, Feb. 6, 2008, courtesy Duke University sports information.

6. Quote from post-game news conference, Feb. 6, 2008, courtesy Duke University sports information.

7. Quote sheet from Duke–North Carolina men's basketball game post-game news conference, Feb. 6, 2008, courtesy Duke University sports information.

CHAPTER 5

Working with the Media

THE DAYS OF pounding out a story on a manual typewriter in a dimly lit newsroom, ripping the paper off the carriage and running it past the copy editor on the way to the typesetter so Sunday afternoon's ball game story could make it into the Monday afternoon edition are long gone. Even the early days of computer-generated stories seem ancient history in light of today's instantaneous delivery of game coverage 24/7 in broadcast, Web streaming and blogs.

Today's sports reporter is one of a team of information gatherers and suppliers working to provide the stories readers crave every day. Theirs is a symbiotic relationship: reporters depend on sports information directors and media relations personnel for access to much of the information they need to produce game and season stories, and sports information directors and media relations departments depend on reporters to get news about their teams, players and programs into the media.

It's a matter of perspective. As journalists, reporters are obligated to produce fair, unbiased stories for their audiences. Media relations personnel, meanwhile, are obligated to their employers to present them in as positive a way possible in any information released to the media. Each needs the other, yet each regards the other with a healthy attitude of skepticism. Both work diligently to build trust and strengthen working relationships that make it possible to meet each other's needs.

Sports Information Directors

Sports information directors and their staffs serve as liaisons between a school's athletic department and the media and public. General duties include assisting media with coverage by providing statistics, notes and information on a school's teams, arranging interviews with athletes and coaches and organizing game-day operations.

Some colleges and universities prefer the title of sports media relations director. The job description is the same, although the specific responsibilities of sports information directors, also known as SIDs, may vary. "You might get 20 different answers if you asked 20 different SIDs," said David Plati, associate athletic director/ sports information at the University of Colorado.

Sports information staffs at larger schools, like Colorado, generally include five or six full-time staff members, one or two graduate assistants and a host of undergraduate student assistants. Each person is assigned one or two sports, sometimes more.

Plati's office is responsible for media guides, weekly and daily news releases, game and meet programs, statistics, record maintenance, game and match administration, general correspondence, and speaking engagements. But, as Plati writes in his 19-page office manual for student assistants, every office has its own way of running its show.

Colorado's sports information office issues, on average, more than 350 news releases or information updates per year. When Plati began his current position in 1984—he was the nation's youngest sports information director—that meant coming in on Sundays, typing four to eight pages of football notes, copying, folding and stuffing them in envelopes, and rushing them to the post office. "And everybody was seemingly happy when they got it in the mail on Wednesday. Now, if somebody called on Sunday and said, 'Hey,

Photo 5.1
One responsibility of sports information directors is arranging player interviews.
Sometimes, that means arranging a news conference, too.
©REPRINTED WITH PERMISSION FROM THE LINCOLN JOURNAL STAR.

I need your stats,' and we said, 'You'll get them on Wednesday in the mail,' that would not fly." Plati said.

Thank e-mail and the Internet. But now, not only are sports reporters able to quickly receive and access the most recent information for their stories, fans are also able to keep up-to-date by reading news releases and statistics online.

Writing for Sports Information

Plati, who teaches a course in sports public relations, says weaning students from a grandiose style of writing is usually his first challenge. "It's like they're writing for highlights on ESPN. They're trying to build this crescendo to get to the score. State your case in the first paragraph, what it is, and throw in what I call the grabber, that one fact that spices it up. Whether it's the guy on the Internet reading it on our Web site, or if you're sending your story to a sports editor, do you want to read seven paragraphs in before you find out what the hell this is about?"

Don't overwrite, either, Plati advises in his office manual. A release full of mundane and useless information is filed in the wastebasket or deleted from e-mail.

Sports information writers generally take a positive approach, even when that task may seem difficult. "You lose a football game 70-3, there's no way to put lipstick on that pig," Plati said.

Pointing out the negatives, in those cases, is sometimes necessary and should be done carefully and tactfully. "You've got to be smart, but don't be critical of your own team."

If your team goes 6-of-20 from the free-throw line and loses by three points, it's hard to ignore the fact that poor free-throw shooting

Photo 5.2
A player interview.
©REPRINTED WITH PERMISSION FROM THE LINCOLN JOURNAL STAR.

was to blame. Sports information staffs emphasize to their writers that they should, if possible, try to get a coach or player to say something about the free-throw shooting so it can be used as a quotation. "If none of them say it, you can point it out by saying, 'The major difference in the game was CU missed 14 free throws and had their worst night of the year at the free-throw line.' That's perfectly acceptable," Plati said.

Highlighting or dwelling on the negatives, however, isn't acceptable. Plati said he remembers taking his class to see the NBA's Denver Nuggets play. The students' assignment was to produce three pages of game notes. Some students put two negative notes on the first page. "In my class you'd get a D or an F. You know what you get from [Nuggets owner] Stan Kroenke? The pink slip. You don't make fun of your own product."

Media Guides

One of the biggest projects for any sports information department is writing and designing media guides for each sport. Media guides also serve as recruiting guides for prospective student athletes, so information is vast.

For media members, media guides contain records, biographies, game and season summaries, schedule information and general media information, such as how to arrange interviews, apply for game-day credentials, or find a motel in the area.

Media guides vary in length depending on the sport. For many years, football media guides were known to be the largest. Before the National Collegiate Athletic Association began mandating that all media guides be no longer than 208 pages, some guides had grown to four times that size, with most of the information designed to lure recruits. If nothing else, those guides made good doorstops.

Here's a breakdown of some key information Plati recommends be included in a media guide, with suggestions on how to approach writing certain areas.

Biographies

- use basic questionnaires for athletes, coaches and staff
- research bios of the person and any other information that can be accessed
- research and maintain a record of accomplishments since that form was submitted
- provide accompanying photographs (mug shot, action picture)

Last season/season in review

- game summaries (do as they are played; don't wait until the year is over)
- statistical summary
- key pictures

Opponent section

- schedules/results/pertinent information for each opponent
- all-time series results (and trends)
- bests against and by the opponent

Record book

- "The Last Time"; perhaps the pages to answer the most common questions
- career leaders
- year-by-year leaders
- select circles/longest plays
- single-season/game bests
- individual and team records
- opponent records/bests
- home venue information and records

- attendance records
- records by season
- coaching records
- year-by-year results
- program milestones/chronology
- honors/awards
- All-American and all-conference nominations
- all-time letterwinners
- players in the pros/draft picks
- postseason history
- bowl, playoff games/tournament results
- postseason records
- all kinds of miscellany
- —vs. the nation
- —vs. ranked teams
- —television appearances
- —season/conference openers
- —all-time comebacks

Media Information

- general information (credentials, parking, access, services, interview policies, etc.)
- Web site information (links, procedures, passwords, etc.)
- media outlets (major organizations that cover the program on a regular basis)
- media hospitality (listings of hotels, restaurants, rental cars, taxis, etc.)

Credential Requests

One responsibility of sports information directors is granting credential requests for media members and assigning seats or locations for coverage of games.

Each school sets guidelines on what media outlets are eligible to apply for credentials. For example, beat writers from daily newspapers will receive credentials, whereas freelance writers for fledging monthly magazines might need to cross their fingers.

One unique stipulation at the University of Colorado: Any Web site that sponsors anonymous message boards is not eligible for credentials. (An exception is made if a printed publication accompanies the Web site.)

It's part of Plati's fight against anonymous Internet posters. "If you want to criticize us, if you want to rip us, that's fine. But you know what? When newspaper people do that, their names are on it. On sports talk shows, when somebody calls in with an asinine rumor or accusation, you cut the caller off in a second. You never stop criticism. But we want sites to be responsible."

If those sites want to be credentialed to Colorado athletic events, Plati makes them identify their posters to him. That includes rivals.com and scout.com sites that focus on Colorado athletics. "And if they don't identify them, the agreement is that if I call them and say, 'Who's Stokes27?' they have to tell me to keep their credentials."

News Releases

A news release, whether on paper, in an e-mail or online, is the primary communication tool used by organizations, colleges, businesses and nonprofit groups to send information to the media. News releases represent the interest of the sponsoring organization and contain a message the source thinks is news or might be an idea for a news story.

E-mail is the delivery method of preference for news releases today, with fax a close second and mail a distant third.

Contrary to popular belief and to the implication in its name that it is news, a news release *does not* communicate news to the public. The goal of a news release is to attract the interest of the media—one editor, news director or reporter at a time.

Media want stories with local angles that will interest their audiences. If a news release presents the possibility of such a story, journalists will consider it. If the news release does not make a local connection in the headline or the lead, or contains more fluff than fact, the media are less likely to pursue it.

Why Send a News Release?

Information conveyed through news releases serves three general functions:

- It announces events and personnel changes.
  A professional sports team or a university athletic department might issue a news release when a coach is hired or fired, a player signs or is drafted, a conference affiliation changes or a building project is planned.
- It promotes citizenship and good causes.
  Athletes partnering with youth service programs, reading to elementary school students or sponsoring a middle school soccer camp are events that promote them as good citizens in their communities.
- It builds a person's or organization's image.
  Scholarships, awards, promotions and hall of fame recognitions promote a positive image for recipients and sponsors.

Sometimes it's necessary to release news that's not positive. A player is arrested, a coach has been fired, members of a team are killed in a van crash or a franchise is moving to another city. A news release makes the official announcement in straightforward, factual language as quickly as possible following the action.

Senders should never use news releases to mask an issue or to cover up facts, but they can and do approach the topic from a perspective that makes them look as good as possible.

Reporters who receive news releases know the information is generated and distributed by biased sources not obligated to represent both sides of the story.

A news release is not a news story and is not meant to be used as such. Reporters check the information carefully and verify the quotations in the release. A sports story or gamer based on information in a news release is rewritten and expanded to present an objective, balanced and fair message. It is converted to AP style as needed.

The media view a news release that does not have a newsworthy point, or is filled with puffery in place of fact, as an attempt to get free advertising. If a fresh, newsworthy topic is not the reason for sending a release, don't send it.

Factual information is the most helpful. If the topic has news value, present it in a straightforward news style (see chapter 7). Chances are better that a release will be considered if it presents facts and is written in journalistic style than if it is laced with puffery and overblown superlatives à la P. T. Barnum's "Greatest Show on Earth." Not everything can be the newest, the best, the fastest, the most coveted or the only one of its kind.

Journalists also read news releases looking for future stories or photos. The announcement of a women's rowing team being started at a local university may generate a news story. The reporter may also file the release as a reminder to check back for a story on the changes the university is making to accommodate practices and schedule competitions. The dates of the first practice and first meet are noted on the photographer's assignment sheet.

Who Cares?

The topic of a news release may get the attention of one media person because it's of interest to the audience of a station or Web site with a specialized format. It may not get a second glance from another whose audience has no need for the information or depends on another medium for news. A news release about a figure skating camp for 7- to 9-year-olds would be of more interest to the local newspaper upon which parents depend for local news than it would to the hip-hop station in town.

Stressing a local angle in the subject line, the headline, and the lead helps draw attention to a news release. Who or what about the story is of special interest to people in the area? Whether it's the local Parks and Recreation Department announcing sign-ups for summer softball leagues or the International Olympic Committee announcing the location for the winter games, the story can have a local angle.

The police department might send a release reminding the media that local officers who worked security at the Salt Lake Winter Olympics are available for interviews. A business might be sponsoring an Olympics competitor. A feature or sidebar about them would add human interest and a local angle to the news story.

Writing the News Release

A professional news release is a mini version of a news story with a direct lead and facts organized in inverted pyramid structure. The more the writing conforms to AP and journalistic writing styles, the more apt it is to be considered (see chapters 7 and 8).

Do everything possible to accommodate media deadlines and make it easy for the media to use the information. Accommodating the media may mean writing and sending a news release in both e-mail and print formats, preparing a radio script, making B-roll (generic background video) available for television and Web sites, cutting a DVD or providing a link or disk with high-resolution photos.

Find out the names of the people to whom news releases should be directed. Ask how they would like to receive messages and send them by the preferred means in the preferred format to the most direct source. Weekly newspapers and community newsletters may not be set up to receive electronic news releases and will prefer to receive them by mail. The more localized and personalized the message, the more likely it is to be used.

Electronic News Releases

Electronic news releases are posted on Web sites or sent via e-mail or fax. The majority of journalists say they prefer to receive news releases by e-mail or fax. Twenty-five percent prefer mail, and just over 10 percent like to receive information by phone, according to a study by Jerry Walker in Jack O'Dwyer's Newsletter.[1]

An electronic news release may have B-roll, downloadable audio and video files, or links to supplementary information embedded in the release. Links are preferable to attachments that have the potential for carrying viruses.

An organization sponsoring a basketball camp for middle school students might post a news release and make B-roll of a previous camp available for media to use in promoting this year's camp. A taped collection of season highlights, shots of fans entering the stadium, cheering and watching the halftime show is B-roll that stations could use with any story about an athletic program all year.

Organizing News Conferences

Among the duties of a sports information director is organizing news conferences. Some news conferences are planned days in advance, and some are hastily arranged. In either case, SIDs must follow some basic guidelines for conducting news conferences.

1. Decide who will be present and who will announce what. If more than one person is to speak, decide:
   Who speaks and in what order?
   Who will open the news conference and introduce the speakers?
   What do you want them to wear? Standard dress for all (e.g., players in uniform)?
2. Decide on the format. Will the speakers take questions after their general comments? Or will they just say what they are prepared to say and exit immediately?
3. Prepare handouts. News releases, press kits, progress reports, backgrounders—whatever materials you choose to support your speaker—should be available to the media. NOTE: Allow enough time to properly prepare the handout materials because you may not have much time once you've announced you're having a news conference.

4. Select a location. Will the room accommodate the media who are coming? Is the room suitable? Make sure there's proper seating for the media, work space, and enough electrical outlets to support the media equipment.

   You will need a mult box (a box into which the media can plug microphone feeds, so the speakers have one microphone in front of them instead of a dozen). Is the room well lit or do you need extra lighting? Are there telephones and wireless Internet access for the media to utilize?

   What background do you want behind the speakers for the TV cameras? Perhaps something with a team or corporate logo or your sponsors' logos?

   What is in proximity to the location where you're holding your news conference? Will there be any noise issues (traffic near a road if windows are open, noisy corridors with people talking, or even a dance or music class in the next room)?

5. Arrange for adequate parking. Is it easy access from the parking area to where you're holding the news conference so television photographers don't have to walk too far with all their equipment?

6. Choose the time of day. The earlier, the better—don't make the media scramble to cover your event. Make it as convenient as possible for your media audience. Allow time for outlying media to be able to reach the news conference site. Late in the day works if it's a crisis situation; otherwise, plan to hold your news conference one day to one week in advance. If you're planning ahead, arrange for food and beverages to be available.

7. Follow up immediately. Send a news release to those media from whom you'd like coverage but who didn't show up for the news conference.

© Reprinted with permission from the University of Colorado

Accommodate the Media

Having a solid knowledge of what information the media want and how they prefer to receive it is an ongoing challenge for message makers. The difficulty with sending information electronically is determining the format each receiver needs: CD, DVD, MP4, digital tape, or whatever the next wave of technology brings—options abound and quickly become outdated.

Check with contacts at least annually to see that they are receiving messages in a usable format. Some editors appreciate a call a day or two after an e-mail is sent so they don't miss an important story because of an unopened or misfiled e-mail. On the other hand, receiving too many follow-up calls is a pet peeve of those journalists who would rather call than be called, so again, it pays to know the preferences of your contacts.

Today, most media want a multimedia presence in the marketplace. Training or experience in producing electronic messages is beneficial to those preparing for careers in sports news. Reporters and media relations professionals are expected to know how to shoot video and create short news or promotional packages. They're asked to host videocasts and talk shows from studios in their offices or to provide streamed audio and video live on company Web sites.

E-mail News Releases

A survey of 400 journalists showed 70 percent read every e-mail release they receive (except the obvious spam).[2] Twenty-three percent indicated they read the e-mails with the most compelling subject lines.

One of the respondents who said she reads every e-mail she receives is Kristen Stieffel, a news assistant for the Orlando (Fla.) Business Journal. Stieffel said she "looks at the ones with good subject lines first."

The subject line is the e-mail reader's cue that a message is waiting. In four to six key words a subject line jumps out of the long list on the screen and captures the reader's interest—or it doesn't.

The subject lines that get attention are brief, succinct and provocative, according to public relations expert Fraser P. Seitel.[3]

Work the local angle into the subject line, advises Deann Stumpe, news director at the Hastings (Neb.) Tribune. "I always look for the local angle first. If it's plain from the subject line, I will open it."

Writing an attention-getting subject line is akin to writing a headline. Select short, concise, targeted key words.

Specific, short: Top 100 football recruit rankings

Specific, but too long: Versus coverage of Mountain West College Basketball continues: Utah vs. BYU Saturday

Generic: Notes idea

"Notes idea" is short, but it doesn't give any information. "Versus coverage of Mountain West" is about all that can be seen on a subject line at one time, and even though the headline as a whole tells the story, the first four or five words aren't enough to tell the receiver what the story is about. "Top 100 football recruit rankings" is specific, interesting and the right length.

The body of an e-mail news release should also be short and to the point. Online readers read about 25 percent slower than newspaper readers, according to Web usability research by Jakob Nielsen, and two to three screens is about as far as an online reader will read.[4] Take advantage of the first page to pull readers in with an engaging headline and a first paragraph packed with the five Ws: who, what, where, when and why.

Print News Releases

Writing a print news release is like filling in the blanks. A template is all a writer needs to get started.[5]

As with electronic news releases, shorter messages are better. One page is more apt to get read than two or three, but don't skimp on information just to squeeze it onto one page. Make the message long enough to include the vital information.

Tips for Writing Electronic News Releases[6]

- One reporter per "To" line.
  Nobody—least of all reporters—likes to be lumped in with everybody else . . . so don't group journalists together on the "To" line of an e-mail release. Listing one reporter per "To" line will deliver the personalization that journalists prefer.
- Limit subject line headers.
  Most reporters are cursed with a daily e-mail box that runneth over. They're swamped with e-mail releases, just as their latter-day counterparts were swamped with print releases. Therefore, enticing them with a provocative subject line is a necessity if you want your release to be considered . . . limit subject headers to four to six words.
- Boldface "FOR IMMEDIATE RELEASE."
  With this advisory on the first line of the release, right above the date and dateline, reporters will know instantly that this is news to be used right away. As is true with print releases, "embargoing" news for later publication is rarely honored in a day of 24/7 breaking news and round-the-clock Internet publicity.
- Hammer home the headline.
  E-mail release headlines are as important as print headlines to attract immediate interest and subsequent coverage. E-mail headlines should be written in boldface upper- and lowercase and, as in all e-mail writing, should be limited . . . to 10 words or less.
- Limit length.
  E-mail news releases should be shorter than print versions. PR Newswire reports that the average print release is about 500 words. E-mail releases should generally be shorter.
- Observe 5 W format.
  E-mail news releases should observe traditional news release style, leading with the 5 W format, to answer the key questions of who, what, where, when, why, and even how. The

limited length of the e-mail—to say nothing of the attention span of the e-mail reader—mandates that the writer get to the point immediately, right in the first paragraph.

- No attachments.
  Never. Never. Never. Journalists wish neither to face the risk of a virus nor take the time to download. So don't attach anything. Rather . . .
- Link to the URL.
  Accompanying information, such as photos, bios, backgrounders and the like should be linked in the e-mail to the organization's URL. This negates the inconvenience of downloading and allows reporters the opportunity to link at their leisure.
- Remember readability.
  E-mail releases must balance information with readability. That means using short paragraphs, varied sentence length, bullets, numbers, lists—devices that make the release more eye-friendly and scannable.

Reprinted with permission of Pearson Education, Inc., from Fraser P. Seitel, "The Practice of Public Relations," 10th ed., p. 343.

An average news release is about 500 words, the equivalent of two pages of double-spaced 12-point Times or Times New Roman copy.

Tips for Writing Print News Releases

Heading: Use business letterhead that includes the name, address, phone, fax and e-mail contact information for the source sending the news release.

Date: Date the release at the top or in the dateline at the beginning of the copy. This tells the recipient when the release was written and how "new" the news is.

Release Terms: State publication terms above the headline. Most are "FOR IMMEDIATE RELEASE." Information not to be published until later (award winners, for example) is marked "Embargoed until (date)" or "Hold for release (date)," which tells the media not to release the information before the date specified. This gives the media time to prepare a story to release as soon as the event happens.

Contact information: Because the majority of journalists prefer to call the sender rather than be called, make it as easy as possible for them to contact someone who is available to answer questions, set up interviews or send press credentials. List contacts' names with phone numbers and e-mail addresses in the heading, at the end of the release or both. Use phone numbers that will reach people at whatever time the journalist may need to call, including evenings and weekends.

Headline: Begin with a headline that tells the reader exactly what the message is about. On a news release, the headline should be as long as necessary to tell specifically what the content is about.

Specific, informative:

2009 USA Rock Paper Scissors Championship, March 10–31, Panama City, Fla.

Winner will receive $20,000 for college tuition

Less informational:

USA Rock Paper Scissors contest worth $20,000 to lucky college student

Generic:

College students flock to Florida for competition

Center the headline one or two double spaces below the heading and one double space above the text.

Dateline: Begin the copy with a dateline, usually the location of the corporate headquarters, using AP style: CITY, State—. Use English abbreviations, not postal abbreviations, for states. The date the news release was written may be included in the dateline. Check the AP Stylebook for a list of cities that may be used without the state name in datelines.

Examples: GREEN BAY, Wis.—
                     AMES, Iowa—
                     ATLANTA—

Example with date: BATON ROUGE, La., April 7, 2028—.

Text: Write short sentences and paragraphs, and use short, specific words. Double-space the text. Stop at the end of a sentence or paragraph at the bottom of each page. Use only one side of the paper.

Organization: Begin with a direct lead containing most or all of the five Ws. Organize the information in most-important-to-least-important order. (See chapter 7 for an explanation of leads and story structure.)

Closing: The last paragraph may be a standard boilerplate statement about the sponsor.

End marks: Mark the bottom center of each page —END— or ### if it is the end of the document, or —more— if text continues on the next page. —END—, ###, and ?more? are standard end marks indicating whether the story is complete or continues to another page.

Options for the media: Note special instructions or options for the media after the end mark of the release. Notes might include photo options, set-up times, interview arrangements, technical instructions, rain dates and numbers to call for information.

Subsequent pages: A *slug* containing the subject and page number appears at the top left of each page after the first.

Examples:

Sugar Bowl 2020   Rodeo Advance
2-2-2-2-2   3-3-3-3-3

Include helpful supplementary materials: a list of Web sites, photos, fact sheets, biographies, maps.

Media Advisory/Media Alert

Information traditionally provided in news releases is sometimes offered under the label "advisory" or "alert." Advisories and alerts tend to be short announcements, formatted as bulleted lists or collected in subheads such as *Who, What, Where, When, Why.* They offer reporters in a hurry an even faster way to access information.

Media Kit

A media kit is a collection of information, a "calling card" according to Seitel, to introduce an organization, campaign, merger or other newsworthy event In addition to a news release, a media kit includes any of several communications vehicles for potential use by the media: a media alert or advisory, fact sheets, biographies, advertising information, contact information and Web sites or links to related information such as high-resolution photos, logos and graphics.

Media kits, like news releases, are delivered in print or online and followed by calls to answer questions or offer further assistance to interest media in the story.

Figure 5.2
Red Cross Media Advisory

Media Advisory

Media Contact: Danelle Schlegelmilch, 402.492.2149 x3848
givebloodgivelife.org

Give a Pint, Get a Pint Campaign Supports Local Blood Drives
Culver's to treat guests who donate at Red Cross college blood drives

OMAHA, Neb. (January 29, 2008) – To encourage the act of giving, American
Red Cross and Culver's have teamed up to offer each presenting blood donor
a free t-shirt and a coupon for a pint of Culver's custard at the University of
Nebraska at Lincoln Blood Drives on February 12-14.

Blood supplies tend to be lower during the winter months due to bad weather
and winter illness, but the need is constant. The American Red Cross encourages healthy, eligible blood donors to give blood during flu season to help ensure
blood is available to patients in need. Under normal circumstances, approximately every two seconds someone in America will need a blood transfusion.

WHEN: **Tuesday, February 12 - Thursday February 14**
        11:00 a.m. – 5:00 p.m.

WHERE: **University of Nebraska at Lincoln – Nebraska Union**
         Centennial Room

ABOUT THE RED CROSS
The Omaha, Neb.-based Midwest Region supplies blood products and specialized laboratory services to more than 80 hospitals in Nebraska, Iowa, Colorado
and Kansas. The Midwest Region organizes nearly 2,800 blood drives in an
effort to collect more than 150,000 pints of blood each year for patients in
need. The Midwest Region is one of four regions that make up the Mid-Amer-
ica Division of the American Red Cross Blood Services.

ABOUT CULVER'S
Culver's restaurants are independently owned and operated in more than 350
locations. With the opening of Culver's first restaurants in Arizona, Arkansas
and Tennessee, they have since grown to operate in 19 states across the
nation. Culver's invests deeply in partnerships and programs, including its VIP
scholarship program, Culver's Cares™ charitable program.

###

Saddle Up

Ted Harbin spent 20 years in the newspaper business, primarily in sports. A native of western Kansas, he's also long had a passion for rodeo.

Harbin decided to combine his sports writing, layout and editing experience with his love for a nontraditional sport by beginning his own business: Rodeo Media Relations.

Among Harbin's goals is to not only promote rodeo and its athletes, but to help sports writers better understand a sport some may have a difficult time grasping. Harbin knows it's not an easy sport to cover.

"Most sports writers understand baseball. They understand basketball. They understand football. A few understand soccer, most can wade their way through other sports, like golf and wrestling, but they can't grasp the difference between bareback riding and a saddle-bronc ride."

To that end, Harbin writes what he calls nontraditional news releases. They are more feature-oriented.

"Most of the newspapers I'm sending these things to are going to be your small daily newspaper, where I'm trying to entice editors to say, 'Hey, this is a pretty good story, it's about a local guy.'"

The idea is to inspire local news outlets to follow up with interviews and produce their own stories, although some newspapers, including the Dallas Morning News and Fort Worth Star-Telegram, have used some of Harbin's content verbatim, he said.

Harbin has served as a rodeo correspondent for six newspapers in the Midwest, including the Kansas City Star. He's either written stories or had news releases appear in 32 publications.

> Rodeo Media Relations is a multifaceted business. In addition to helping rodeos market their product—much the same way a sports information director does for a football team—Harbin also represents cowboys and helps them obtain sponsorships.
>
> They're not going to get the $50 million deal, but if I can get them enough money to help them pay for their fuel to get from one rodeo to another, then I'm helping them try to earn more money by making their business decision a wiser decision.

Upon Further Review

1. Interview or job shadow a sports information director for a college or professional team. Prepare a list of questions you don't want to forget to ask. Write a feature news story about the SID.
2. Look at media guides. (You may obtain them from universities or the local sports reporters to whom they are sent.) What content surprised you? What content would you, as a reporter, want to have that was not included?
3. Go to the Web sites of several colleges, universities or professional teams and look for news releases. Or, ask a local television or newspaper sports reporter to save 10 e-mailed or faxed news releases for you. Compare the subject lines, format, length and content. What are the similarities? Differences? Which of the 10 would you find most useful if you were a reporter? Why?
4. On the same Web sites or the Web sites of local media, find their policies and deadlines for formatting and submitting news releases to them. Compile a list of the contact person's name, e-mail address and fax and phone numbers for media to which you would likely be sending information.

Notes

1. Jerry Walker, "Journalists Prefer E-mail Survey," August 25, 2004, at lexisnexis.com.hclproxy.hastings.edu/us/lnacademic/delivery (accessed Jan. 8, 2008).

2. Walker, lexisnexis.com.hclproxy.hastings.edu/us/lnacademic/delivery (accessed Jan. 8, 2008).

3. Fraser P. Seitel, "The Practice of Public Relations," 10th ed. (Upper Saddle River, N.J.: Pearson, 2007), p. 343.

4. Janet Kolodzy, "Convergence Journalism" (Lanham, Md.: Rowman & Littlefield, 2006), p. 192.

5. Press Release Newswire, "Tips, guidelines and templates for writing an effective press release," at prWebdirect.com/pressreleasetips.php (accessed Jan. 7, 2008).

6. Seitel, "Practice of Public Relations," pp. 342–44.

CHAPTER 6

Choosing the Words

EVERY SPORT has rules, and every player knows the penalties. Break an NCAA rule and your team may have to forfeit a game. Make too many fouls, and you will be out of the game. Step out of bounds and the play ends.

Sports writing has rules, too: grammar rules, spelling rules, punctuation rules.

You may not be thrown out of the game for breaking a writing rule, but there is a penalty. With each mistake, you lose credibility with your audience and your employer. Make too many mistakes that someone else has to fix or that get into print, and you will lose your job.

Not only are there rules to learn, there's a sports idiom to master. The sports idiom is a language spoken by insiders and somewhat familiar to followers. It's a combination of sports terminology, slang and cliché that has grown up within the world of sports over the last century or more and has become sports-speak in broadcast, particularly play-by-play. The idiom is so pervasive that some of it has leaked into everyday conversation. *That's par for the course* comes from golf, *to strike out* or *touch base* comes from baseball, and how about that *photo finish* that horse racing chipped in? You *make a pit stop, spin your wheels* or *win by a nose*. Or you might be *thrown a curve, driven up the wall* or find yourself *behind the eight ball*.

Figure 6.1

Professional writers take language rules very seriously because they know their audiences and their editors respect good writing. Bloggers, e-mailers, scriptwriters, news release writers, sports writers and columnists who use correct grammar and spelling in everything they write will be regarded as professionals by everyone who reads their work.

In addition to knowing and using grammar rules, sports writers are challenged by the complexity of their audiences. Sports fans range from the novice to the know-it-all. The sports writer must craft stories informative and entertaining enough for the novice to enjoy and complete, and accurate and technical enough to hold the attention of the die-hard sports fan.

Journalistic Writing Style

Sports reporters are journalists who specialize in writing and broadcasting about sports and the people who participate in them. Sports stories are based on facts and verifiable information and are written in journalistic style.

Look carefully at the structure of sports stories online, in the newspaper and in sports magazines. In general, a journalistic-style story will have:

- facts and information
- short, subject-verb-object sentences
- short paragraphs
- short words with precise meanings

- action verbs
- quotations with attribution
- numbers and statistics

And it will not have:

- misspelled words
- grammatical errors
- misplaced modifiers
- weasel words
- clichés
- euphemisms
- redundant phrases
- gender-biased language or –*isms*

Facts and Information

Sports stories are based on facts, information and quotations. Information is gathered from sources or observed by the reporter. If the information is used in the form of a quotation or paraphrase, it is attributed to the source. Quotations may contain the source's opinion, if the source is identified.

Stories do not include the reporter's opinion. Opinion is reserved for columns and should be clearly labeled as such. In print or online, a column is identified by the writer's column head and byline. In broadcast, opinion segments are introduced as opinion and often delivered by the author in a neutral setting so viewers have audio and visual cues by which to identify opinion as different from game coverage or sports news.

The difference between a fact and an opinion can be as simple as a few words.

Fact: The game went two extra innings, during which the Cubs changed pitchers three times.

Opinion: The game went two extra innings because the Cubs' manager made three questionable pitching changes.

Facts are verifiable. Opinions are often expressed in sweeping generalizations laden with superlatives: most famous, best ever, greatest play.

> *Fact*:   Tom Osborne coached the Nebraska Cornhuskers
>   for 25 years.
> *Opinion*: Tom Osborne is the most famous coach in college
>   football history.

Blogging has opened another venue for expressing opinions, both those of the sports journalist and those of the blogging public. Newspapers and television stations have multimedia Web sites on which they invite people to participate in the community conversation about issues and ideas via written entries, photos and video.

Verify Information

> If in doubt, leave it out.
>
> —Phil Andrews, "Sports Journalism"[1]

The first goal for journalists is to be accurate. Journalists never assume anything. They always verify information before putting it in a story. Verification is checking information by comparing it to information from reliable sources. A generally accepted guideline is to check information with three unrelated sources. If three sources agree, it's probably correct and safe to use the information. Note the word *probably* in the last sentence; if there's any doubt in your mind or you have a gut feeling that something is not quite right, don't use it until you're satisfied that it is correct.

The best way to gather facts and information is to attend the event, observe the activity and the people and take notes or record the action yourself. What you observe may be reported without attribution, but verifying statistics and spelling ensures the accuracy of your story. After the event, verify your notes using data and stats sheets from the sports information office, the news conference with the coaches and your own interviews.

If you cannot attend the event, contact the sports information director ahead of time to get players' names and numbers and background on both teams. Make arrangements with the coaches or media relations director for phone interviews after the game and ask for game stats to be faxed or uploaded as soon as they are available.

Short, S-V-O Sentences

Short sentences make text easier to read according to readability tests. Standard readability, or a level easily understood by most media readers, contains about 17 words per sentence.

Not every sentence will be 17 words. Using a variety of sentence lengths creates writing that is more interesting to read.

Subject-verb-object is the preferred sentence organization pattern in journalistic writing. It's easy to read and understand. It makes the subject do the action, and it helps the reader move through the story quickly and easily. S-V-O sentences pack in enough of the *who, what, where, when, why* and *how* for readers to have an overview of the story in one sentence.

This lead from the USA Today Sports Weekly, for instance, uses 38 words to include all the information:

> Patriots wide receiver Troy Brown [who] spent time playing defensive back [did what] over the last three seasons [when], and it prepared him [why] to make the critical fourth-quarter play [what] that helped turn an apparent Chargers victory into a 24-21 Patriots comeback win [how]. [2]

Daily publications usually break leads into shorter, punchier S-V-O sentences. These 5 Ws and an H leads from wire services tell the whole story.

AUSTIN—Texas' (where) Destinee Hooker, the two-time defending NCAA high jump champion (who), will skip track (what) this season (when) to train with the U.S. women's national volley-ball team (why) before the Olympics.[3]

SALT LAKE CITY—Tag Elliott (who) of Thatcher, Utah, was in critical condition one day after surgery (what) to repair extensive facial injuries sustained in a collision with a bull (why).

Elliott, 19, was riding a 1,500-pound bull named Werewolf on Tuesday (when) in the Days of '47 Rodeo (where) when their heads smacked together (how).[4]

S-V-O is the preferred sentence order in broadcast as well, because it creates easy-to-say units of thought that the listener can understand and absorb while the sportscaster is speaking. Online readers read in chunks: a blurb, a lead or a paragraph. They, too, are looking for easy-to-read, easy-to-understand information, and that's what S-V-O sentences deliver.

Short Paragraphs

Look at the two columns on the next page. Of the two, which would you choose to read first? Why?

At first glance, most readers would choose the column on the right. It just looks easier to read. The short paragraphs, multiple entry points, and added white space within the story give the impression that it's a "fast read."

In journalistic style, one and two sentence paragraphs are the norm. Newspaper and online stories appear in narrow vertical columns with only a few words on each line, making even short sentences fill three or more lines.

Few programs have garnered as much attention in NAIA athletics as the Hastings College women's basketball team. And there's good reason. Under the direction of head coach Tony Hobson, the Broncos have become a perennial power—riding the heels of three national championships in six years.

The team captured its first NAIA Division II national championship on March 12, 2002, with a 73-69 come-from-behind win over Cornerstone, Mich. It was the first team championship in school history.

The Broncos, who found themselves trailing by as many as 12 points in the game, rallied behind the play of All-American selections Trista Mairin, Katie Jade and Cassidy Gail. The team finished that season 34-3 overall.

But the Broncos weren't finished with the national spotlight. One year later, on March 18, 2003, the team became just the second team in NAIA history to win back-to-back women's national basketball titles.

Few programs have garnered as much attention in NAIA athletics as the Hastings College women's basketball team.

And there's good reason.

Under the direction of head coach Tony Hobson, the Broncos have become a perennial power—riding the heels of three national championships in six years.

The team captured its first NAIA Division II national championship on March 12, 2002, with a 73-69 come-from-behind win over Cornerstone, Mich.

It was the first team championship in school history.

The Broncos, who found themselves trailing by as many as 12 points in the game, rallied behind the play of All-American selections Trista Mairin, Katie Jade and Cassidy Gail.

The team finished that season 34-3 overall.

But the Broncos weren't done with the national spotlight.

One year later, on March 18, 2003, the team became just the second team in NAIA history to win back-to-back women's national basketball titles.

Paragraph indentations create small white notches along the left margin that make stories appear easier to read by giving readers frequent entry points. When set in columns, longer paragraphs give the impression of black pillars holding up the headline. Readers tend to skip the longer paragraphs because they are perceived to be more difficult to read.

Writing for Broadcast

Broadcast journalists speak in a conversational tone, but don't be fooled by the ease with which they speak. Conversational does not mean incorrect. Television and radio stories are written with the same care, precision and attention to language as print and online stories. If anything, broadcast is more difficult to write because stories are shorter and each word has to pack so much power.

Spelling and grammar are important in scripts because someone is going to be reading them while speaking the words on air. A misspelled word or incorrect subject-verb agreement can make the reader hesitate or stumble.

Pronouncers, phonetic spellings enclosed in parentheses, are inserted in scripts beside names or words that might be unfamiliar to the speaker. Include a pronouncer with any name or word that can be pronounced more than one way, or is not pronounced with the commonly expected inflections, in a script prepared for someone else to read. It might keep the new sports anchor from pronouncing Cairo as (k-EYE-row) when the residents of the town by that name in your market say (CARE-o).

Broadcast writers use single sentence paragraphs and short sentences, or just a series of short phrases connected by ellipses, to assist the person who will be reading the story on air. Indented entry points help the television sportscaster deliver the story while appearing not to be reading from a script or prompter. The white spaces separate sentences and make it easier to move from one to the next without searching a black block of text to find the next one.

Script format style for television or radio will vary from station to station. Most are divided into columns with the technical cues

Figure 6.2
Television Script

Scripts for Ten PM (04-07-2017)

SO8   CASTING CONTEST   Sun 10 pm
PKG
 00:00:28
Talent
 Hayden Rob
OTS
 147
 Sports Generic

> JUST ABOUT EVERYTHING IS A COM-
> PETITION THESE DAYS.
>
> LIKE RUNNING ON LOGS IN THE
> WATER . . . OR RACING TURTLES.

VO
Locater – Ticker
 Casting Contest
 Tooele

> HERE'S AN INTERESTING ONE FOR
> YOU . . . A FISHING-POLE CASTING COM-
> PETITION.
>
> IT'S SIMILAR TO DARTS . . .
>
> THE COMPETITORS AIM FOR A TAR-
> GET AND ARE AWARDED POINTS FOR
> ACCURACY.
>
> 16 KIDS TOOK PART IN TODAY'S STATE
> FINALS AT THE BOAT DOCK IN TOOELE
> (TWO-WILL-UH).
>
> 11-YEAR OLD TRISTA MAIRIN (MARE-
> en) OF ELM CREEK WON TODAY'S EVENT.
>
> AND SHE'S HEADED TO NATIONALS IN
> LAS VEGAS.

---

on the left and the text on the right. Some prepare scripts in the traditional ALL-CAPS format. Others use the sentence-style capital and lowercase letters. Some double-space copy; some triple-space copy.

If you're writing for specific stations, know and use their preferred styles.

Short Words with Precise Meanings

Newspaper editor Stanley Walker, a proponent of the new, the fresh, the descriptive phrase, thought sports writing had reached new heights during the 1920s and 1930s as young, college-educated

Jargon: On the Air

Actuality	recorded excerpt inserted in audio news story
Lead-in	short phrase or sentence that sets listeners up for the story
Incue	first four words of a sound bite or actuality, written into the script; helps identify correct sound bite
Outcue	last four words of actuality or sound bite, written into script, cue to newscaster to begin speaking
Sound bite	recorded excerpt inserted in an audio or video news story
OTS	over the shoulder; picture or graphic seen behind television announcer
Tag	lines of the announcer's script that close (end) the story
SOT	sound on tape
Still frame	a fixed photo image taken from a video recording
Still store	an electronic memory unit for storing single screens
VOSAT	voice sound over videotape
SFX	sound effects

writers joined the ranks of veterans like Charles Dryden, Ring Lardner, Damon Runyon and Grantland Rice. Walker summed up the dilemma a sports writer faces in his 1934 book "City Editor":

> "The subject matter of sports is pretty much the same. Almost every murder, suicide, shipwreck and train collision is cut on a different pattern, and the reporter does not have to seek outlandish substitutes for common terms. One baseball game, however, is pretty much the same as any other. The few standard verbs and nouns used in writing of baseball, football and boxing become tiresome."[5]

Short, simple words are easier for a reader scanning a print story or someone listening to a broadcast story to comprehend. When there's a choice, choose the shortest, simplest word that does not diminish the meaning of the more difficult word.

Replace technical terms and long words with shorter ones.

abrasions and contusions	= cuts and bruises
torn meniscus	= knee injury
muscle degeneration	= muscle damage

Action Verbs

Close your eyes and picture five-time Wimbledon tennis champion Roger Federer ambling out onto the court to return a 145-mph serve by opponent Rafael Nadal. Next slide: soccer great David Beckham dancing toward the goal. Next slide: horses standing quietly at the gate waiting for the race to begin.

Writing that uses descriptive nouns and action verbs helps readers and listeners visualize. When the verb implies an action not indicated by the rest of the image, it interrupts the reader's expectation and makes the listener pause. It's like the sound of chalk on a blackboard. It draws attention to itself and away from the flow of the story.

Tennis players don't amble when responding to a serve. They sprint, stretch, bound, leap and swing. Soccer players don't dance when moving the ball toward the goal. They may race, run, kick or score, but leave dancing to the ballroom. Horses anxious for a race to begin snort, rear, stomp, strain, almost anything but stand quietly.

Live coverage and video allow viewers to understand the action by seeing it for themselves. Readers expect to feel as though they are seeing the action when they read about a sporting event. Readers rely on the writer's choice of verbs to help them see how the player moved and feel the difference between a stroll, a strut and a sprint. They want to sense what it's like to dive for a ball, to feel the texture of the bat in their hands, to watch the ball approach and hear it connect, to run the bases and slide in to score a run.

Attributive Verbs

An exception to the action verb guideline is attribution. When someone is quoted in a story, quotation marks indicate that the person spoke those exact words. The name of the speaker is linked to the quotation along with a verb of attribution. *Said* is the appropriate attributive verb to use when identifying the speaker. Any other verb carries a shade of meaning that the writer has put on the speaker's words, giving the reader an impression that may not be what the speaker intended. *Shouted, growled, stated, assured, blurted, mentioned, commented* and other words that describe vocal inflections connote meaning beyond the words being said.

Each of these attributive verbs gives a different meaning to the coach's words:

"You are always an injury or two away from being pretty average," the coach explained.

"You are always an injury or two away from being pretty average," the coach sighed.

"You are always an injury or two away from being pretty average," the coach growled.

Words that describe facial expression describe action: *smile, grimace, scowl, wince*. Words are not actions, and they cannot be smiled, cried or growled. Let the reader decide from the content of the quotation and context of the story how the speaker might have sounded saying the words. If it is necessary to indicate both speaking and facial expression, use both.

> *Correct*:   "That play worked well for us," Coach Boeve *said*.
> *Correct*:   "That play worked well for us," Coach Hobson *said with a smile*.
> *Avoid*:   "That play worked well for us," Coach Creech *bragged as he grinned*.

Misspelled Words and Usage Errors

> A misspelled name is second only to an incorrect score—the two most obvious, and unnecessary—errors.
>
> —Steve Wilstein[6]

Spell check and grammar check are your friends. Visit them often. But remember that, like people, they're not always perfect. Spell check will not identify a correctly spelled, but misused, word, even if it makes no sense in the sentence. It won't change *no* to *on*, *how* to *who*, or *tea* to *tee* or *team*.

Unfortunately for journalists, spell check does not work on names. The only certain way to know how to spell someone's name is to ask that person.

Grammar check may identify what it suspects are incorrect uses of a word, but the writer must decide which is the correct word. Homonyms such as *there, they're* and *their* sound alike but are spelled differently and have unrelated meanings. If you have trouble remembering which is which, create a memory trick to help remember the meaning of each word.

When *heirs* inherit money, it is t-*heirs* and *they'(a)re* rich!

They can go here and t-*here* as long as t-*heir* money lasts.

Now it's easy to tell if *there, their* or *they're* is used correctly in a sentence. Are these?

"Our players are not going to have targets on *they're* backs this season. *Their* physically and mentally prepared to win."

"We're a little weak in pitching. *There's* no experience *their* this year."

"*There* the best players in the line-up."

Correct usage would be:

"Our players are not going to have targets on *their* backs this season. *They're* physically and mentally prepared to win."

"We're a little weak in pitching. *There's* no experience *there* this year."

"*They're* the best players in the line-up."

Collective Nouns

Collective nouns describe more than one person, place or thing as a unit: *class, committee, team, group.* A collective noun may represent all those individuals as a single unit, or it may represent those single units as individuals. *Team* is the collective noun most often used in sports.

A team, whether it has two members or 200 members, is one team and requires a singular verb or pronoun when referred to as a whole: *The team is leaving Friday.* If the members of the team are acting individually, team uses a plural verb or pronoun: *The team are expected to work out for an hour each day sometime between noon and 6 pm. and log their times on this form.* For clarity, use *team members* or *players*: *Team members are in the weight room working out* or *The players are warming up.*

The same principle applies to the names of teams. If referred to by the name of the university or the home city, a team is one unit and uses a singular verb or pronoun.

The University of Arkansas *is* favored by 17-21 points.

Miami won *its* season opener.

If the team is referred to by mascot or name, it represents the individuals and uses a plural verb or pronoun:

The Razorbacks *are* favored by 17-21 points.

The Dolphins won *their* season opener.

Misplaced Modifiers

Modifiers should be placed as close as possible to the words they modify. If they aren't, they often distort the meaning of the sentence. At best, the result is confusing; at worst, sadly comical. Dangling participle is a fancy name given to modifying phrases beginning with an "–ing" verb bumping up against the wrong noun or pronoun. For example:

Having summarized the main points of the story in the introduction, the reader should then be provided with the detail in order of its importance.

Did the reader summarize the main points of the story or did the writer do that? The subject who performed the action should immediately follow the introductory phrase. This sentence could be corrected to read:

Having summarized the main points of the story in the lead, the writer should provide the reader with detail in order of its importance.

In sports writing, dangling participles make images like these:

Trailing 14-0, the burden fell on Troy Aikman.

Studying sports writing last fall, my academic performance dropped.

Running down the field, his shoe flew off.

Or headlines like:

Complaints about NBA officials growing ugly

Aging expert joins coaching staff

Weasel Words

fun	a lot	numerous
a little	various	some
very	few	good (as in "it was a good game")
great	many	different

Some words—even short, simple ones—just don't say anything. What is "fun"? An athlete might say "winning." A fan might say "watching my team win." But if a fan said, "Fun is seats on the 50-yard line at the Rose Bowl on a 66-degree New Year's Day watching my team complete the winning touchdown after the clock runs out!" the audience understands "fun."

Weasel words waste space and don't move the story ahead. If each word in the story does not add to the visual image the writer is trying to create through its specific, concise definition, it is a weasel word. Replace it with a definitive word or example:

A lot: sixteen tons; 76,000 fans; 5,280 feet;
          all the blades of grass on a soccer field;
          you saved 1,122 pennies today

Few: the holes-in-one I've made in my lifetime;
          the members of my bowling team;
          the number of blind climbers who have reached the
              top of Mt. Everest

Great: ranks right up there with winning an Olympic gold
              medal; holding a winning lottery ticket

Quotes that don't add information to the story are just bigger weasel words. If a source says "It was a great game," ask what made it great. Ask the source to define "great" in that context or to compare this game to another "great" game. A little more time spent asking for specific details means less time spent trying to write a story that shares something worth knowing with the audience.

Clichés

Down for the count, throw in the towel, snatched victory from the jaws of defeat . . . well, you get the idea, old clichés are dead as doornails and, she went on to say when she sat down with me for an interview, it is interesting to note how a writer's true colors separate the men from the boys when it comes to stringing words together. "If you've heard it or read it 10 times, it's a cliché. Don't use it," master teacher Honey Lou Bonar said.[7]

Clichés are someone else's expressions, often described as trite and overused, repeated by speakers and writers but understood, literally or historically, by few. Recognize any of these?

put the final nail in the coffin	always gives 110 percent
tickled the twine	draw first blood
hit it through the uprights	a nail biter
sat down with (interview)	turn the tide of the game
off to the races	gut-check time
all over but the shouting	get that monkey off his back
go out and leave it all on the ice	records are made to be broken
step up to the next level	always come through in the clutch

Cliché Speak

Sometimes as writers we have our backs against the wall. We have editors who expect our A-game every time we metaphorically lace up the cleats. That's when I revert to what has been working: clichés.

But you can't win them all. Your editor would have a field day with your work, and your readers would think you've gone to the well once too often.

Unfortunately, there are days like this. But what can you do? Sports are all about winning, and clichés are a proven winner.

Who hasn't ever drained the buzzer beater shot to clinch the win in OT? Who hasn't wanted to punch one across the goal line for six?

And who else but the media can add onto the excitement with such bland, overused terms?

Don't get me wrong. Scored, made, missed, run—they all tell what happened, but they hardly take your writing to the next level.

Some of us are wily veterans of the sports writing world and don't have to try the "Hail Mary" when we're down and out.

But we freshmen phenoms want to dive into the playbook for something fantastic.

We try to describe the things that don't show up in the stat column. We try to bottle up the emotion and capture the moment in words.

Covering sports is a team effort and I'm happy making my contribution, but there has been a lot of trash-talking out there.

Some bad words between writers have caused some extracurricular activity to take place on the field. I tip my hat to them. They made a point that clichés can be boring and useless.

I don't want to point fingers. I only have to look in the mirror to see who is to blame. I couldn't get it done in the clutch, and I shied away from the pressure.

You just have to put the past behind you. My old arm isn't what it used to be.

I hope I can become a living legend, go out on top. But you know, you win some, you lose some, and a tie is like kissing your sister.

So the moral of the story? Throw those old clichés out of your news stories.

And if you're keeping score at home: 34 clichés.

—Isaiah May[8]

The more a cliché is used, the less power it has to engage people's imaginations. The goal is to write the expression that becomes the new cliché (oops, sorry, that's an oxymoron), or to put a new twist on one as this headline does:

Third Tynes a Charm for Giants

Even two-word combinations become clichéd if people recognize them.

> Alexandre Vinokourov and Andreas Kloeden, Team Astana's top two title contenders, were injured in *nasty spills* Thursday in the *thrilling* and bumpy stage through the Burgundy winemaking region.[9]

The names of the cyclists and the fact that they are the top two title contenders can be verified. That they took "nasty spills" is the clichéd opinion of the writer and says little to the reader about the falls or the condition of the men or their injuries. The section of the route through Burgundy can be comparatively bumpy or smooth, but that it is "thrilling" is also the opinion of the writer. It may be scary to one person, challenging to another, and yes, "thrilling" to some.

Euphemisms

A sports writer is like the reporter who was assigned to write a feature about bananas. He thought readers would tire of reading *banana, banana, banana*, so he substituted *that elongated yellow fruit*. The sports writer, too, searches for new ways to write about the same old things and ends up with a euphemism instead.

The sports page is the birthplace of many euphemisms. Little has changed since editor Stanley Walker wrote "the few standard nouns and verbs . . . become tiresome." Thus did a left-handed pitcher become a "southpaw," although, Walker observes, "For some reason, right-handed pitchers never were 'north-paws.'" A pitcher's throwing arm was his "salary wing," . . . and . . . "a baseball became 'the old apple.'"

A euphemism is a word substitute used to make something sound nicer, fresher or just different. It's a way of sugarcoating reality, making it taste better or sound more exciting. Euphemisms are created when sports writers are trying to find a new, lively, colorful way to say the same old thing.

football	=	pigskin
goal posts	=	uprights
basket	=	hoop
football field	=	gridiron
wrestlers	=	grapplers
cross country runners	=	harriers

Using a euphemism to replace an accurate action verb is the equivalent of using attributive verbs other than *said*. The euphemism substitutes a verb that is subject to interpretation by each person who sees or hears it.

In most sports, for example, players run. If the ballcarrier ran, he ran. He didn't plow, gallop, break loose or trot because he's a human being, not a horse. If she made the shot, she scored. She didn't drain, sink, nail, knock down, swish or put two on the board.

Euphemisms for *run* or *ran* permeate the sports idiom. Use them sparingly. Here are just a few euphemisms for run:

rambled	rumbled
rattled	broke loose
plowed	bounced off
skipped	danced
flew	galloped

Redundant Words and Phrases

Redundant phrases say the same thing twice or attempt to qualify a word that, by definition, stands alone. Take the commonly used *all-time record*. *All-time record* is a way of trying to make a *record* sound more important than, by definition, it already is. The *record* is the highest, fastest, most or best for as long as data have been kept on that activity or event. *Set a new record* is also redundant because only one record exists at a time.

Jargon: On the Page

Flag	name of the paper or Web site as it appears on the first page
Headline	summary of story content, above story
Subhead/ secondary head	second headline, also called a deck
Byline	reporter's name, run with a story
Dateline	the place, and historically the date, a story happened
Cutline/ caption	words describing a picture
Photo credit	source or photographer's name run with a picture
Copy	body of story as written
Rule	lines used to separate elements on a page
Jump	continuation of a story to another page
Slug	label given to a story in process
Double-truck	spread that covers two facing pages, including gutter
Gutter	narrow strip of white space between columns of text; especially center of double truck
Pagination	assembling page layouts on a computer screen
Morgue	place archived issues are stored, may be newspapers, film, tapes or electronic files

An *old record* is no longer a record. It is now second place. Hank Aaron held the most-home-runs-hit in Major League Baseball record at 755 for more than 33 years. But as soon as Barry Bonds hit his 756th home run, that became the record. The number hit by Aaron will forever be Aaron's best, but it is no longer the record for number of home runs hit by one player.

Redundant terms like these often appear in sports contexts:

a team of 12 players	ultimate outcome
close proximity	new record
completely outplayed	new recruits
end result	true facts
favored to win	totally destroyed
free passes	future draft choice

Even the football staple *sacked the quarterback* is redundant. The quarterback is the only position that can be sacked. It pays to study the terminology for the sport you're covering.

The Language of *-isms*: Sexism, Racism, Ageism

Forget you ever heard the cliché "throw like a girl." It's kid stuff compared to the *-isms* some broadcast personalities have been using on the air.

Radio talk-show host Don Imus was fired in April for using a racial slur in reference to members of the Rutgers University women's basketball team. But it took a week and a public outcry to make his employer, CBS radio, take action against Imus.

Imus had violated one of the *-isms*: sexism, racism, ageism.

The *-isms* have changed the language significantly in the last five decades. Historically, the white male has been assumed superior in U.S. society and in its written documents. "We hold these truths to be self-evident, that all *men* are created equal." Two constitutional amendments and more than two centuries later, women and minorities are still struggling against sexism and racism to achieve equal treatment. Sports, where female and minority ath-

letes have long excelled and been recognized for their achieve-
ments, may be the exception. Or maybe not. In many U.S. cities,
in California, and in the world as a whole today, whites are the
minority.

But be careful of the alternatives. Don't describe people by what
they're not. If *non-whites* covers all persons of color, are whites
non-colored? Is a redhead a *non-blond*? Is a shortstop a *non-
pitcher*? The authors of "When Words Collide" suggest writing sen-
sitively and accurately about people in any collective such as age,
race or gender; think of people in terms of individuals, not as rep-
resentatives of, or exceptions to, a group.[10]

Generally, ageist language reinforces stereotypes by expressing
surprise over those who do not conform to them. The focus of this
story implies Brett Favre's accomplishments are "sensational," an
anomaly for someone past *"his prime."*

DETROIT—Brett Favre was asked to
throw 17 straight passes at one point.
The way he was completing them, the
Green Bay Packers didn't need to hand
the ball off.

Favre set a franchise record with 20
consecutive completions and finished
with a season-high 381 yards and three
touchdowns in the Packers' 37-26
Thanksgiving Day victory over the
slumping Detroit Lions.

"You never think he is going to
miss one," Green Bay coach Mike
McCarthy said.

The three-time MVP put together
another sensational performance that
made the 38-year-old Favre look as if
he's back in his prime. His seventh 300-
yard game of the season matched a
team mark he set 12 years ago.

> "I've played against him since
> 1996, and he's playing as well as I've
> ever seen him," Lions coach Rod
> Marinelli said.
>
> —Larry Lage, Associated Press[11]

Straightforward, factual writing devoid of descriptive adjectives and stereotypical allusions, or labels that indicate a person is a member of a specific gender, race or age group, is the best way to eliminate accusations of *-ism* bias in writing.

Oh, yes. Imus was back on the air before the end of the year.

Proofreading

"Accuracy, accuracy, accuracy" was Joseph Pulitzer's mantra for reporters and copy editors when he was the editor of the New York World in the 1880s.

He might have added that a simple way to achieve accuracy is to *proofread, proofread, proofread.*

Proofreading begins with the writer who should correct errors before filing a story. Some errors only you will recognize because you're the one who asked the sources to spell their names or saw the coach put an arm around the shoulders of a player who was

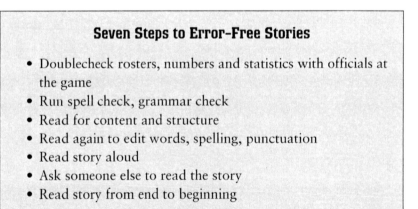

Seven Steps to Error-Free Stories

- Doublecheck rosters, numbers and statistics with officials at the game
- Run spell check, grammar check
- Read for content and structure
- Read again to edit words, spelling, punctuation
- Read story aloud
- Ask someone else to read the story
- Read story from end to beginning

having a bad day. Which player was it—number 23 or number 32? Was the player's name Cheri, Shari or Sherry?

Try these six strategies for achieving error-free stories:

1. Use spell check and grammar check. Even if there's no time to do any other editing, take advantage of these helps built into your software. Even an eagle-eyed copy editor will never be as fast at finding and fixing errors as these electronic checkers.

    But look carefully at the suggested corrections before making a change. The computer-generated correction may change the content in such a way that the message is no longer what you intended.

    Spell check won't flag a correctly spelled word, but you will know if the word is *would* when it should be *wood* or *king* when it should be *kind*.

2. Read the story from beginning to end just to get a sense of what it says. Do not stop to make corrections.

    The goal at this stage is to analyze the story: Does it have all the necessary information? Does it flow easily—that is, will readers be able to follow the story and understand what they've read? Are quotations in appropriate places to explain points you were trying to make? Is it organized appropriately for the content? Does it need a conclusion, or does it have a conclusion but needs a wrap to the lead?

    This is the time to add information, reorganize paragraphs or insert a quote.

3. Print the story and read it again, this time penciling in corrections in sentence structure or punctuation, changing words that are misspelled or don't seem quite right for the context.

    This is where you'll catch errors spell check didn't. Only the writer will recognize a misspelled name or know if the game was Friday or Saturday or whether the score is reversed.

4. Read the story aloud. You may see mistakes because your eyes have to look at each word long enough for your brain to get the message and send it to your vocal chords. You may hear mistakes in sentence structure or find sentences that need to be

shortened. If a sentence is too long to read aloud without taking a breath, it's too long.

The author of "AP Sportswriting," Steve Wilstein, calls this the *mumble method*. "I read sentences and stories aloud to myself, kind of mumbling along the way, so that only I can hear what it's about and whether it makes any sense. By mumbling just loud enough, I can pick up the sound of sentences and the connections between them and better spot errors."[12]

5. Read the story to someone. Better yet, have someone read it to you. If the reader stumbles over a word, hesitates, or stops midsentence, those places are going to be a problem for others, too.

6. Read the story aloud *backward*. Start with the last word and read from right to left, enunciating each word. This is the ultimate test to make your eyes focus on each word. In reading from left to right, readers see phrases or groups of words and may not realize one word is repeated or missing, or that there's an *-s* on the end of a word that should be singular. By forcing your eyes to look at each word, you are more apt to recognize an error.

Upon Further Review

1. The sports idiom is a language unto itself used by insiders and fans with total understanding. Discuss some words and phrases you think are a necessary part of the idiom and some that are truly meaningless clichés and euphemisms. Where should a reporter draw the line in a game story? In live play-by-play? In game analysis?

2. Find stories where euphemisms or clichés are used. Revise the sentences, replacing the euphemisms and clichés with more accurate, precise language.

3. As language evolves, usage changes. In some contexts, including newspapers, the plural possessive pronoun *their* is becoming acceptable with a singular noun or pronoun antecedent. Example: *A player should work on their skills in the off-season.* Read sports stories from several newspapers paying particular attention to sentences containing *their*. Is the antecedent in each

use singular or plural? How important do you think it is for writers to adhere to the rules of grammar? Why? Is it acceptable to use *their* in media writing as a substitute for the gender-specific *he* or *she*? Why?

Notes

1. Phil Andrews, "Sports Journalism" (London: Sage Publications, 2005), p. 74.

2. Jim Corbett, "Chargers get lesson in playoff pressure," USA Today Sports Weekly, Jan. 17–23, 2007, p. 15.

3. "Texas' NCAA high jump champ to skip track season for volleyball," www.usatoday.com/sports/college/2008-01-22-texas-hooker-volleyball _N.htm?csp=34 (accessed Jan. 23, 2008).

4. "Bull rider critical with head injury," Dallas Morning News, July 27, 2007, p. 2.

5. Stanley Walker, "City Editor" (New York: Frederick A. Stokes Company, 1934), p. 119.

6. Steve Wilstein, "Associated Press Sports Writing Handbook" (New York: McGraw-Hill, 2002), p. 112.

7. Isaiah May, "Cliché Speak," Hastings College Student Media, Jan. 2006.

8. Honey Lou Bonar, adjunct professor, Hastings College, Hastings, Neb. Interview on August 26, 2007.

9. Jerome Pugmire, "Vinokourov, Kloeden crash in Tour de France," Associated Press, Hastings (Neb.) Tribune, July 13, 2007, p. 3C.

10. Lauren Kessler and Duncan McDonald, "When Words Collide" (Boston: ThomsonWadsworth, 2008), p. 182.

11. Larry Lage, "Favre leads Packers past Lions," Associated Press, Hastings (Neb.) Tribune, Nov. 23, 2007, p. 1B.

12. Wilstein, "Associated Press Sports Writing Handbook," p. 182.

CHAPTER 7

Writing the Story

At a glance, Richmond Country Club, just north of Oakland and directly across the bay from San Francisco, appears no different than most other private clubs in the United States. There is a sturdily built stucco-and-brick two-story clubhouse, in the Tudor style; rich green, kempt grounds; a quiet, unhurried air.

In the men's locker room, however, there are photographs on the walls indicating that in this place a bit of golf history was made. They are pictures of Sam Snead, Toney Penna, George Schoux and E.J. "Dutch" Harrison when they won the Richmond Open, a tournament played from 1945 through 1948 as part of the pro tour's winter West Coast swing.

Then again, if a picture that was never taken also dressed the wall, it would peg the club as the site where a considerably more significant historical event took place than the likes of a Sam

Snead winning a golf tournament. It would show two black pros who were denied the chance to compete in the 1948 Richmond Open because of the color of their skin.

And as a result, it was there where one of those two men, Bill Spiller, opened the struggle to change that order of things.
—Al Barkow, originally printed in Golf World[1]

PORTS WRITERS are storytellers. They tell action stories and human interest stories about real people. They share information in the form of facts, quotations and numbers, but their ultimate goal is to create detailed pictures of athletes as human beings with whom readers and viewers can identify. As in this feature story lead, they explain events and explore issues.

To a true sports storyteller, it's not enough to say who won, who lost and what the score was. The storyteller focuses on how people interacted to reach that end and uses descriptive details to bring the event to life. To decide what makes the event worth a story, the sports writer considers its news value to the audience. On the 60th anniversary of Bill Spiller's "struggle to change the order of things," Al Barkow decided it was time to tell his story.

What makes Spiller's story news now? It has conflict, a timely anniversary, prominence, consequence and human interest. And for golfers and blacks everywhere, it has emotional proximity. All the values that make a sports story newsworthy are wrapped up in the story of a black man who sued the PGA of America (not today's PGA Tour, which did not exist at that time) for $315,000 because its constitution allowed membership only to Caucasians.

Sports News Values

- conflict
- timeliness
- prominence

- proximity
- consequence or impact
- human interest
- unusual

Sports and news share a common set of values that make stories news to a specific, identifiable audience. The values are the same in print, on air and online. Sports fans want to read and hear about their favorite teams. They're interested in stories about games they've seen to compare their ideas of what happened during play and what it means to the team through the eyes of the players and coaches. Fans also want to know about the games they've missed and how those performances will affect their seasons. They want to know more about their favorite athlete's life away from sports. Sometimes they just want to see or hear their child's name in the news.

Conflict

- Who played?
- Who won?
- Was someone injured?
- Was personal conflict involved?
- Was a rule or law broken?

Sports competitions are based on conflict: two or more competitors, one winner. A record holder is out to beat his or her personal best. A competitor develops a health problem. Competitive eating champion Takeru Kobayashi won Nathan's Famous Hot Dog Eating Contest six years in a row. The seventh year, Kobayashi swallowed 63 hot dogs and buns in the allotted 12 minutes, beating his own record of 56 the year before, but it wasn't good enough. He lost the title to Joey Chestnut, who downed 66 dogs in the same time to win the contest.

Game coverage describes the conflict and breaks it down into individual plays, moments of heartbreaking defeat, and dramatic, adrenalin-pumping victory. Preseason and pregame stories anticipate the conflict. Postseason and postgame stories analyze the conflict.

Conflict also makes news off the field or court. A player is charged with a crime. An unpopular coaching change is made. An athlete is involved in an accident. Basketball star Kobe Bryant faced rape charges, and the story made headlines for months before the case was dismissed. When Tour de France winner Floyd Landis was determined to have used performance-enhancing drugs during the race, both the Tour's and Landis' reputations suffered.

Timeliness

- When did or will the event happen?
- When will the audience know about the story?
- What is the deadline?
- What does the audience know about the subject before seeing this story?
- Is this new information or an update to an existing story?

As a news value, timeliness is the first time a story is published or broadcast. The same story is not timely again unless new information is added. The continuous deadlines of online media and live coverage have boosted timeliness from anything that's happened since the last edition or newscast to what's happening in real time.

Timeliness may also be seasonal. A preseason story is timely shortly before play for that sport's season begins. Signings, training camps, and the Super Bowl are subjects for seasonally timely stories.

Timeliness is relevant to the medium and influences the perspective from which the story is presented. Timeliness for newspapers can be as little as an hour or as long as a week for the next edition. Timeliness for broadcast is live coverage, the next regularly scheduled newscast, or, if the news is important enough, "We interrupt this broadcast for. . . ."

Timeliness for online stories is immediate, with updates as often as new information becomes available. Reporters and bloggers upload game commentary in the online equivalent of play-by-play. Each story and update is marked with the exact time it was posted.

Deadline differences dictate content differences. A game played tonight will be a game story on tonight's sportscast. The same game online has been updated several times during the game with a complete story as soon as it's over and another update after interviews with the coaches and players. Tomorrow's newspaper will carry a detailed game story with quotes from the coaches, statistics and an analysis of how this game changes the season for the team or the rankings for the tournament.

Consider these leads for the same story collected from print, broadcast and online. The indication of when the event happened and the content varies with each medium's deadline. The time of the announcement and the names of the candidates were released in advance so reporters had time to gather background for the story before the moment the winner was announced.

Following the 6 p.m. ceremony in New York where the winner of the Honda-Broderick Cup was announced, usatoday.com posted this lead at 6:36 p.m. (ET) Monday:

> Nebraska volleyball star Sarah Pavan maintained a 4.0 grade-point average in biochemistry while leading the Cornhuskers to a 33-1 season and the NCAA title. Those achievements earned the junior from Kitchener, Ontario, the 31st annual Honda-Broderick Cup as the nation's female college athlete of the year Monday.[2]

At 7:18 p.m. (ET) Monday, after the post-announcement interview or news conference, usatoday.com updated the lead to reflect Pavan's response:

> Nebraska volleyball player Sarah Pavan was shocked to win the Honda-Broderick Cup, which was announced Monday in New York.[3]

Viewers of the 10 p.m. (CST) local sports report in Nebraska Monday heard this lead:

Even before she was named 2007 Collegiate Woman Athlete of the Year, University of Nebraska volleyball player Sarah Pavan had already won some great honors. Pavan helped lead the Huskers to the 2006 National Championship and was selected NCAA Volleyball Player of the Year and the Academic All-American Player of the Year.

Today Pavan won the Honda-Broderick Cup Award. . . .[4]

A central Nebraska daily newspaper ran this lead Tuesday afternoon:

She has achieved "celebrity status" in Nebraska, UNL volleyball coach John Cook said.

"When she shows up to speak to grade school kids in her (Nebraska) sweats, the kids shut up and listen."

Nebraska's Sarah Pavan on Monday won the Honda-Broderick Cup becoming the nation's female athlete of the year and the first Nebraska athlete to be named in the 31-year history of the award.

Since coming to UNL from Kitchener, Ontario, the 6-5 junior has led the team to three national titles. . . .[5]

Prominence

- Will people recognize the name of the person or team?
- Is the person or event locally, nationally or internationally known?
- Is the championship or award commonly recognized and respected?

Prominence is having name recognition among the audience. Local athletes have prominence in their communities' media, professional teams and athletes have national prominence, Tiger Woods and Lance Armstrong have international prominence.

A story about Tiger Woods becoming a father is news because it's happening to a well-known sports figure, not because it is about sports.

Jackie Joyner-Kersey was just another promising runner before she gained prominence as a three-time Olympic gold medalist.

Few recognized the name Lance Armstrong before he won the Tour de France in 1999, but by the time he won his seventh consecutive Tour, Armstrong had become an internationally prominent athlete.

At age 17, Hawaiian golfer Michelle Wie was the first woman named to Sports Illustrated's annual list of the 50 top-earning American athletes. Wie was No. 22.

Proximity

- Did the event take place close to home?
- Were people the audience knows involved?
- Does the local audience have an emotional connection to a story happening elsewhere?

Proximity is nearness in place, time or allegiance, and it may be geographical or emotional. Sporting events that happen in your community and involve people your audience knows are news in your community's media. College teams have proximity in the state or region. Professional teams have local proximity in their hometowns and national proximity because their loyal fans are dispersed throughout the country and their games are televised regularly.

For years, the Boise State Broncos won a few and lost a few on the famous blue artificial playing surface in Bronco Stadium in front of loyal hometown fans. The Idaho Statesman covered Bronco games and charted their rise to win the Western Athletic Conference championship five times. Then came the season when, with a first-year head coach and a perfect record, they earned a trip to the Fiesta Bowl. More than 20,000 fans followed the Broncos to Arizona, but, for the fans at home watching their Broncos face-off against the Oklahoma Sooners on television or online, the game had emotional proximity. Even though the game was a thousand miles away, they were there in spirit to see their team become the Fiesta Bowl champion in a 43-42 upset in overtime.

Consequence or Impact

- What will change as a result of this?
- How many people will be affected?
- Will this action result in legal, financial, emotional or ethical change for players, teams or fans?

Consequence is gauged by the impact an action or change will have on a number of people, and consequence stories explain the impact so people will understand what it means to them. Talk shows and blogs often focus discussion on the possible impact of an action by an individual or a governing organization.

A rules change, a policy shift, a salary negotiation or a change in ticket prices has the potential to change behavior or circumstance far beyond the initial act. If ticket prices go up, some fans may attend fewer games or not purchase the season tickets they have always had. The program loses income, the concessionaires sell fewer hot dogs, the printer prints fewer tickets, and employees collect less trash in less time. Eventually people lose jobs and the program has to make cuts because the dollars aren't coming in to cover expenses.

That's an extreme example, but reactions and repercussions invariably follow any change, and it's the reporter's job to keep the public informed of the impact beyond the official action.

The adoption of the Bowl Championship Series as a method of identifying the top college football teams in the United States overturned a century-old bowl game system. The NCAA Division I-A's action had a direct impact on colleges and their football teams.

Implementation of the BCS had an impact on fans, pollsters, the media, bowl game organizers, budgets, host sites and the economy. The BCS calculation system will continue to be a topic of discussion in the media and in locker rooms and living rooms where people debate its financial, emotional and ethical implications.

Feature Stories

Features are timeless human-interest stories that tell about people doing something special or out-of-the-ordinary stories that entertain as they inform. The best feature stories tug at the heartstrings.

Features May:

- stand alone or run as a sidebar to a news story
- run any time
- be hooked to news or season
- inform, educate or entertain
- profile a person
- explore innovations, trends or issues.

Lead

- delayed
- anecdote, picture that sets up story
- 5 Ws and an H

Structure

- circular, tells story
- longer, space planned ahead of time
- quotations: subject, sources tell story
- conclusion usually ties back to lead

Language

- picture words show subject, setting
- news story: fact, not opinion or analysis

Human Interest

- Does this story tug at the heartstrings?
- Is this story about personal emotional trauma or triumph?
- What has the athlete overcome or the family sacrificed?
- How does an athlete or coach spend time away from work or sports?

The human interest value fills people's natural curiosity about other people. From pictures on cave walls to text messaging and tweets, human beings have communicated to learn how others think, feel, overcome obstacles and succeed. Human interest stories stir emotions and make people feel the urge to take action, if only by blogging their opinions and support.

For instance, bloggers sided with Oscar Pistorius, a double amputee with a big goal, after he appeared on ABC's morning news show. Pistorius, a sprinter dubbed "the blade runner" because of the shape of his prosthetic legs, wanted to run in the Olympics.

He had already earned gold medals and set records in the 100-meter, 200-meter and 400-meter races at Paralympics competitions. But when the South African athlete announced that he intended to try out for the Olympics, the International Association of Athletics Federations said Pistorius' prosthetic limbs might give him an advantage over runners with legs and proposed a rule that would prohibit him from participating in Olympic competition.

Approximately 85 percent of readers who wrote comments about the abcnews.com story in the two weeks after it was posted sided with Pistorius, commending his accomplishments and defending his right to compete against "able-bodied" athletes in the summer Olympics.

In player profiles, sidebars and sports features, readers and viewers expect to hear the human interest side of the story: whose side of the field the grandmother sits on when she has a grandchild on each team, what kind of therapy it took to rehab a player's injury, how it feels to play the last game of a collegiate career, what a player's hobbies and favorite charities are, how a man with prosthetic legs reacts when he's told he's not allowed to compete in the Olympics.

The IAAF ruled Pistorius ineligible to compete in the Olympics because "his carbon fiber blades give him a mechanical advantage. The IAAF based its decision on studies by German professor Gert-Peter Brueggemann, who said the J-shaped 'cheetah' blades were energy efficient."[6] "I was pretty surprised by the outcome . . . and I was pretty disappointed," Pistorius said.

This time, those who posted comments on abcnews.com were divided almost evenly between Pistorius' supporters and those who sided with the committee or commented on related issues.

In the end, the Court of Arbitration for Sport overturned the IAAF ruling and said Pistorious could compete in the Olympic games, if he qualified for the team. Pistorious failed to qualify. He went on to triple-gold-medal in the 100-meter dash, 200-meter dash and 400-meter dash in the Beijing Paralympic Games.

Unusual

- Is this story out of the ordinary on sports pages?
- Has this rarely or never happened before?
- Is it so unusual that people will be amused or entertained by it?

Most of the starters in a car race eventually cross the finish line with four tires on the track. That's why when NASCAR driver Clint Bowyer's No. 7 Chevrolet slid across the finish line upside down and on fire at the Daytona 500, it was unusual. Even though Bowyer placed eighteenth, his finish was the most visual image to emerge from the race and stole the headlines from winner and teammate Kevin Harvick.

French tennis player Tatiana Golovin's choice to wear red shorts during play at Wimbledon was unusual enough to attract attention from the audience, the referee and the media. The referee consulted the rule book before declaring the red shorts underwear, not a visible part of Golovin's white tennis dress, and therefore acceptable attire for Wimbledon's all-white dress code.

Advance Stories

Pre-game stories prepare readers for what they may see during a sporting event.

Advance stories:

- are timely
- appear a day or two before the event

Lead

- direct
- 5 Ws and an H

Structure

- inverted pyramid or Model T

Content*

- name of event, e.g., U.S. Tennis Open
- place and time of event
- names of opponents, conference, division
- names, accomplishments of key players
- comments from the coaches, players
- strategies or plays to expect
- strengths, weaknesses of opponents
- history of rivalry
- results of previous competitions
- season records, past and present

*Order of content will vary with story

Leads

The lead is the beginning of a media story. It sets the scene and tells readers and viewers what happened. On a sports news story, the lead introduces the teams, players, competition and score, and at least hints at how play led to the outcome. On a sports feature, the lead focuses on the person or topic, drawing the audience in with examples, anecdotes, word pictures or an unusual circumstance.

A well-written lead on a well-organized story assures readers that no matter where they exit the story, even after the first paragraph or two, they will have enough information to know what happened.

News values help sports writers determine the lead and structure for their stories. If a fight breaks out on the court, the conflict will almost certainly be the lead. If a record is broken, the consequence or impact is likely to be the lead. If it's a game story, timeliness (when) will be a value, but more important, the result of the conflict—the score—will be in the lead. So will prominence (who), and maybe the human interest. If a well-known player is involved, whether it's a game story or a news story, the name (prominence) will be in the lead, usually connected to another news value such as conflict or consequence.

Think of the lead as a basketball at the moment it reaches the high point of the official's toss. At that moment, all eyes are on the ball. Fans hold their breath for a millisecond. Arms stretch, fingertips poised to direct the ball as it descends. Eyes, then bodies, turn and follow the ball into play. At that moment no one knows who will win, what the score will be, or who will be injured or foul out. What they do know is that an unpredictable sequence of plays will become a game and their team has a chance to win.

The tip-off is when the real story begins. Some of the fans will watch every play intently. Some will watch for a quarter, then go out for popcorn, come back, go out to get a drink, come back. Some will watch the cheerleaders, the people in the next row, the instant replays or the scoreboard more than the game. Some will leave and never return.

Readers and viewers focus on the lead of a game story with just as much interest and intensity as they did the basketball as it went into the air to start the game. The lead should give them enough information so they know what game they're reading about, and it should create enough intrigue that they want to read more. But readers and viewers are like fans at a game. Some will read or listen to every word. Some will pay attention for a few paragraphs or comments before they go out for popcorn. Some will leave and never return.

The major difference between a toss and a lead is that the toss is only the beginning of something. The lead also reveals the outcome. Game story leads tell the end first, but the best ones tell it in such a way that even someone who saw or listened to the game will be curious enough to pay attention.

Here's how Shirley Povich of the Washington Post & Times Herald captured readers' attention for a story about a 1956 World Series game:

> The million-to-one shot came in. Hell froze over. A month of Sundays hit the calendar. Don Larsen today pitched a no-hit, no-run, no-man-reach-first game in a World Series.[7]

Writing the Lead

Readers will decide in seven to 14 words whether to read on or move on. That makes writing the lead one of the biggest challenges a sports writer faces.

The lead sets the tone for the story. It must convey enough information to tease readers and viewers into the story while not giving away so much that they are content to know who played, who won and what the score was.

The writer's goal is to craft a lead that exudes the importance and energy of the event. An allusion lead written in 1924 by New York Herald Tribune sports writer Grantland Rice to describe the Notre Dame–Army football game is considered by many to be the most famous lead in sports-writing history.

Photo 7.1
A Notre Dame student publicity aide staged this photo of the "Four Horsemen of Notre Dame." L-R: Don Miller, Elmer Layden, Jim Crowley, and Harry Stuhldreher.
ASSOCIATED PRESS

Rice captures the tension and energy of not-just-another-football-game by casting it in deep historic shadows where ominous mounted personas with cyclonic power ride onto the battlefield to challenge a fighting army.

Outlined against a blue-gray October sky, the Four Horsemen rode again. In dramatic lore they are known as Famine, Pestilence, Destruction, and Death. These are only aliases. Their real names are Stuhldreher, Miller, Crowley and Layden. They formed the crest of the South Bend cyclone before which another fighting Army football team

was swept over the precipice at the Polo
Grounds yesterday afternoon as 55,000
spectators peered down on the bewildering panorama spread on the green
plain below.[8]

Notre Dame defeated Army 13-7 that day. Coached by Knute
Rockne and led by the four linemen who played from 1922 to
1924, Notre Dame went on to a 10-0 season. Rockne's student
publicity aide arranged a photo of the four uniformed players
mounted on horses. The photo was picked up by the wire services,
cementing Rice's lead, and the Four Horsemen, in the annals of
sports-writing history.

Sometimes the lead is written first; sometimes it is written last.
When sports reporters are covering a game or a news conference
and have short deadlines following the event to file the story, they
often write the body of the story as the game unfolds and add the
lead at the conclusion of the game or event.

When writer's block strikes, as it does for every writer at some
time, the cure may be to write the rest of the story. The lead usually reveals itself as the story develops. A forced or contrived lead
always sounds like what it is: the writer attempting to make the
story fit the lead instead of the lead setting up the story.

The job of the lead is to

- capture the attention of the audience and make them want to
  know more
- establish the theme or essence of the story
- reflect the tension and energy of the event
- summarize key information.

Summarizing the key information is easy once the reporter identifies the 5 Ws and an H:

Who   =   the UC Irvine Anteaters
What   =   defeated Arizona State 8-7
Where =   College World Series

When	=	Tuesday
Why	=	the Anteaters are serious about winning a national championship
How	=	in their final at-bat in the tenth inning

Some of this information is known before the game begins, but some isn't known until it ends. Once the facts are identified, compare them to the news values. Which component has the highest news value to the audience? Is a prominent person or team playing? Was it the tournament championship game? Was there a key play that clinched the game?

From this the reporter should be able to summarize the story in a sentence or two beginning with the word or words with the most audience appeal.

> The UC Irvine Anteaters won in their final at-bat for the third time in four games on Tuesday night, knocking off Arizona State 8-7 in 10 innings in an elimination game at the College World Series.[9]

The why and the how are included in this lead, but often they are found in the next paragraph or two. Seldom is the day the factor with the most audience appeal, but it should be in the lead, as it is in AP writer Eric Olson's story. Olson could have written:

> Tuesday night the UC Irvine Anteaters defeated Arizona State 8-7 in 10 innings in a College World Series elimination game.

Or he could have written:

> Tuesday's College World Series elimination game went 10 innings before the UC Irvine Anteaters sent Arizona State home with a loss.

In the first example, Tuesday night is an accurate descriptor. In the second example, it is not correct if more than one game was played on Tuesday.

Both are acceptable leads, but in neither case is Tuesday the most important or engaging word. If the reader's eye skips to Anteaters or College World Series, there's a chance that reader will stay with the story at least long enough to read the lead.

Two Types of Leads

Leads fit into two general categories: direct and delayed. The lead can be as short as the first sentence of a story, or it can be as long as several paragraphs. Advances, gamers and briefs usually have short, direct leads while features, profiles and in-depth stories are more likely to have longer, delayed leads. But they're not mutually exclusive: gamers may have delayed leads and in-depth stories may have direct leads.

Direct Leads

Direct leads, also called summary leads, are timely and present information quickly. If readers stopped at the end of a direct lead, they would know who played, who won, what the score was, and where and when the event happened.

Game story reporters on deadline use direct leads because they're quick and easy to compose. Readers and listeners like direct leads because all the key information is readily available to help them decide whether to continue with the story or move on to the next. Editors like direct leads because they know if there's not enough room for the whole story, it can be shortened from the bottom without losing important facts or a conclusion necessary to the understanding of the story.

Direct leads are appropriate for most sports stories. They are also used in news stories about trends in sports, advances in sports medicine, sports and politics or government or sports and the courts. These stories are more likely to appear on news pages, where direct leads dominate, than among the gamers, sidebars and box scores on the sports pages. Direct leads are also standard for the first story posted online as a game ends and newspaper stories written on tight deadlines for newspapers.

A complaint about direct leads is that they all begin to sound like fill-in-the-blank boilerplate. The last thing readers want in a sports story is dull and boring. If it's an important game the first thing they want to know is who won. One way to pique curiosity is to add a short teaser sentence that entices viewers or readers to stick with it to find out what the reporter knows that they don't.

The College World Series story about the Anteaters' win ran on the AP wire with this lead:

> That team with the funny nickname is serious about winning a national championship.
>
> The UC Irvine Anteaters won in their final at-bat for the third time in four games on Tuesday night, knocking off Arizona State 8-7 in 10 innings in an elimination game at the College World Series.

Now it is clear why winning the game was so critical and how hard the Anteaters had played to reach this point.

Delayed Leads

Leads that do not summarize the event immediately are called delayed leads. Delayed leads are good for stories that could run any time. They use visual descriptions and emotional appeals to show the subject of a profile doing something unrelated to sports or to introduce the subject of a sports feature. In a delayed lead, the 5 Ws and an H are not all clear until several sentences, even paragraphs, into the story.

A delayed lead may take the form of an anecdote, a short, presumably true story with a point to make about the subject. The lead might set up a scene that invites readers or viewers to imagine themselves becoming part of it, or it might create a portrait of the subject engaged in some activity. The point of the anecdote may be completed in the lead or not revealed until the end of the story, but the lead should transition into the body of the story by telling the reader what focus the story is going to take.

Al Barkow's lead on "One Man's Mission" at the beginning of this chapter is an anecdote that transports the reader into the men's locker room at the Richmond Country Club. Hanging on the wall are photographs of golf greats Sam Snead, Toney Penna, George Schoux and E. J. "Dutch" Harrison when they won the Richmond Open more than 60 years ago.

Then Barkow introduces the intrigue: the photo that was never taken of two black men denied the chance to compete in the Richmond Open because of a membership rule allowing only Caucasians to play in PGA of America–sponsored events. Suddenly the story isn't about a picturesque golf course across the bay from San Francisco; it's about Bill Spiller and his crusade to get the rules changed.

An anecdote sets up this story about one of the nation's best 70-and-over slow-pitch softball teams. It transports readers to the field where they feel the summer heat, meet the players, and ultimately want to stay to watch the game.

LIBERTY, Mo.—Think heat, motion-stifling, odor-producing, nap-inspiring heat. Think of sitting in an attic in the Sahara with a space heater under your rump. Think of eating Grandma's chili with her wool quilt over your head.

Records will show the temperature on July 6 in this Kansas City suburb topped out at 93, but if you think it was a day to swing a bat instead of playing pinochle down at the coffee shop, somebody poured a few shots of something in your chili.

Think heat, Great Depression–era heat. You can ask the guys on the diamond about that kind of heat. They're

Photo 7.2
They call themselves the Omaha Spirit and they don't just play, they win enough to earn distinction as one of the nation's best 70-and-over slow-pitch softball teams.

primary sources. They started playing ball in that heat in the 1930s and '40s when baseball was the thing.

Most never really stopped.

"You know every spring the robins come hopping along," said 71-year-old Lee Leriger of Norfolk. "Well, it's the same thing with us. We'll play 'til we can't."

They call themselves the Omaha Spirit and they don't just play, they win enough to earn distinction as one of the nation's best 70-and-over slow-pitch softball teams.[10]

— Dirk Chatelain, Omaha World-Herald. Copyright 2008. All rights reserved.

Nut Graf

The nut graf is the sentence or paragraph that tells the reader what the story is about and what slant the writer will take. In the slow-pitch softball lead, it is the last paragraph. Readers now know the story will be about a team of men age 70 and older preparing to compete in a national tournament, and it will have a light-hearted tone.

The nut graf may be the first sentence in a story with a direct lead, or, as in the Bill Spiller and slow-pitch softball stories, it may be the sixth or seventh paragraph in a feature story with a delayed lead. If a story does not have a clear nut graf, the reader will become confused by the story or lose interest after a few paragraphs.

Leads to Avoid

Asking a question would seem an easy way to pull readers into a story. Reporters formulate questions to ask before interviewing sources or to answer before beginning to write a story. Readers have the same questions, but they expect answers from the reporter, not more questions. It's too easy for a reader to answer a question with "yes," "no," or "I don't care," and move on without reading the answer the reporter worked so hard to find.

Readers like to know what people said, and that makes quotations tempting to use as leads. Sometimes a source puts the whole story, the intrigue, in one colorful, concise sentence, and it is worth risking a quotation to introduce a delayed lead. Finding a quote that captures the essence of the story without an introduction is rare. It's better to use the quotations to embellish the lead.

If the lead is a quotation, use the next sentence to explain the situation and add enough facts so the reader knows why the quotation is significant. In this example, the writer used the quotation first to capture some of the anguish and disappointment team members might be feeling, but it would also have explained the lead if it had followed the first sentence.

Finding the Nut Graf

Delayed

If you listened closely to the women's basketball games this week, some say, you could actually hear the records breaking.

En route to a 20-3 season, the Blue Jays were led by senior co-captain Tamara Bunner who broke the school's 26-year-old career scoring record with 1,967.

Senior Jeanne Egan smashed the record for rebounds in a season with 311 for an average of 11.6 per game.

Along the way, the team played some heart-stopping games including Friday's conference tournament championship match that ended the Davenport Tigers' season.

With the score tied and 1.7 seconds remaining, a three-pointer by Bunner put the Blue Jays up 59-56 for the championship.

Direct

The Wildcat freshmen came up with a clutch performance for the women's basketball team during Wednesday's 69-64 win over conference rival Sundown State.

The win keeps the No. 8 Wildcats in a tie atop the conference standings, while No. 11 Sundown drops two games back.

"They kept their heads about them," coach Abby Wood said of the freshmen. "They hit some free throws and took care of business. Next time we're in that situation, they should be less nervous."

Try the "cut" test on these stories to find the nut graf. Starting at the bottom, cut one paragraph at a time until no more can be cut without losing information necessary to understanding the stories.

"It's frustrating. But it is what it is. That's what I told the team. . . . It's gotta hurt," Buffaloes coach Trace Tool said.

The Cardinals flew into the Sports Center on Saturday and squeaked out a 72-70 victory over a Buffaloes team desperate for a conference win.

Game Stories

Game stories tell readers what the reporter saw and what the numbers show happened at the game.

Game stories

- are timely
- appear soon after the event

Lead

- direct
- 5 Ws and an H

Structure

- inverted pyramid or Model T

Content*

- score
- name of event, e.g., U.S. Tennis Open
- names of opponents, conference, division
- specific location of event
- key plays, key players' impact
- unexpected factors affecting outcome: injuries, penalties, weather
- comments from coaches, players
- impact of strategies or plays executed
- strengths, weaknesses of opponents
- results of previous competition
- season records, past and present
- next contest if significant, e.g., tournament

*Order of content will vary with story

Story Structure

Sports writers use the same structure patterns as news writers to organize stories. Once the facts have been identified, the background research done and the sources interviewed, the writer plans how to tell the story.

Inverted Pyramid

The most used organization pattern for media stories is the inverted pyramid. An unwieldy, top-heavy triangle looking more like a diamond solitaire than a pyramid, the image is an appropriate way to show the most-important-to-least-important arrangement of information in a news story. Sports news stories, game stories and some features and sidebars use the inverted pyramid because of its reader-friendly organization that allows the reader to stop at any point after the lead knowing what the story is about.

"Who won?" and "What was the score?" are the first questions asked by someone who hasn't yet heard about the game. After they know the end of the story—the score—they may ask, "What happened?" Most people would tell the story beginning from the end and moving through the game from highlight to highlight in a descending order of importance as they remember it. You might tell the story this way:

> "Did you see that game? Wow! Tied with 2 seconds on the clock!
>
> "The Dogs were down 13-7 with 1:02 to go, and then they pulled a fancy zig-zag play nobody's seen before— Brooks passed to Pratt, and he actually caught it on the 30. He tossed it off to Wood—he hasn't caught anything all season, but he was awesome—just grabbed it out of the air like it was nothing! Then he has to get rid of it before they take him out.
>
> "So he aims in the direction of the end zone and lets it fly. You shoulda' seen it! Doerr was standing there with his hands up and this smirk on his face just like he was waiting for it all the time.

"No pressure on Kramer! He laid one on that pigskin, dead center on the posts, his best kick all season, puts us up 14-13. Man, our Dogs barked all the way home!"

If you were writing the story, your lead might be something like this:

> Jack Kramer's extra-point kick was good. Some might even say perfect.
>
> With two seconds left on the Memorial Stadium clock, Kramer slipped in the final point giving the University Dogs a 14-13 win over the College Wildcats on Saturday.

Subsequent paragraphs, in the appropriate order of importance to the audience, would

- explain the new play
- quote the coach on the play and on the performance of key players
- quote players who participated in the touchdown and extra point plays
- review earlier scoring
- show how this game affects both teams on the season
- wrap with a look back at Kramer's extra-point kick or ahead to next week.

Most readers already know who won, may even have seen the game or television footage of the last play, before they read the story. But sports fans are insatiable, especially if their team is winning. It doesn't matter how many times they've seen it or read it, they'll do it again, sometimes for years. They're ravenous media consumers where their favorite teams are concerned. They want to relive the high points of each game again and again and to know what the coach said, how Kramer felt as his toe connected with the ball and what fans thought about the last minute turnaround their team finessed.

That's the concept illustrated by the inverted pyramid organization pattern. The first questions fans would ask are the most important to them and should form the base upon which the rest of the story is built. Without a solid base, a pyramid would not stand. Without a solid lead, the story will not make sense. The base of the story is at the top with the supporting information flowing from the most-interesting-to-the-largest-number-of-people to the least-interesting-to-the-smallest-number-of-people below.

Figure 7.1
Inverted Pyramid
GRAPHIC BY ISAIAH MAY

Readers, reporters and editors like inverted pyramid stories because they are quick and efficient to read, to write and to place on the page. The information of most interest to the most people is in the first paragraphs or on the first screen. The least necessary information is at the end so the reader who doesn't scroll to the second screen won't miss a key point. The newspaper story can be cut from the bottom if space is limited without losing vital information.

Sports reporters like inverted pyramid for the same reasons and more. It works for game stories and news briefs. Sports reporters working on short deadlines or continuous online updates find the pattern especially helpful because they can start the story during the event and insert information anywhere in the story as it becomes available. The lead changes as the story develops, but it isn't complete until the clock runs out.

Inverted Pyramid Online

Online readers scan for chunks of information, according to converged media writing expert Janet Kolodzy.[11] The pyramid becomes a stack of blocks separated by white space descending from a larger square or rectangle representing the lead. Each chunk may stand alone, presenting a small part of the story but being a complete thought in itself for readers who just want to scan the page for interesting tidbits.

A stripped-down version of the inverted pyramid, the Model T organization pattern introduced by MSNBC.com, is gaining popularity with online news writers. Online readers move quickly from story to story, spending only seconds deciding whether to read anything more than the lead. A direct lead forms the horizontal top of the T. It gives the reader a quick overview of the story and a reason to keep reading. The vertical line represents the rest of the story told in whatever order best supports the lead.

Circular

Broadcast media predominately use a circular organization pattern for their stories. Each story has a beginning, a middle and an end,

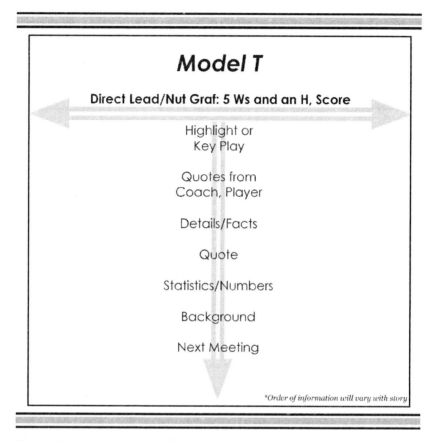

Model T

Direct Lead/Nut Graf: 5 Ws and an H, Score

Highlight or
Key Play

Quotes from
Coach, Player

Details/Facts

Quote

Statistics/Numbers

Background

Next Meeting

Order of information will vary with story

Figure 7.2
Model T
GRAPHIC BY ISAIAH MAY

and it must tell the whole story in a strictly controlled time. Game stories, for instance, begin with a direct lead, add details or sound bites in the middle, and end with a wrap that ties content back to the lead to complete the story line. The wrap might anticipate the next step, such as when the teams will meet again, or it might restate the outcome of the event or finish a theme begun in the lead. If circular stories need to be shortened, they must be carefully edited in the middle so the tie-back is not lost.

The circular pattern is also good for features and profiles in all media. Because features and profiles are planned ahead and can run

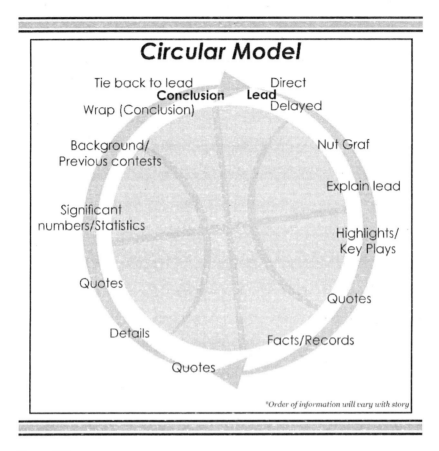

Circular Model

Tie back to lead
Conclusion **Lead**
Wrap (Conclusion)

Direct
Delayed

Background/
Previous contests

Nut Graf

Explain lead

Significant
numbers/Statistics

Highlights/
Key Plays

Quotes

Quotes

Details

Facts/Records

Quotes

Order of information will vary with story

Figure 7.3
Circular Story Structure
GRAPHIC BY ISAIAH MAY

most any day, they can be longer and still run without editing for length. Features and profiles look and sound like short stories because of their delayed leads and circular structure, so readers anticipate an ending. They are disappointed if the story ends abruptly without some conclusion. The ending does not have to wrap up the plot line, only refer back to something in the lead. The lead should not give away the ending if the writer chooses an organization pattern that leads to a conclusion.

One college reporter circled the track postseason story this way:

P. I. T.

Passion. Intensity. Team.

P.I.T. became the mantra for the indoor and outdoor track teams this season. Few on the team actually thought this acronym, designed to inspire individuals and create team unity, would really produce results.

However, as the season progressed, it seemed this new mentality helped propel the athletes to record-breaking heights.

Together, nine members of the track teams broke 14 school records, two members were named conference athletes of the week, and 13 earned All-American status.

. . . (body of story) . . .

Sounds like the P.I.T. crew doesn't need much fine-tuning.[12]

Columns

Columns and editorials provide the personality and passion that news reporting doesn't show, according to Tim Harrower in Inside Reporting.[13]

It's OK to take a position if you're a columnist. It's acceptable to analyze and criticize. It's the one place you can use your imagination, paint pictures, create a persona, say what you think—based on the facts—and still be respected as a sports journalist. Becoming the staff columnist is the pinnacle of sports writing, and the title has to be earned.

Columns are the most read part of the sports page. Readers and viewers find sports columns appealing because they add color, interest and perspective to the sports section. Fans like to know what those on the inside, the columnists, think. They're also attracted to

Follow-Up Stories

Follow-up stories reflect upon the game and analyze the results. They focus on players, strategy and the long-term impact of the event.

Follow-Up Stories:

- are timely
- appear a day or two after the event

Lead

- direct or delayed
- may be reflective or anecdotal
- 5 Ws and an H

Structure

- inverted pyramid or Model T
- circular

Content/Analysis*

- recap of score, occasion, location
- name of event, e.g., U.S. Tennis Open
- names of opponents, conference, division
- reflective response by coaches, players
- key plays, key players' impact
- unexpected factors affecting outcome: injuries, penalties, weather
- impact of strategies or plays executed
- strengths, weaknesses of opponents
- effect on teams' seasons
- next contest if significant, e.g., tournament

*Order of content will vary with story

columns with a voice, a style, a personality that comes through consistently in a columnist's writing. Readers or viewers who identify with a columnist become regular followers and begin to think of the columnist as a friend, someone who shares similar ideas or makes them chuckle. Mike Babcock, freelance sports writer and columnist, noted,

> "When you're a reporter, your words have an impact on your audience. Columnists especially. People listen to you. I would never call for the firing of a coach, because it's not my place. Readers believe what they read. It's not my job to tell them what to do."[14]

Sports writers who know their beats and their communities well have long-term familiarity with their audience and with their subject—sports—and they have practiced their craft long enough to be at ease with the language. The best columnists are reporters who know how to use the language and are comfortable with words, Babcock said:

> "I have a tremendous regard for the English language. When a reporter sits down to write on deadline, the goal is to pound it out as quickly as you can. The most important thing is to get it done. When a sports writer covers a game, the first goal is to get the score and get it right.
>
> "OK, but I get perturbed when people are careless with the language. The writing is important; the grammar is important. When a columnist writes, there's no short deadline pressure, no excuse for not getting it right."

The position of staff columnist is a coveted one earned over time as a beat reporter. Media give columnists space on the page or on the air and time to write on topics of their choice because their columns draw readers and viewers.

Opinion and commentary are clearly labeled to visually separate opinion from sports stories. Each has a column logo, a byline and usually a photo, also called a sig pic, of the writer. Some are set in different type or are justified ragged right to emphasize the difference in the content.

Functions

Columns entertain, educate, editorialize or comment. Some persuade, some inform, some encourage action or question ethics. Consumers today expect columns to make a point, Babcock said.

Online opinion options such as blogs, personal Web pages, and instant messaging have increased peoples' expectations that columnists will help them understand how to think about issues and people.

- Entertaining columns deliver their messages through humor or slice-of-life experiences. They help people look at life from the sidelines and laugh at themselves.
- Educational columns address issues: Should college athletes be paid? Should runners with prosthetic legs be allowed to participate in the Olympics? Is the BCS working as a system for identifying the best college football team?
- Educational columns take an inside look, present facts or ideas as food for thought or explain the impact of an issue.
- Editorial columns express opinions, attempt to persuade, recommend an action or take a stand. Facts and quotations interpret and support the columnist's position.
- Brief comment columns are a collection of comments on unrelated topics. These crazy-quilt columns are often presented in a bulleted list.

Form

Although there is no set structure for columns, starting with an outline similar to that of a news story helps columnists organize what they want to say.

- lead
  introduces the topic, usually an anecdote or delayed lead

- nut graf
  focuses the position of the column in one clear statement
- support
  uses facts, quotes, statistics and other material to explore the
  topic and support the position
- conclusion
  draws a conclusion from the data that restates the message
  encourages an action
  completes the set-up begun in the lead

Upon Further Review

1. Find a sports story for each news value. Select one story that is
   news primarily because it is timely, one that is based on a conflict, one that is unusual, one about a prominent person, and
   so forth. Also, find one story in which all the news values are
   represented and explain why you think it represents each.
   Which news values do most of the sports stories you read contain? Why do you think those values are the ones upon which
   news stories are most often based?
2. Choose three stories you think are written in inverted pyramid
   structure. In each, circle the paragraph you think is the nut graf.
   To see if a story is written in inverted pyramid, use the "cut"
   test. Starting at the bottom, cut off one paragraph at a time
   until you reach the point where the reader must have the information in that paragraph to know what the story is about
   (knows the 5 Ws). That paragraph should be the nut graf, and
   it may be the first paragraph if the story has a direct lead. If the
   story can be "cut" to the top two or three paragraphs, it's written in inverted pyramid structure.
3. Choose three online stories you think are written in Model T
   structure. Run the same "cut" test. A Model T story has paragraphs that might stand alone as "packages" of information,
   but each should be supplementary to the 5 Ws in the lead
   rather than integral to the understanding of what the story is
   about. A reader should know what the story is about, the 5 Ws,
   in the lead.

4. Find three sports stories you think are written in circular structure. Try the crop test on circular stories. What's the difference? What kinds of stories are written in circular structure: Gamers? Follow-ups? Profiles? Features? What news values do these stories represent?

5. If you were a columnist, what would your column say to readers? Would it entertain, educate, editorialize, or comment? Describe the tone or persona your column would take, and choose a column head and tagline for it. Write four columns based on the selections you have chosen. Ask someone to read your columns and tell you what purpose and persona the columns seem to have. It takes practice to write a consistent column that readers look forward to reading, so keep writing and asking for feedback until you feel confident enough to submit samples to an editor.

Notes

1. Al Barkow, "One Man's Mission," Golf World 61 no. 21 (Jan. 18, 2008), p. 18.

2. Drew Costley, "Nebraska volleyballer Pavan takes Honda-Broderick Cup," June 25, 2007, at usatoday.com/sports/college/2007-06-25-pavan-honda_N.htm (accessed July 18, 2007).

3. Costley, "Nebraska volleyballer."

4. Ed Littler, KHAS-TV, 10 p.m. newscast, June 18, 2007.

5. Eric Olson, "NU's Pavan is female college athlete of the year," Associated Press, Hastings Tribune, June 26, 2007, p. 1C.

6. "Double amputee ruled eligible for Beijing," May 16, 2008, at nbcsports.msnbc.com/id/24665015/ (accessed June 19, 2009).

7. Melvin Mencher, "News Reporting and Writing" (New York: McGraw-Hill, 2006), p. 99.

8. Associated Press. "Four horsemen of Notre Dame." Reprinted by permission.

9. Eric Olson, "UC Irvine wins extra-inning thriller to eliminate Arizona State," Associated Press, Hastings Tribune, June 20, 2007, p. 1B.

10. Dirk Chatelain, "Spirit of the 70s," Omaha World-Herald, July 15, 2007, p. 1C.

11. Janet Kolodzy, "Convergence Journalism: Writing and Reporting across the News Media" (Lanham, Md: Rowman & Littlefield, 2006), p. 194.

12. "P.I.T. Crew racing toward top finish." Bronco 90 (Hastings, Neb: Hastings College, 2005), p. 112.

13. Tim Harrower, "Inside Reporting: A Practical Guide to the Craft of Journalism" (New York: McGraw-Hill, 2007), p. 130.

14. Mike Babcock, freelance writer. Personal interview, Jan. 15, 2008.

Answers to the Cut Test:

1. Direct: can be cut to the first paragraph.
2. Delayed: cannot be cut.

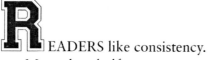

CHAPTER 8

Following the Style

READERS like consistency.

More than half a century ago, the Associated Press created a stylebook because the news service organization recognized the need for a consistent style among stories from AP bureaus worldwide. Today, the "Associated Press Stylebook" is the standard in American journalism.[1]

It offers guidelines on spelling, usage, grammar and punctuation, and supplies formats for information that appears frequently such as scores, times, distances, dates, addresses, names and titles.

AP Style

Using a standardized style makes writing easier and faster for reporters once they learn the guidelines. It makes grasping information easier and faster for readers (who may not even realize a standard is being applied). It becomes a habit for the writer and a comfort zone for the consumer.

The Associated Press is committed to accuracy, clarity and conciseness in sports writing. The AP made guidelines that strive to be fair and not to offend any individual or group of people, according to Dr. Mike Sweeney, head of the journalism graduate program at Ohio University. The AP Stylebook also contains many entries intended to keep writers from making errors in fact, grammar and punctuation. It aims at "a general audience with a tone that is neither too elite nor too common,"[2] Sweeney said.

Most publications have in-house stylebooks in addition to the AP guidelines. Local stylebooks add rules for situations or preferences unique to that medium. The New York Times, for instance, has such a complete set of guidelines that it publishes its style manual.

Scores, times, distances, measurements—anything that recurs in news stories—are easier to read and understand if they appear in the same format every time. The date an event takes place, for example, might be written as a day of the week or as a date depending upon the writer's habit, whim or mood. It could be written:

Sunday, January 17, 2048

Sunday, Jan. 17, 2048

Sunday, Jan. 17

Sunday

January 17

Jan. 17

Yesterday

Today

Tomorrow

Even more variations may be used for dates if the publication has weekly or monthly editions.

Using AP style, the date would be written:

Monday, Tuesday . . .	—within one week either way of publication
Jan. 17	—if the month is used with a day

Jan. 17	—if more than one week from date of publication but within the calendar year, omit the year
Jan. 17, 2048	—if outside the current calendar year, include the year
January 2048	—if used without a specific date, write out the month; do not separate with a comma

The words *yesterday*, *today* and *tomorrow* make readers pause to calculate when the story appeared in relationship to *today* or *tomorrow*. If a story is delayed, such time references become inaccurate and require further editing before publication. Unless specified otherwise in the local newsroom's stylebook, use the day or the date.

Online sports news sites solve the problem of potential confusion by marking each story with the exact minute, hour and day of publication. Each time the story is updated, however, the time references within the story have to be adjusted accordingly, thus another reason for using the day of the week instead of *yesterday*, *today* or *tomorrow*.

Is Reggie Jackson "Mr. October," "Mister October" or "Mr. Oct."? Check the rules on courtesy titles, names and nicknames. Courtesy titles—Mr., Mrs., Miss or Ms.—are not commonly applied in sports, except in special situations such as Reggie "Mr. October" Jackson.

The style guide on names and nicknames is to write them the way the person prefers to be addressed. Nicknames, such as Laurence "Kool-Aid" Maroney, are always placed in quotation marks.

Numbers are all over the place in sports stories. So are the rules for writing them. In news style, single digit numbers are written as words, and double digit and above numbers are written as numerals: one, nine, 10, 19, 119. Unless it's an exception, and there are many of those. When Mark Twain said, "Let the student beware the changes," he must have been contemplating numbers for sports stories.

Exceptions include: ages, dates, heights, measurements, percents, proper names (Big Ten), scores, times, statistics and weights, which are always written in numerals whether they're single or double digits. The stylebook specifies the order in which scores and statistics are organized in stories and stats boxes and gives examples of the format.

The AP Stylebook has a separate sports style section. This section indicates how scores, times and distances should be written, defines sports terms and offers help with spelling and punctuating sports terms. (See appendix A: AP Sports Guidelines and Style.)

Whether it's an editor, a sports reporter or the sports information or media relations director, anyone who writes for print or online media should know and use AP style. An editor or news director recognizes immediately whether the writer is a professional by the style used in a story or news release. Much less editing is required to prepare a story for release when it already conforms to AP style. That alone may make the difference in whether a story or news release is used or rejected by the journalist who reads it.

Broadcast sports departments also have stylebooks. Style changes when the reporter is writing for listeners who only have one chance to hear and understand the information. Because broadcast stories are shorter, it is even more important to omit extraneous words that take up airtime when it could be used to report significant information.

Headlines

The Chicago Bulls were preparing to play the Utah Jazz for the NBA Championship. It would be the Bulls' sixth championship in eight years if they won. Amid the tension and excitement, the Chicago Tribune was preparing for the front page that would run the morning after the championship game. Win or lose, readers would expect a big headline.

Bill Parker, assistant managing editor, canvassed the newspaper's headline writers and gathered a list of ideas about what the headline should incorporate. He knew he had four to six words to capture the spirit of a sports-crazed city.

The Bulls won 87-86 on a steal and shot in the last five seconds. The streets of Chicago "erupted in an all-night celebration,"[3] according to James Glen Stovall in "The Complete Editor," and waited for the Tribune's morning headline which "summed up the feelings of the Bulls fans at the moment with a wink toward another type of physical activity":

The joy of six

Headlines are ads that sell stories to potential readers by promising a benefit for reading the story. That little "wink" of an allusion to the famous book by almost the same name implies the benefits of happiness, humor and satisfaction for the reader who reads on.

Some readers are looking for stories they expect to be there: last night's big game, who made the cut for the next round of the play-offs, or who's favored to win the Super Bowl. Some readers are in the market for any story about favorite teams or players. Some readers are just grazing, looking for a good story to read.

Each decides whether to read the story based on the headline. Information, entertainment, mystery and amusement are among the benefits a headline may offer as a value for time spent reading.

The popularity of online news sites has made headlines even more critical in getting readers' attention and drawing them into the story. The Poynter Institute conducts Eyetrack studies using sophisticated technology to follow the eye movements of print and online news readers to find out, among other things, whether readers were attracted first by the headlines, the photos or something else.[4]

The first Eyetrack studies showed that online readers notice and scan headlines first.[5] They check out the first two or three words of a headline or text block before making a decision to read on or leave. The majority of online readers in the most recent study, however, looked at the navigation bars and tools before reading the headlines. Print readers looked first at headlines and then at large photos.

Figure 8.1

Writing Headlines

Names appear to be the secret to writing sports headlines. Names of teams. Names of mascots. Names of players and coaches. An informal survey of sports stories in newspapers and on sports Web sites showed more than 90 percent of the headlines begin with the name of a team, a mascot, a player or a coach.

Typically, newspaper headlines are written by copy editors or page designers during the pagination or uploading process and not by the reporter who wrote the story. Newsletter editors, news release writers and promotions designers usually write their own headlines.

Headline writers have the task of reducing each story to a few words that will fit in the space left above the text when the page is designed. A one-column story will accommodate one or at most two very small words per line—and present one very big challenge for the headline writer. Columnist Mike Sweeney wrote in the Fort Worth Star-Telegram:

> "Names like Moe Iba fit well in headlines and are appreciated by copy editors. When Iba was an assistant coach at the University . . . the college newspaper ran a story saying he had turned down a job elsewhere. An editor who drew the page called for a headline so tight that only three little words would fit, and '*Iba rejects job*' was too long."[6]

"The solution? '*Moe no go.*'"

Tips for Writing Headlines

- Represent the story accurately
- Use specific, concise words
- Use conversational language
  This: *Four Horsemen of Notre Dame trot across goal line*
  Not: *Quad of equestrians flay flanks in battle for pigskin*

- Use present tense for past and present events
  This: *UNK crunches Mental State in Popcorn Bowl*
  Not: *UNK crunched Mental State in Popcorn Bowl*
- Use action verbs
  This: *Yeager earns new position*
  Not: *Yeager in new position*
- Replace *a, an* and *the* with information
  This: *Olympian carries torch, lights flame*
  Not: *An Olympic runner carries the torch*
- Replace *and* with comma
  This: *Kenyan, Australian qualify for semifinals*
  Not: *Kenyan and Australian qualify for semifinals*
- Do not split: subject-verb, preposition-object, modifier-noun
  This: *Dottseon wants fans*
  with team in bowl momentum
  Not: *Dottseon wants fans with*
  team in bowl momentum
  This: *Baseball commission adopts*
  new policy to control drug use
  Not: *Baseball commission adopts new*
  policy to control drug use
- Avoid double meanings
  This: *Commission gets complaints about NBA officials*
  Not: *Complaints about NBA officials growing ugly*
- Omit *to be* verbs
  This: *Summer Olympics headed to China*
  Not: *Olympic games are headed to China*
- Use infinitive form of verb for future tense
  This: *Boerigter to receive Hall of Fame honor*
  Not: *Boerigter will receive Hall of Fame honor*
- Fit space
  Headline should fill at least 90 percent of allowed space
- Read aloud
  Emphasize a different word each time to hear rhythm, double meanings, bad splits, awkward phrasing

Most headlines have the luxury of room for four to six words, maybe more if there is space for more than one line. In those few words, the writer is challenged to summarize the story in such a way that it is specific and accurate while selling the story to the reader and not misrepresenting the reporter's work or distorting the meaning of the story.

The sentence, or down style, headline is the most common style. The first word is always capitalized, but no end punctuation mark is necessary. A sentence headline uses the English rules of capitalization, contains a subject and a verb and conveys a complete thought.

UNK hammers Arizona State

Knights trample King's men

Rain washes out Cup practice, jumbles schedule

Headlines omit articles (a, an, the), conjunctions (and, but, or) and most adjectives and adverbs. Articles and conjunctions may be used if needed to help make a headline fit, but they're always optional. Question marks and exclamation points are the only terminal punctuation used. Those are rare, but they do make the headlines on special occasions.

A question mark in the Omaha World-Herald[7] wonders of Notre Dame:

Will Irish eyes smile in '08?

Another uncertainty led to this Idaho Statesman[8] headline:

Pacman Jones getting ready to . . . wrestle?

And this special-section label headline in the Honolulu Advertiser[9] celebrated the University of Hawaii's come-from-behind win over Washington for a chance at the BCS playoffs:

Perfect!

'Perfect!' timing and a lot of hustle

The Advertiser's special four-page edition with the headline "Perfect!" made it onto ESPN and local television stations just seconds after the Warriors' come-from-behind victory against Washington.

The idea of a front page printed in advance and handed out right after the game is not new, but to do it right and get it on the field in front of the cameras requires a lot of luck and perfect timing.

We printed 16,000 copies of the section on the morning of Saturday's game and kept them under wraps in two Advertiser vans until the end of the game. When it was 21-0 Washington after the first quarter, it looked like our time and effort had been wasted. But by halftime, the Warriors had managed to stay within a touchdown of the lead.

With 10 minutes left in the game, Lester Kodama, our single-copy manager, called together his crew of about 40 teenagers who usually hand out our Bowtime football programs and hid the papers in garbage bags. The teens remained outside the gates to hand the papers to departing fans while Kodama went inside with a bundle of 300 papers.

Only two minutes remained

AFTER DEADLINE
By Mark Platte

when I called Kodama from the sidelines. When I got his voicemail, I started to get nervous. It was important that the papers get into the hands of players just as the game ended so they could get maximum exposure.

With 44 seconds left, Colt Brennan connected with Ryan Grice-Mullins for the lead, and I connected with Kodama. But with the stadium roaring, we had a hard time hearing each other as we tried to arrange a meeting spot. I was at the 10-yard line on the mauka side, and I needed Kodama to meet me at the 20-yard line. Just then, I saw Alvin Karahara, our market development director, and Jay Higa, our classified advertising director, arrive and ready to help.

Kodama appeared from the stands just in time, and we raced toward him, tearing into the bun-

dle. Fans were eager to get copies, and someone grabbed four from the stack. But by the time we turned to the field, Washington had a first down at the Hawai'i 4-yard line. It appeared the Huskies were going to tie the game, and Kodama grabbed two of the papers back. The other two made their first appearance on national television.

We hid 200 papers as best we could while praying Washington would not tie the game. Ryan Mouton's interception with three seconds remaining had everyone swarming the field, and the papers felt safe to hand out. I approached coach June Jones with a copy but he was hustling everyone off the field because there was still time to play.

Mayor Mufi Hannemann got the first copy and UH athletic director Herman Frazier got the second. Then the players and coaches got the next batch. The players must have thought we literally printed the paper on the spot, judging from their puzzled looks.

Kodama was mobbed in the stands as he passed out about 100 papers. Then he got word back to the teens to break open the garbage bags and man the gates

for the cheering fans leaving the game. Kodama, Higa and I remained on the field as players started mugging for the cameras and holding the pages aloft.

But there were 1,000 papers left that Katahara smartly held back for the next day's rally at the Stan Sheriff Center.

Five minutes after the gates were open that Sunday, the papers were gone. Only a few precious copies remain in our possession.

"It was good to see the fans were so passionate about what the team has done," Katahara said. "They were hungry for something that was a souvenir of a memorable season."

Mark Platte is senior vice president/editor of The Honolulu Advertiser. Reach him at mplatte@honoluluadvertiser.com or 525-9680. Or post your comments at honoluluadvertiser.com.

Figure 8.2
©REPRINTED WITH PERMISSION FROM THE HONOLULU ADVERTISER.

'Perfect!' timing and a lot of hustle

The Advertiser's special four-page edition with the headline "Perfect!" made it onto ESPN and local television stations just seconds after the Warriors' come-from-behind victory against Washington.

The idea of a front page printed in advance and handed out right after the game is not new, but to do it right and get it on the field in front of the cameras requires a lot of luck and perfect timing.

We printed 16,000 copies of the section on the morning of Saturday's game and kept them under wraps in two Advertiser vans until the end of the game. When it was 21-0 Washington after the first quarter, it looked like our time and effort had been wasted. But by halftime, the Warriors had managed to stay within a touchdown of the lead.

With 10 minutes left in the game, Lester Kodama, our single-copy manager, called together his crew of about 40 teenagers who usually hand out our Bowtime football programs and hid the papers in garbage bags. The teens remained outside the gates to hand the papers to departing fans while Kodama went inside with a bundle of 300 papers.

Only two minutes remained when I called Kodama from the sidelines. When I got his voicemail, I started to get nervous. It was important that the papers get into the hands of players just as the game ended so they could get maximum exposure.

With 44 seconds left, Colt Brennan connected with Ryan Grice-Mullins for the lead, and I connected with Kodama. But with the stadium roaring, we had a hard time hearing each other as we tried to arrange a meeting spot. I was at the 10-yard line on the mauka side, and I needed Kodama to meet me at the 20-yard line. Just then, I saw Alvin Katahara, our market development director, and Jay Higa, our classified advertising director, arrive ready to help.

Kodama appeared from the stands just in time, and we raced toward him, tearing into the bundle. Fans were eager to get copies, and someone grabbed four from the stack. But by the time we turned to the field, Washington had a first down at the Hawai'i 4-yard line. It appeared the Huskies were going to tie the game, and Kodama grabbed two of the papers back. The other two made their first appearance on national television.

We hid 200 papers as best we could while praying Washington would not tie the game. Ryan Mouton's interception with three seconds remaining had everyone swarming the field, and the pages felt safe to hand out. I approached coach June Jones with a copy but he was hustling everyone off the field because there was still time to play.

Mayor Mufi Hannemann got the first copy and UH athletic director Herman Frazier got the second. Then the players and coaches got the next batch. The players must have thought we literally printed the paper on the spot, judging from their puzzled looks.

Kodama was mobbed in the stands as he passed out about 100 papers. Then he got word back to the teens to break open the garbage bags and man the gates for the cheering fans leaving the game. Katahara, Higa and I remained on the field as players started mugging for the cameras and holding the pages aloft.

But there were 1,000 papers left that Katahara smartly held back for the next day's rally at the Stan Sheriff Center.

Five minutes after the gates were open that Sunday, the papers were gone. Only a few precious copies remain in our possession.

"It was good to see the fans were so passionate about UH and what the team has done," Katahara said. "They were hungry for something that was a souvenir of a memorable season."

Mark Platte is senior vice president/editor of the Honolulu Advertiser. Reach him at mplatte@honoluluadvertiser.com or 808-525-8080. Or post your comments at honoluluadvertiser.com.

Action Verbs

Action verbs are the lifeblood of sports headlines. "Erickson takes lead" or "Erickson leads" would state the fact, but "Erickson *grabs* lead" gives a stronger sense of the intensity and momentum.

When choosing an action verb, make the action it implies appropriate for the subject in the situation. A horse in the final leg of the race *gallops* to the finish line, but a soccer player does not *gallop* to the goal. A baseball player *slides* home, but a basketball player does not *slide* to the bucket.

Cats can pounce, and a player can be *jazzed* if he's just been traded to the Utah Jazz.

Wildcats pounce on depleted Tigers

Korver's Jazzed, joins team on the road

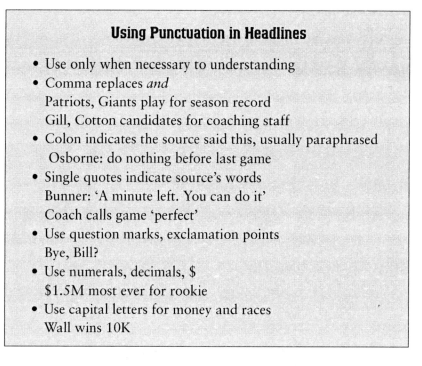

Using Punctuation in Headlines

- Use only when necessary to understanding
- Comma replaces *and*
  Patriots, Giants play for season record
  Gill, Cotton candidates for coaching staff
- Colon indicates the source said this, usually paraphrased
  Osborne: do nothing before last game
- Single quotes indicate source's words
  Bunner: 'A minute left. You can do it'
  Coach calls game 'perfect'
- Use question marks, exclamation points
  Bye, Bill?
- Use numerals, decimals, $
  $1.5M most ever for rookie
- Use capital letters for money and races
  Wall wins 10K

Secondary Headlines

Secondary headlines add layers of information between the headline and the text. They serve two quite opposite purposes: to encourage readers to read the rest of the story, and to give readers enough information to know some facts about the story if they decide not to read more.

Secondary headlines are set in type smaller than the headline and larger than the text. They may be longer phrases or complete sentences that convey additional facts and details. More than one may be used with a story.

Power grabs lead, Jennings misses cut
Senior Chad Power sinks 4-footer on 14th
in Saturday's Crooked Creek Classic

Broncos prepared to make history
The Broncos will travel to face
the Prairie Wolves in their
final battle for a perfect season.
Taking the Conference lead
after besting the Wolves 77–76
in their last match at home,
the Broncos are raring to go.

Punctuation and Style

Headline syntax and punctuation differ from standard English grammar rules because of space limitations. Periods are not used, commas replace *and*, and a colon connects a speaker's name and message.

Seattle stymies Washington's rally, wins in NFC playoffs

Lenson recovers to win sprint finish; Dawson leads overall

Richardson: Landis fills stat sheet all the way across

Single quotation marks replace double quotation marks around words quoted in the story.

'Once-in-a-lifetime' shot sends Deuel to top

Texas QB 'ready to go' for KC

Cicotello chasing 'Hawai'i Slam'

The dollar sign is the only symbol used in text, but symbols such as &, @, # and % appear in headlines as space-saving devices or for graphic illustration of a subject.

¢ turn into $ for baseball retirees' fund

Martini to earn $1.1M first year

Numbers may be written as words or numerals.

#1 or not, Pepperdine has best finish

Woe and 2 for the Pacers

Coach has five-year deal

Blurbs and Links

Blurbs (also called intro headlines or talk heads) are the online equivalent of secondary headlines. Like secondary headlines in print, blurbs tell online readers what's in the news and help them decide what stories to read. More than one blurb may appear with a story or brief.

Eyetrack research showed that half of online readers are scanners who move quickly from one headline or blurb to another, seldom

---

Checklist for Headlines

- ☐ Is it accurate?
- ☐ Is it a complete thought?
- ☐ Does it sound conversational?
- ☐ Does it use active voice?
  This: Ruth bats in three
  Not: Three batted in by Ruth
- ☐ Does it have an action verb?
- ☐ Does the punctuation further understanding?
- ☐ Can *a*, *an*, *the* and *and* be replaced by more informative words?
- ☐ Are grammatical constructions on the same line?
  subject and verb
  preposition and object
  noun and modifier
- ☐ Does it fit without altering publication font or size style?
- ☐ Are the largest headlines at the top of the page?

returning to read a story once they move away from it. By scanning the visual chunks created by headlines and blurbs, these readers gain an overview of the news.

Links connect online readers with even more layers of information and access options. Online stories have the added advantage of being able to use embedded links to lead readers to sites about related topics and give them more choices in selecting the information they want. An online reader may never finish reading a news story yet have a more thorough understanding of the event or subject than someone who reads the whole story because of the ability to follow the thread of information from link to link through more sources.

An online reader who wants to know more about that 1998 NBA championship game might link to the NBA Encyclopedia Playoff Edition to read a retrospective story about the game, to YouTube or Moviefone to watch video of the final shot, to Amazon to buy a book or the video "Unforgettabulls" from the NBA Championship Series, or to the New York Times archives for stories published about the series.

Captions

Today's newspaper is tomorrow's history. Even if most people would recognize the person in the photo today, a researcher would be unable to track the photo without names for identification. The significance of the event would be lost if the caption did not provide the information.

Caption and *cutline* are interchangeable terms meaning the words that describe what's happening in a photo. Before photography and printing press technology converged in the 1800s, the only way to get an illustration in the newspaper was to carve or "cut" the image into a wood block that could be inserted alongside the type on the printing plate. Images became known as "cuts," and the name has stuck through all the technological advances in photography and printing.

Every photograph, including mug shots, needs a caption. Whether it's online, on a page in a newspaper or magazine or in a company newsletter, a photograph is just a graphic design element unless it's accompanied by a caption explaining *who* is in the photo, *what* is happening, *when* and *where* it took place and *why* it's newsworthy. The sports editor may know by looking at a photo that it's quarterback Tom Brady sweating out the last few minutes of the game that gave the New England Patriots a 16-0 season, but do not assume everyone who sees the photo will have the same instant recognition.

Captions identify the people in the photo. As a general guideline, journalists go by the "rule of five": if up to five persons are recognizable in a photograph, and they are all involved in the action, each should be identified by name. In a shot of four players sitting on the bench with their heads down as the opponent makes the winning point that knocks them out of the playoffs, each should be named.

If the coach is pictured standing on the sideline shaking his fist at the officials and four players on the bench behind him are identifiable, only the coach needs to be identified because he is the center of the action. The bench provides background that establishes the environment in which the action is taking place. The players are just part of that environment. It would not be wrong to name them, but it is not necessary.

This "rule of five" is flexible. If six or seven people wearing hard hats and holding shovels poised to break ground for the new stadium are pictured, they should all be named. If two or three players are shown making a key play and faces in the crowd behind them could be identified, only the players need to be named.

Photographers are responsible for gathering the information about the photographs they take, including the correct spelling of names, and filing it with the photographs for future reference.

Captions should also tell readers what they cannot see by looking at the photograph. The groundbreaking is a ceremony formalizing a process that has taken months, maybe years, to reach this moment. The reader wants to know why these particular people are breaking ground for the Morrison-Reeves Athletic Complex, how much construction is going to cost, and whether it will be ready in time for next season.

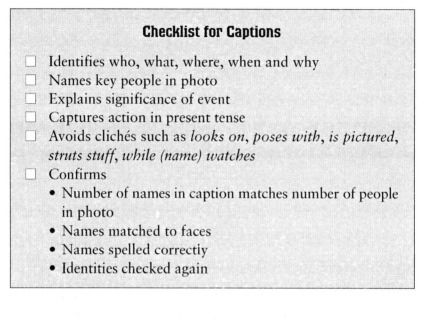

Checklist for Captions

☐ Identifies who, what, where, when and why
☐ Names key people in photo
☐ Explains significance of event
☐ Captures action in present tense
☐ Avoids clichés such as *looks on, poses with, is pictured, struts stuff, while (name) watches*
☐ Confirms
  • Number of names in caption matches number of people in photo
  • Names matched to faces
  • Names spelled correctiy
  • Identities checked again

Avoid grip-and-grin handshakes and posed photos, even if that is the CEO of an athletic shoe manufacturing company presenting a multimillion dollar check to a local university. The caption can explain in great detail the significance of that handshake, but readers will probably not stop to read it. Staged or studio photos, including mug shots, draw relatively little attention from readers, according to the Eyetrack study.

Posed team photos appear in special preseason sections and on posters. Every player, coach and team assistant is named in the caption. The in-house stylebook defines when and how team photos are published and how the caption will be written: first initial and last name, first and last names, last name comma first initial or another way.

Captions can be as long as necessary to make the photo understandable without stating the obvious. "Coach Big Shot poses in his office" is easy to see from looking at the photo, but the reader wants to know more: Why is the coach in his office? What's newsworthy about this photo? "Coach Big Shot prepares to watch films and take notes for next week's game before meeting with the team Sunday evening" explains why the coach is taking notes as he watches the screen on the corner of his desk.

Photos capture the action as it is happening. Captions describe the action as though it were happening at the present time, in present tense. "Coach Big Shot watches . . . and takes . . ." says he is doing it as the reader watches. The next sentence or sentences may be past tense if they explain the background leading up to this moment.

Libel and Other Legalities

Sports writers are subject to the same laws as all journalists when it comes to saying or writing words that are untrue or harmful to others. Writers are responsible for knowing and abiding by federal and state laws and the codes of ethics of their profession.

A commitment to accuracy is the best protection a journalist can have. Failure to check facts, or the inability to support those facts, is the cause of most libel suits. At the very least, publishing an incorrectly spelled player's name or the wrong score damages the credibility of the reporter and the publication. At most, reporters lose jobs and courts order millions of dollars paid to persons who have been libeled or whose privacy has been invaded.

Here is a brief overview of the legal terms sports writers should know.

Libel

Libel is printed defamation of character, an untruth that damages a person's reputation or hinders that person's possibility of getting or holding a job. The statement must be untrue and be about an identifiable person to be grounds for libel.

A generalization such as "golfers are crooks" is not libelous because it does not identify an individual. "Dick Krapff is a crook" would be libelous if it damages Krapff's reputation as golf cart manager at the local country club or keeps him from getting another job. If Krapff sold used golf carts from the course and pocketed the money, he might be a thief. But until or unless he is convicted of stealing from his employer, it would be libelous to say he is a crook.

Newspapers, magazines and Web sites are considered sources of print text, as are broadcast scripts. Live, unscripted broadcasts, preserved in a tangible form such as video or digital recordings, are also subject to allegations of libel.

Slander is spoken defamation of character and is subject to the same laws as libel. If based on unscripted speech, however, slander is treated as a lesser offense because its effects are less permanent. A script or a recording of the speech would constitute publication, making the charge libel.

One defense for libel is truth. The information must be provable and not used with malice. If the printed information can be proven, through documentation or court record, it is a statement of fact and not libel. Most questions of libel are the result of the reporter's negligence. Always verify information before using it. False information reported as fact, even if used as a quotation and attributed to the source, is libelous and is the reporter's responsibility.

Use of the word *alleged* and not identifying a person by name are not defenses against libel. If the number of persons to whom the libelous information might apply is small enough that one or all of the individuals feel they could be singled out as the injured party, say members of a college tennis or softball team, each may file charges.

Public Figures and Private Persons

Public figures are persons who have voluntarily put themselves in the public eye in such a way that they gain prominence, fame or notoriety. By virtue of their voluntary and intentional action to earn a living through an activity that is supported by the public, professional athletes and coaches, like entertainers, are considered to be public figures.

Access to media is also a factor in determining a public figure. A person who has regular and open access to the media through news conferences with reporters, or whom the media seeks out to interview because of the person's newsworthiness, is likely to be considered a public figure.

For a public figure to bring a libel charge against a reporter or the media, that person would have to prove the information was false and that the media publishing the material knew it was false before it was published. If that is true, the reporter or media acted with malice, intentionally defaming the public figure.

Private figures, persons who are not paid to perform their roles as athletes or coaches, have more protection under the law than do public figures, according to the Supreme Court. Most high school, college and amateur athletes do not have to prove cause when they believe they have been libeled. Negligence, which usually results from carelessness on the reporter's part, is cause enough for the court to acknowledge libel on the part of a private person.

Corrections

Mistakes happen, and they should be corrected as quickly and as publicly as possible. Truth, and the fact that the error is acknowledged quickly and without prompting, is often enough to calm the injured person and prevent a libel suit. A show of good faith on the reporter's part does not undo the damage done to someone's reputation, but it may be looked upon favorably in court.

Privilege and Fair Comment

Journalists are protected in expressing opinions, even if the comments are negative or critical, by *privilege*. Privilege covers the right of a journalist to report information and statements made in official governmental proceedings, such as courts, without fear of being sued even if the information is false or the statements would be libelous in another context.

Privilege also protects journalists' right to express opinion. It does not protect inaccurate or false information masquerading as opinion. A columnist who writes that a coach made a stupid decision at a critical point in the game or an official made a bad call that caused a team to lose a key game is protected by privilege because those are opinions and the topic of many a post-game debate. If, however, a columnist says the coach is stupid because he bribed players, that columnist is not protected by privilege and had better have proof to show that, in fact, cash and cars were made available to players.

Fair comment allows journalists to publish columns and editorials commenting on professional players, coaches and athletic directors for things they do, directly or indirectly, if the action is a matter of public interest. When a coach at a state university gets a big raise paid for with tax dollars or a prominent athlete attacks a woman walking her dog along a residential street and leaves her unconscious and bleeding, it's a matter of interest to the public's pocketbooks and personal safety.

In turn, the journalist's obligation is to write commentary and analysis that is factually accurate.

Open Records and Open Meetings Laws

Sports reporters occasionally have reason to attend a court session where an athlete is being arraigned or sentenced. They may need to see the police report on a traffic violation or an accident to gather or verify information.

Each state has *sunshine laws*, so called because they allow the "sun to shine in" on public records, public meetings and court proceedings. Laws vary from state to state, but almost all court proceedings and court records are open to the public. It's a matter of finding them. Some traffic violations and accident reports may be on file at the courthouse and others at the police station, firehouse or city hall.

Not every public official or government agency is willing to hand out information on a moment's notice, so plan ahead. Know where the information is located and get acquainted with the people in the offices.

Even a sports reporter can benefit from reading the state and local statutes. A tour of local public offices will make finding the right place and the right piece of paper much faster when a deadline looms and the only way to get the official information is to go look at it.

More public records are available online every day, but be aware that the Web sites may not be up-to-date or fully archived.

© Copyright

Copyright is a symbol. Copyright is a law. Copyright is an attempt to keep people from stealing the work others have created and claiming it as their own, usually for profit. For journalists, presenting accurate information in a news story is the main reason for wanting to use the work of others. Law allows the use of limited amounts of copyrighted work in news contexts. However, if a journalist used the same material in a book without securing permission, that would be a violation of copyright.

Copyright protects any creative work in a tangible form including written words, art, photographs, music, video, film and online works such as podcasts and blogs. From the moment an idea is put into words or on canvas or recorded digitally or sent in an e-mail, the creation is copyrighted. Depending upon the date the work was created, it may be legally protected for 100 years or more. The law establishes copyright as the life of the author plus 70 years.

All the work done by someone employed to write or produce material, such as photos or video, is known as work-made-for-hire. A sports reporter employed by a newspaper, broadcast station or Web site, for instance, does not own the copyright on work done for the medium; the employer owns the right to the work. The copyright on work-made-for-hire is 95 years.

It's safest to assume that any quotation, graphic, photo or recording a sports writer might want to use is copyright protected and permission is needed to use it in any new way. However, the law permits a few exceptions. In addition to news reporting, the law allows limited use of copyrighted work for purposes such as criticism, comment, teaching, scholarship or research without infringing on the owner's copyright.

Determination of a violation of copyright will be decided by the court based upon

- the intended character and use (commercial, educational, news reporting)
- the nature of the copyrighted work
- the portion of the work used in relation to the work as a whole
- the effect of the use on the potential value of the original work.

Both the words *Super Bowl* and the logo are copyright-protected trademarks. The name Super Bowl, for example, may be used in a story without permission as long as it is written as two words, each capitalized (AP style). The trademarked Super Bowl logo may also be used in editorial copy such as a feature page or an infographic, with the proper trademark symbol, but it may not be reprinted in any commercial or promotional context without securing written permission and paying licensing fees. A sports bar advertising a special event on the day of the Super Bowl must call it "The Big Game Day Bash" or the "Game of the Year Gathering," rather than "Super Bowl Extravaganza."

The same applies to all trademarks whether they are the names of companies such as Nike and Adidas or the names and logos of schools.

Securing written permission from the owner is the fair and safe way to use any copyright-protected work. Finding the current owner of a copyright may not be easy. Copyrights are sometimes sold with the work, or the owner might have died, making it difficult to find the family members who own it. If the request is to use the material for personal profit or commercial use, expect to pay to use it. And be aware that the process itself takes time.

Commercial Use

Use of copyrighted material in an advertisement or promotion without written permission is a violation of copyright. This includes words, photos, trademarks, logos and graphics.

The use of photos and endorsements in commercial advertising requires the signed consent of the person or persons pictured or named. The use of an athlete's photo to promote a product without that person's consent would be unlawful. The easiest way to

The Fair Use Question

Case law and statutes affecting copyright and the media are constantly changing and open to interpretation by the courts on a case-by-case basis. Overall, court decisions provide guidelines that interpret the fair use doctrine as it applies to news and sports in the media.

In light of those decisions, fair use would probably be applied as in these examples. When in doubt, ask for permission.

Acceptable Fair Use

- a few lines of a song or excerpts from a book in a review
- a drawing of a copyrighted cartoon character in a staff-drawn editorial cartoon in a college publication
- a limited amount of copyrighted material in a parody, just enough to cause a reader or viewer to recognize the original
- news video in which copyrighted music provides ambient sound at a newsworthy event
- attributed quotes from a copyrighted work in a news story
- up to one minute of copyrighted audio or video in a news setting such as an obituary of a famed athlete

Violation of Fair Use

- copyrighted material, including logos and trademarks, used in an advertisement or promotion
- a cartoon taken from a newspaper reprinted in a school or business publication such as a sports program
- copyrighted music used as background in video segments on recruiting DVDs
- photos from a Web site republished in a media guide

—From "Sifting through the legal issues of ©Copyright," by James Tidwell, printed in College Media Review[10]

avoid a commercial use suit is to have signed permission forms on file for everyone in any photo that could potentially be used in advertising or promotion, including promotion of the school student athletes attend.

Online Media Issues

Internet users are still exploring the frontiers of media and communication law. Online discussion groups, blogs and citizen journalist Web sites were of concern to Internet service providers until the Supreme Court ruled that service providers are not responsible for messages posted by users. Thus media Web sites that encourage public participation in blogs and instant messaging cannot be held responsible for comments posted by users.

Libel, copyright and commercial use laws applying to print and broadcast media apply equally to online media whether the source is a company Web site, a Facebook page or a personal e-mail, according to copyright expert James Tidwell, professor of journalism at Eastern Illinois University.

Reporters who record interviews for rebroadcast at a later time, or broadcast telephone conversations live without the knowledge of the person speaking, open themselves up to libel and invasion of privacy charges. Consent laws determine whether the state is a one-party consent state, in which a conversation may be recorded without the knowledge of both parties, or a two-person consent state, in which both parties must be aware that the conversation is being recorded.

A general rule of operation is to document all calls by recording acknowledgment and permission from the person being called before beginning an interview or live broadcast. Call-in shows are an exception. Participants call with the intention of speaking live on the air and are personally responsible for what they say.

Code of Ethics

Although no industry-wide code of ethics exists for journalists, most newsrooms have ethics guidelines in their policies or stylebooks. The Associated Press Sports Editors has adopted such guidelines specifically for sports journalists. In principle, the APSE guidelines address the issues and situations that might compromise the integrity and obligation of reporters and editors to produce fair and unbiased sports news, including, but not limited to, those in the box below.

- Accepting tickets, travel, gifts and gratuities.
  The media source should pay travel and meal expenses for staff, even when they travel on a charter flight or dine with a team they are covering. Gifts of more than token value should be declined, returned or given to charity.
- Participating in athletic events, including serving as an official stats or scorekeeper.
  Writers should avoid involvement with outside activities that could be viewed as a conflict of interest, including serving as a scorekeeper for a team they may at some time be assigned to cover.
- Using credentials and press box communications equipment.
  The media source should pay for the use of on-site communications equipment at events, and, outside of established reciprocal relationships, for tickets and press credentials for staff members.
- Endorsing commercial trade names and sponsorships.
  In editorial matter, avoid using product names or endorsements except where necessary to properly identify an event.
- Outside employment.
  Reporters should not accept outside employment that would create a conflict, or the perception of a conflict, in the publication's coverage.

— Adapted from Associated Press Sports Editors Ethical Guidelines[11]

Media relations writers, freelancers, and sports information directors whose employers do not have stated ethics policies may choose to adopt the Society of Professional Journalists' Code of Ethics as a standard for all communications with the media and the public.

The SPJ Code sets forth four simple principles.

- Seek truth and report it.
  Journalists should be honest, fair and courageous in gathering, reporting and interpreting information.
- Minimize harm.
  Ethical journalists treat sources, subjects and colleagues as human beings deserving of respect.
- Act independently.
  Journalists should be free of obligation to any interest other than the public's right to know.
- Be accountable.
  Journalists are accountable to their readers, listeners, viewers and each other.

—Adapted from the Society of Professional Journalists' Code of Ethics[12]

For a sports writer, these guidelines mean being extra careful to represent both teams equally in a story even though you're a homer at heart; making just one more call after trying all day to reach a player and give her the chance to defend herself against allegations of steroid use before the story goes to press; and encouraging the public to express their opinions to and about the media openly via e-mail, blog or call.

It means not accepting tickets, meals or gifts that might obligate you to someone who expects a favor in return; avoiding putting yourself in situations that might be perceived as a show of support for one team over another; not marching in that protest demonstration even though you strongly agree with the sentiment; and not giving in to the temptation to make a couple of calls to get enough information to write your story because you'd just really rather stay home than travel to the game.

It means treating sources, colleagues and the public with respect, and admitting and correcting mistakes when you're wrong.

Upon Further Review

1. Read the AP Sports Guidelines and Style in appendix A. Compare stories about your favorite sport in a newspaper or on an online sports news site with the AP guidelines. Is the source consistent in its use of the guidelines? What exceptions did you find? Look at several stories to see if the same guideline is applied in all stories. Why do you think the source uses a different style for the exceptions?

2. Ask for a copy of a local media style guide (each newsroom has its own style rules in addition to AP). Ask the reporter or news director to explain why the newsroom formulated the specific guidelines in its book. If your office or newsroom does not have a style guide, make a list of guidelines you would want to have included and ask others to contribute ideas. Discuss the suggestions with your colleagues or your employer. Draft a style guide and add to it as you find yourself questioning the way in which something should be written.

3. Study the headlines on sports stories in five sources. What similarities do you notice among the sources? Differences? Make a list of the most descriptive action verbs and figure the percentage compared to those with understood or nondescriptive verbs. Rewrite some of the not-so-interesting headlines using higher interest verbs. Count the number of headlines that begin with the name of a team, mascot, player or coach and calculate the percent. Compare the percent on news pages. Why the difference?

4. As a sports reporter, what would you want to have included in a code of ethics for sports journalists? Should it be different from a code for all journalists? Explain your rationale. If your office does not have a code of ethics, or has one that has not been reviewed recently, draft a list of topics that might be included and circulate it among your colleagues for their input. As a team, discuss the need for a formal code and the suggestions for what it should include. Draft or revise a code for your workplace.

Notes

1. Norm Goldstein, ed., "Associated Press Stylebook and Briefing on Media Law" (New York: Associated Press, 2007).

2. Michael Sweeney, "The guide to AP style," Aug. 27, 2007, at http://web.archive.org/web/20071024002142/www.usu.edu/journalism/faculty/sweeney/re (accessed June 19, 2009).

3. James Glen Stovall and Edward Mullins, "The Complete Editor" (Boston: Allyn and Bacon, 2006), p. 134.

4. Sara Quinn, "Eyetrack07 ASNE presentation script," March 28, 2007, at poynter.org/content/content_print.asp?id=120470&custom= (accessed Jan. 12, 2008).

5. Nora Paul and Laura Ruel, "Early lessons from Poynter's Eyetrack07," April 14, 2007, at ojr.org/ojr/stories/070414paul/print.htm (accessed Jan. 13, 2008).

6. Sweeney, http://web.archive.org/web/20071024002142/www.usu.edu/journalism/faculty/sweeney/re.

7. "Will Irish eyes smile in '08?" Omaha World-Herald, Jan. 3, 2005, p. 1(C).

8. "Pacman Jones is getting ready to . . . wrestle?" Idaho Statesman, Aug. 7, 2007, p. 3 (Sports).

9. Mark Platte, "'Perfect!' timing and a lot of hustle," Honolulu Advertiser, Dec. 9, 2007, p. 3B.

10. James Tidwell, "Sifting through the legal issues of ©opyright," College Media Review, Summer 2001: pp. 18–21.

11. Associated Press Sports Editors, "APSE ethics guidelines," April 21, 2009, at apse.dallasnews.ccm/main/codeofethics.html.

12. Society of Professional Journalists, "Code of Ethics," Indianapolis, IN: Society of Professional Journalists, 1996.

CHAPTER 9

Making Numbers Count

> Baseball statistics give many of us our first sense of mastery, our first (and for some of us our last) sense of what it feels like to really understand something, and to know more about something than our parents.
>
> —George Will[1]

Look at the beginning of a not-so-unusual sports story:

> BLOOMINGTON, Ind. (AP): There was a tense second in the final minute of Iowa's one-point victory over No. 1 Indiana.

In a game full of thrilling emotions, this writer devoted the bulk of his lead to numbers: one second, the final minute, one point, and number one ranking. That sort of preoccupation is not unusual among sports writers. In fact, many of them, and fans for that matter, seem determined to quantify every aspect of their favorite game.

Baseball is perhaps the most notorious example of this obsession. You could probably find, for example, the statistical likelihood of a batter getting a hit in a Tuesday night game at home against a southpaw in July with the bases loaded. Who needs to watch?

From the shelves of bookstores and on the airwaves, telecasts and Web sites, the number crunchers are out in force. We may be in the golden age of sports statistics. Two companies, the Elias Sports Bureau and Sports Team Analysis and Tracking Systems (STATS), compile data for fans, professional teams and print and broadcast media around the world. They can tell you worthwhile trivia, such as the fact that a pitcher can reduce the chances of a stolen base by throwing over to first—as well as ridiculously esoteric non-information, such as which player hit the most foul balls.

What do all these numbers add up to? In sum, they do three things for the intrepid sports writer: they provide new and interesting ways to understand and interpret the game, they provide lots of filler and fodder for radio and TV broadcasters, and they help us make smarter bets. Whoops, scratch that last one. Instead, let's say sports statistics help whether we're fans wanting to improve our chances in a fantasy league or players seeking to make a better arbitration case.

Understanding the Game

If historians were sports writers, we would probably know:

- How long it took Washington to cross the Delaware, depending on whether the wind was blowing up or down the river;
- What size of rock David used to beat Goliath, not to mention the brand of his slingshot; and
- Why Gen. Custer, given his career record against the Indians, should have thought better of participating in the Battle of the Little Big Horn in 1876.

It may seem odd to spend this passion for minutia on a game, but here we are, in a new era of statistical curiosity. There is a statistic for virtually every situation, and a number of astute observers have figured out how to apply all this numerical data to gain a better understanding of their sport.

Keeping Track

First, though, let's consider how those numbers get compiled in the first place. Most of the time, sports writers try to keep "the book," that is, they keep their own statistics. At a basketball game, for example, they might keep track of shooting percentages, rebounds, and free throws.

One of the best things about keeping your own stats is that the process forces you to pay close attention. You learn to be intent on every play and at every moment. Who can know, after all, when the game's turning point will come or what play will signal a shift that turns the game around?

It's true that the home team provides an official scorekeeper, but in the case of high school games, that scorekeeper might be the coach's wife, a teacher, the town dentist or the bus driver. These people are probably reputable, but they may only keep track of made baskets and total points. The scorekeeper might leave, too, before you have finished talking with the players and coaches. If the sports writer wants to look under the hood, so to speak, to see the hidden story of the game—the steals, assists and so on—she or he will need to keep track individually.

In college games, the situation changes. The home sports information staff will likely provide a bevy of scorekeepers, each one responsible for a different statistic. One person, for instance, might record the time each point is made. These statisticians often work in pairs, one reporting the result out loud while the other records it. That way, the scorekeeper never needs to take his eyes off the game, lest he miss something.

Competing Philosophies

Believe it or not, statistics actually play a role in two competing philosophies of sports coverage. On the one hand, we have the

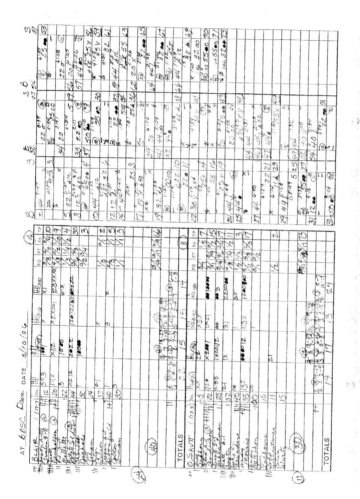

Figure 9.1

This page from a basketball scorebook shows how Omaha Central defeated Kearney, 68–58

RYLY JANE HAMBLETON, LINCOLN JOURNAL STAR

sports writer who is intent on finding the story in the numbers. This writer would typically keep close track of several key statistics, and then, as you might suspect, base the story mainly on those numbers.

Many fans appreciate this kind of writing, but there's a risk that the writer may rely too much on numbers. You may use a stat, for example, when you don't really need one, when a telling quote or sparkling description might work better.

For example, notice all the numbers in the following description of a girls' basketball game:

> For as cold as Southeast was in the first half, then again in the fourth quarter, it was as hot in the third period. Houser hit three three-pointers, Kastanek tallied six points, Katie Birkel chipped in four, and the Knights made good on 11 of 15 shots from the field while rolling up 26 points and streaking to a 41-26 lead after three periods.

That many numbers might make the reader's head spin. Why not just a quote from the coach:

> "I don't know how you can play good in one quarter and not good in three and still win."[2]

A sports writer with a different philosophy, however, might spurn press row altogether and sit in the stands with a box of popcorn, hoping to catch the flavor of the game in a different way. This is the writer who notices what the kid on the end of the bench is doing or gauges the emotions of the fans on each sideline. For this writer, the story is more about people than numbers.

Take, for example, this sentence from the renowned writer Murray Kempton, describing a young Cassius Clay (later to become Muhammed Ali) about to enter the boxing ring against the champ, Sonny Liston:

> "They met in the center of the ring with Clay looking over the head of that brooding presence; then Clay went back and put in his mouthpiece clumsily like an amateur and shadowboxed like a man before a mirror and turned around, still catatonic and the bell rang and Cassius Clay went forward to meet the toughest man alive."[3]

Neither approach is sufficient by itself. The best method is to blend some of each, discovering the key thread of the story through the players themselves and then supporting that concept with facts based on the game statistics.

But don't worry if you feel a bit challenged by the numbers game. As we've indicated, other people are keeping track too, and generally, they will provide the media with frequent updates. At halftime of a basketball game, for example, you will get an update on who's scored, how much, and who's in foul trouble. And after the final buzzer, you've got a box score to examine.

Box Scores

A box score is a detailed summary of a game, usually in the form of a table listing the players and their individual performances. An abbreviated version called a line score basically duplicates the scoreboard on the field.

Baseball box scores may look, on the surface, like nothing more than a list of names and a jumble of figures. But if you know how to read them, you can gather some genuine insights into how a game was played. Many fans check the box scores daily to see how their favorite players are doing or why their team stumbled in the ninth inning to lose a close game.

Where's the Biggest Classroom?

Students may not get a letter grade for the hours they spend in the weight room and on the running track, but they often swear by the lessons they've learned through sports. The key is finding a good mix between papers and practices, between exams and games. Done well, an intercollegiate athletic program can enhance the lives of all students at the college, whether they suit up for a game or not. "What's the biggest classroom at Carleton?" asks college president Robert Oden, Jr.

> "People often guess Olin 149, the concert hall, or Skinner Chapel. Almost nobody gets the answer I'm after: Laird Stadium. My point is that lots of teaching and learning happens in athletics."

Varsity athletics tend to teach lessons that are difficult to learn in the classroom. Says athletic director Leon Lunder,

> "Some of the most important things you'll do in life will be done under pressure and in public. You'll have to make decisions without debating or taking time to vote. These are important skills, and you can learn them by participating in sports,"

Michael Armacost, president of the Brookings Institution, a Washington, D.C., think tank, notes,

> "I learned the importance of subordinating individual aims to what was good for the team. I learned to hang in there when things got tough, to win with modesty and lose with grace, that luck often played a large role in the outcome of games, and that you can increase the odds of getting lucky by preparing more thoroughly and thoughtfully than your opponent."[4]

Study the box score printed below and then answer the questions that follow.

1. What was the final store of the game?
2. In which inning did the winning team score the most runs?
3. Who were the winning and losing pitchers?
4. How many runners did Mudville leave on base?

MUDVILLE	ab	r	h	bi	SPRINGFIELD	ab	r	h	bi
Orson, rf	4	0	1	0	Colbert, 1f	3	1	1	0
Lesco, ph	1	0	0	0	McHale, cf	4	0	2	2
Wylie, cf	4	1	0	0	Kerr, 2b	3	1	2	0
Madden, 3b	4	2	1	1	Carr, 1b	4	2	1	0
Thomas, 1b	3	1	2	0	Van Dyke, rf	3	1	0	0
Kane, 1f	3	0	1	1	Lathrop, rf	1	0	0	0
Panza, c	4	0	0	1	Peterson, 3b	4	0	1	2
Gomez, 2b	4	1	1	2	Polson, c	4	0	2	2
Davis, ss	4	0	2	1	Jones, ss	3	1	3	0
Roberts, p	1	0	0	0	Andre, p	2	0	0	0
Minello, p	1	0	1	0	Knight, p	1	0	0	0
Clayton, p	0	0	0	0	Quinn, p	0	0	0	0
Gray, ph	1	0	0	0	**Totals**	32	6	12	6
Totals	29	6	9	6					

Mudville   000 200 120—5
Springfield   011 003 10X—6

E—Davis, Kerr. DP—Mudville 1, Springfield 2. LOB—Mudville 5, Springfield 6. 2B—Carr, Polson, Jones. 3B—Colbert. HR—Gomez (1). SB—Jones (14). HBP—by Andre (Roberts). T—2:53. A—30,649.

Mudville	IP	H	R	ER	BB	SO
Roberts (L)	5.3	8	5	3	3	3
Minello	1.6	3	1	1	2	1
Clayton	1	1	0	0	0	0

Springfield	IP	H	R	ER	BB	SO
Andre (W)	6	5	2	2	1	5
Knight	2	5	3	2	2	0
Quinn	1	0	0	0	0	2

5. Which batter had the most hits? Who did the most to raise his batting average?
6. Who were the pinch hitters?
7. How long did it take to play the game?
8. How many fans attended?
9. Who was the only batter to hit a triple?
10. Whose performance is most significant to use in writing a lead?

It's All Japanese to Me

In 1992, Kansas State opted to have its home football game against Nebraska moved to Tokyo for the Tokyo Bowl—for a $1 million guarantee for both teams.

While staying in Tokyo for six days, I got a feel for the city. I was assigned to do a Christmas shopping story in downtown Tokyo for the news side. I explained that Japan was not a Christian country to my editor, but to no avail.

But back to the game.

It turned out that my stats would be the official stats for the game since nobody involved in the game, from the Japanese side, understood that stats were important. Thank goodness, I had a long history of keeping my own stats at high school games.

The other "hardship" was the fact that there were five flights of stairs and no elevator between the press box and the locker rooms.

Deadlines being what they were—the game was over at 3 a.m. Lincoln time—it meant writing a running lead and sending. Then, down five flights of stairs for quotes from coaches Tom Osborne and Charlie McBride. Back up the stairs, a side bar and quotes inserted into the lead. Back down the stairs for another side bar on players Tommie Frazier and Calvin Jones. But they had left.

I ran outside the stadium, into this open market, and spotted them. After a loud whistle, they came, provided the quotes I needed for a side bar.

All was peaceful.

—Ken Hambleton, Lincoln Journal Star

Interpreting the Game

Everything about America seems to be getting larger, from the portions in fast food restaurants to the size of a chocolate chip cookie. And it's no different in the National Football League. Consider this: the average weight for pro players in 2006 was 248 pounds, 10 percent higher than in 1983. More remarkably, in 1976 just three NFL players tipped the scales at 300 pounds; by 2006, 570 players, or one in five, weighed that much.[5]

Do these numbers tell us anything beyond the fact that almost everything is getting bigger? They may, if we know how to interpret them, and interpreting numbers has been a lifetime obsession for Bill James.

James is a baseball statistician who has written more than two dozen books devoted to an objective analysis of how baseball could and should be played. The Boston Red Sox raised a few eyebrows when they hired James in 2002, hoping to somehow end a streak of 86 years without winning a World Series. Guess what? Since James has come on board, the Red Sox have won baseball's championship twice.

Sometimes called the "professor of baseball" or the "sultan of stats," James began trying to work out baseball puzzles at his job as a night watchman in a pork-and-beans plant in Kansas. It was a good job, in the sense that it gave him a lot of time to keep to himself and think about baseball. Each day, he lugged his "Baseball Encyclopedia" and a stack of box scores to his boiler-room post, and compiled evidence that began to challenge baseball's sacred cows. He concluded, for example, that starting pitchers have no effect on attendance, and that ballplayers peak in their late twenties.

By hiring James to be their senior baseball operations adviser, the Red Sox joined the ranks of several teams—such as the Oakland A's and the Toronto Blue Jays—which are now emphasizing mathematical data as an alternative to relying on weather-beaten scouts with radar guns and seat-of-the-pants hunches. James calls the effort "the search for objective knowledge about baseball."

In his first "Baseball Abstract," James wrote that he wanted to approach the subject of baseball "with the same kind of intellectual rigor and discipline that is routinely applied, by scientists great and poor, to trying to unravel the mysteries of the universe, of society, of the human mind, or of the price of burlap in Des Moines."[6]

He treated his readers to an egghead's theory of winning baseball, in which outs should be avoided at all costs and walks are really as good as hits. The result of this analysis indicates, James says, that sacrifice bunts are almost never worth the price, confounding a century of baseball's received wisdom.

Do the Math

Remember that algebra you did in high school? Dust off those old formulas because sometimes you will have to plug some numbers into your calculator. Give these a try:

1. Julie Martinez, star shortstop for the Spitwads, has been at bat 77 times this season and gotten 24 hits. What's her batting average?
2. In 37 games, knuckleball pitcher Slim Dickens has thrown 186 innings and given up 47 earned runs. What is his earned-run average? (Hint: ERA is the number of earned runs given up per nine-inning game.)
3. Javon Wilson, North High's star tailback, has gained 812 yards rushing in the first six games of an 11-game season. If he continues at the same pace, in what game will he break the school record of 1,406 yards gained in a season?

Numbers to Note

In putting together a package for an upcoming girls' state basketball tournament, writers compiled a column of "numbers to note." Some of those numbers include teams' winning percentages, number of sophomore starters, returning state champions, unbeatens, first-time qualifiers, top scoring average per player, average margin of victory, and longest winning streak. The column was helpful both to sports fans and other sports writers.

Feeding the Fans

So who needs to know this stuff, anyway?

Basically, television and radio broadcasters need it to fill the dead air between pitches, plays and serves. According to statistician Gary Gillette, more than 500 stats were discussed by network announcers or displayed on the screen during just one World Series game.[7]

Reading a stat sheet has become an occupational requirement. Besides a dictionary and a thesaurus, many sports writers now study an endless stream of numbers, charts, diagrams and box scores. Those box scores, by the way, have doubled in size as statisticians have added more and more items to measure.

So while most sports fans probably don't know how to fix the plumbing or where their septic tanks are, they can prove that a certain player's first pitch will be a strike more than 60 percent of the time. Some know their favorite baseball player's batting average to a thousandth of a point.

Dollars and Cents

Although "Show me the money!" was just a catchphrase from a Tom Cruise film, it's now a common refrain among sports writers. You may find yourself writing about contracts, buyouts, lease arrangements, and the cost of field turf, to mention just a few.

Take this interesting example: college towns have become desirable places to live. People love the pageantry, tradition and idyllic settings of these towns and like to connect with the nostalgia they feel for their own happy college years. So, if you decide to write a feature about this topic you might wonder which college town has the most expensive houses and which has the cheapest.

The answers, according to Coldwell Banker, are Stanford and Ball State. A modest four-bedroom home with a double garage in Palo Alto, California, home of the Stanford Cardinal, will set you back about $1.7 million. Meanwhile, a similar house in

Muncie, Indiana, home of the Ball State Cardinals, would only cost $150,000.[8]

Arbitration Suits

Certainly sports writers and fans love their stats, but, it turns out, lots of players do, too. Awash in numbers, mesmerized by details such as pitch counts and runners in scoring position, some players have found their value escalating, depending on how the numbers play out. "We'll sometimes get involved in arbitration. Players want stats that will make them look good while teams provide some stuff that will make 'em look not so good,"[9] said Don Zminda, who writes the STATS Baseball Scoreboard.

Players haven't always been the masters of their sums. Columnist George Will recalls the more innocent days of the past: "Honus Wagner, the greatest shortstop ever, rejected a salary offer from the Pirates of $2,000 by declaring: 'I won't play for a penny less than fifteen hundred dollars.'"

An NFL running back got those numbers confused not long ago when he said his goal was to gain 1,500 yards or 2,000 yards, "whichever comes first."[10]

For the Record

Compiling a sports record book at your school can be a tremendous resource for future reporters. Such a book includes team and individual records for each sport your school participates in, over time. For example, suppose you wanted to know the fastest time anyone at your school had ever swum 50 meters, or the highest anyone had ever vaulted or the farthest someone had thrown a discus. The record book should be able to provide the answers.

It's often fascinating to look back in history and discover that your tiny college once played Notre Dame in football (or perhaps the local high school). Remember, too, that records are made to be broken. Your sports record book will need to be updated each season as new marks are established.

Itsy-bitsy

Can sports writers get carried away with minutia? It seems so. Reporters covering a college football team's opening game thought they had asked just about every possible question until someone asked the team captain if he would be calling heads or tails at the pre-game coin flip.

The captain took the question in stride and said he had been practicing since "I messed it up in church softball this summer." For the record, the captain said "Tails never fails."

Answers to Do the Math

1. .312
2. 2.27
3. the last game (11th)

Upon Further Review

1. How large a role should statistics play in how a reporter covers a story?
2. How can statistics be used to interpret or better understand a game?
3. List ten different statistics you could compile for a sports event at your college.
4. Discuss which statistics seem most significant when analyzing a game.

Notes

1. This quote appears in "The Pythagoras of Winchester, Kansas," a chapter in George Will's book "Bunts" (New York: Scribner, 1998), p. 54.

2. This game was reported in the Lincoln Journal Star.

3. This quote is reprinted in "The Best American Sports Writing of the Century" (Boston: Houghton Mifflin, 1999), p. 700. More on the Clay-

Liston fight can be found in Kempton's article "The Champ and the Chump," New Republic, 1964, also reprinted in "The Best American Sports Writing of the Century."

4. "Fair Games?" by Erin Peterson, Carleton College Voice, Summer 2006.

5. More information about how everything is getting bigger in America, including the size of NFL players, can be found in "Livin' Large," compiled by Jess Blumberg, Katy June-Friesen and David Zax in Smithsonian, Sept. 2007.

6. This quote appears in "The Professor of Baseball," by Ben McGrath (New Yorker, July 14, 2003). The first "Bill James Baseball Abstract" appeared in 1977.

7. Gary Gillette is co-editor of both "ESPN Baseball Encyclopedia" and "ESPN Pro Football Encyclopedia." He has written or edited more than 50 baseball books.

8. Coldwell Banker ranks the affordability of housing in major college football towns annually. The study can be found at http://hpci.coldwellbanker .com.

9. Zminda writes for STATS, one of the world's leading sports information companies. Its work can be found at www.stats.com.

10. "Bunts" by George Will, p. 57.

CHAPTER 10

Highlighting the Greats

NOT LONG AGO, a young reporter had a challenging assignment: he was to do a story on a varsity team. But Grant Damon of Larkspur, Calif., had a brainstorm. What better way to get the inside scoop on the team than by joining it? His personal experience would give him a microscopic look at what really happens during practice and games.

Choosing lacrosse was easy, too. As Damon put it, its "sportitude" was unquestioned. Lacrosse, he noted, was "the only sport that combines football's we've-got-pads-and-helmets-for-a-reason toughness with basketball's speed and agility, soccer's run-till-you-puke endurance, hockey's vicious body checks, and baseball's fascination with balls and sticks."

Playing lacrosse meant learning to throw a ball with a stick, catching passes left-handed, spinning, and switching hands. It also meant learning a new vocabulary—line drills such as "v" and "down ball."

The culmination of Damon's effort was to stand on the sidelines of a big game, thinking "if only I were on the field." Of course, Damon quickly realized that if he were out there, "I'd probably lose my breath after a minute or two, get distracted, and pass the ball to the other team's defender."[1]

Damon eventually filed an interesting and informative story, but he apparently didn't realize he was walking, or running, in the footsteps of another noted sports writer, one who took the idea of participatory journalism to the highest level.

What can we learn from the great sports writers of the past? Certainly we all stand on the shoulders of those who went before us. Knowing some of the great writers of the past, and a few contemporary masters, will help you step up your own game.

Participatory Journalism

Once upon a time, George Plimpton pulled off something the rest of us have only dreamed about. In 1963 Plimpton pretended to be a 36-year-old rookie quarterback in the Detroit Lions' training camp, turning his experiences into the best-selling book "Paper Lion." In the process, Plimpton helped fans imagine what it would be like to suit up with their gridiron heroes.

Plimpton was able to capture the inside story of a professional football team, from the drudgery of classroom sessions to the hijinks of men playing a boys' game. He wanted to share the special secrets of athletic competition, the ones you could only find in the huddle. Plimpton called himself the "last-string quarterback" and, appropriately, wore the number zero. He said,

"There are people who would perhaps call me a dilettante because it looks as though I'm having too much fun. I have never been convinced there's anything inherently wrong in having fun."[2]

Since that time, the relationship between NFL teams and the press that covers them has become, in many cases, frosty. Thus, it seems unlikely that Plimpton's feat will be repeated in today's multi-billion-dollar, win-at-all-costs NFL. Fortunately, Plimpton was a gifted storyteller. His engaging and thought-provoking style made his adventures all the more enjoyable.

For example, here is what he wrote about playing quarterback:

"Everything fine about being a quarterback—the embodiment of his power—was encompassed in those dozen seconds or so: giving the instructions to ten attentive men, breaking out of the huddle, walking to the line, and then pausing behind the center, dawdling amidst men poised and waiting under the trigger of his voice, cataleptic, until the deliverance of himself and them into the future."[3]

Playing for the Lions was only one of Plimpton's many insider stories. In 1960, Plimpton pitched against the top National League hitters preparing for baseball's All-Star game. Later, he sparred for three rounds with boxing greats Archie Moore and Sugar Ray Robinson, and trained as a hockey goalie with the Boston Bruins.

Plimpton's classic "The Bogey Man" retells his attempt to play professional golf on the PGA Tour. Among other challenges for Sports Illustrated, he also attempted to play top-level bridge and spent some time as a high-wire circus performer.

As a "participatory journalist," Plimpton believed that it was not enough for writers to simply observe; they needed to immerse themselves in whatever they were covering to fully understand what was involved. For example, he believed that football huddles and conversations on the bench constituted a "secret world, and if you're a voyeur, you want to be down there, getting it firsthand."

The ability to see the game from the inside has become a hallmark of sports journalism. Readers expect to be taken inside the huddle, the meeting at the pitcher's mound, even the locker room, to gain insights into coaches' strategies and learn the personalities of their favorite players.

Just days before his death in 2003, Plimpton reunited with veteran players to mark the book's 40th anniversary. "We had a good time last weekend. I got to roast him a bit," said former Lions star Roger Brown. "I told him how he was a light in my life."[4]

Giants of the Past

Plimpton is one of the figures who have helped transform sports writing into its current form, and there are many others, including novelist Ernest Hemingway, that we will consider soon. But first let's take a trip back in time to find out what sports writing looked like a century ago.

America's first noteworthy sportswriter was Grantland Rice, famous for his "Four Horsemen" lead for the 1924 Notre Dame-Army game and a poetic couplet that forever established the code of sports:

> " . . . when the one Great Scorer comes
> to write against your name
> He marks—not that you won or
> lost—but how you played the Game."[5]

Rice joined the Nashville News as a sports reporter for $5 a week and then worked in Atlanta and Cleveland before finally reaching New York. There he became the country's best-paid, best-known sports writer, earning as much per year as Babe Ruth. But the style of those days strikes us now as hopelessly extravagant.

Consider, for example, the work of one of his colleagues who covered a baseball game between Detroit and Washington (reported in the New York Times on Oct. 1, 1907, without a byline). Notice the long sentences, extended descriptions, and florid prose. Note, too, some early signs of greatness from a certain "Tyrus Cobb":

> Detroit's pennant aspirations were placed in jeopardy this afternoon when the Washingtons got an early lead on their opponents and looked to be almost certain winners of a battle that deeply interested the whole baseball world.
>
> Detroit responded with superb gameness and Tyrus Cobb, a new star among baseball men, who took up his mighty cudgel and opened the way to victory. His liner to safe territory inspired others, and before the last man in the sixth inning was declared out, the Tigers had saved the day for themselves.

That "mighty cudgel" and "liner to safe territory" hint at the mountains of sports jargon to come, and the whole scene smacks of Homeric hyperbole. Indeed, in the early days of sports writing, games were reviewed as if they were performances and were often covered by theater critics.

But things would change. By 1910, almost every daily newspaper had a sports section and by 1920 sports stories were appearing regularly in general interest magazines. Here is Heywood Broun's 1921 description of a Babe Ruth home run:

> In the fourth inning Ruth drove the ball completely out of the premises. The ball started climbing from the moment it left the plate. It was a pop fly with a brand new gland and, though it flew high, it also flew far.
>
> When last seen the ball was crossing the roof of the stand in deep right field at an altitude of 315 feet. We wonder whether new baseballs conversing in the original package ever remark: "Join Ruth and see the world."[6]

Talking baseballs, however, would soon disappear. The powerful influence of Hemingway's style began to stimulate a more muscular, stream-lined prose. It was a style polished, too, by World War II correspondents, many of whom had been pulled by their papers from the sports section.

Hemingway loved boxing and bullfighting, but it wasn't just his sports writing on those subjects that appealed to others. It was his stripped-down style. Here is the beginning of his celebrated novel, "A Farewell to Arms":

> In the late summer of that year we lived in a house in a village that looked across the river and the plain to the mountains. In the bed of the river there

> were pebbles and boulders, dry and
> white in the sun, and the water was
> clear and swiftly moving and blue in the
> channels. Troops went by the house and
> down the road and the dust they raised
> powdered the leaves of the trees.

Apparently, the reader is expected to assume that he knows what the speaker is talking about. Very little is spelled out; instead, the reader must bring past knowledge and experience to bear on the passage. This is a tough talker, an insider, a man's man. This is the voice of someone who doesn't need to tell us what village, what river, or what mountains because he assumes we know. We have left the days of epic language far behind.

A More Muscular Prose

One of the best sports writers in the generation inspired by Hemingway was William Bryson, father of current best-selling author Bill Bryson. In "The Life and Times of the Thunderbolt Kid," a story about growing up in the 1950s, Bill Bryson described his father's life as a sports writer for the Des Moines Register.

Every year for nearly 40 years, from 1945 until his retirement, Bryson's father went to the World Series, where he got to witness many of the most memorable moments of baseball history. One of those moments came in 1960 when Bill Mazeroski of Pittsburgh hit a ninth-inning home run to beat the Yankees. Most of the papers in the country reported the news in the usual sober fashion. Here, for instance, is the opening paragraph of the story that ran in the New York Times:

> The Pirates today brought Pittsburgh its
> first World Series baseball championship
> in thirty-five years when Bill Mazeroski
> slammed a ninth-inning home run high
> over the left field wall of historic Forbes
> Field.

But people in Iowa got to read something different:

> The most hallowed piece of property in Pittsburgh baseball history left Forbes Field late Thursday afternoon under a dirty gray sports jacket and with a police escort. That, of course, was home plate, where Bill Mazeroski completed his electrifying home run while Umpire Bill Jackowski, broad back braced and arms spread, held off the mob long enough for Bill to make it legal.
>
> Pittsburgh's steel mills couldn't have made more noise than the crowd in this ancient park did when Mazeroski smashed Yankee Ralph Terry's second pitch of the ninth inning. By the time the ball sailed over the ivy-covered brick wall, the rush from the stands had begun and these sudden madmen threatened to keep Maz from touching the plate with the run that beat the lordly Yankees, 10 to 9, for the title.[7]

The attention to physical detail—the dirty gray sports jacket, the steel mills and ivy-covered brick walls—are all echoes of Hemingway, as is Bryson's description of the umpire. He sounds almost like a matador, "broad back braced and arms spread," as he holds off the crowd. Bryson's story was free of sentiment and grandiose overtones, but it also gave a hint of an important future trend in sports writing. He turned his attention to the side, away from the spotlight, to find those telling details and fascinating sideshows that have delighted sports fans ever since.

As Bill Heinz, another of the era's top sports writers put it, "I eventually discovered that there was a lot more dandruff to that world than stardust," speaking of the glamorous world of professional sports.[8] Yet if it proved to be a less romantic world than he expected, he was never bored. The athletes of that day were exceptionally accessible to the enterprising reporter, and often unguarded in their comments. Who could forget, for example, these memorable quotes from Yankees' catcher Yogi Berra:

- You can observe a lot just by watching.
- It ain't over 'til it's over.
- Half the lies they tell me aren't true.
- If people don't want to come out to the ballpark, nobody's going to stop them.
- Pitching always beats batting—and vice versa.
- You don't hit with your face. (Yogi's standard response whenever someone told him he wasn't good looking.)[9]

Sing Along with Harry Caray

"Take Me Out to the Ball Game" is baseball's most popular song, a catchy little number sung during the seventh-inning stretch. Of course everyone at the ballpark stands and sings along.

Surprisingly, neither of its composers had ever been to a game. Jack Norworth wrote the words in 1908, inspired by a sign that said "Baseball Today — Polo Grounds" outside his train window. They were set to music by Albert Von Tilzer, whose wife made the song popular through her vaudeville act. It's really a pitcher's song, former Brooklyn Dodger ace Carl Erskine liked to say, with its "one, two, three strikes you're out" lyric. Today fans sing only the chorus, but that still makes it the third-most-often-played song in the United States, after "The Star-Spangled Banner" and "Happy Birthday to You."

Modern Masters

An important change in the modern era is the rise of women's sports, thanks largely to the passage of Title IX, federal legislation in 1972 that guaranteed women an equal chance to participate in varsity sports. And as women's sports have grown, so, too, has the presence of women sports writers.

Women Invade the Locker Room

In the mid-90s there were about 10,000 sports reporters in print and broadcast; about 250–300 were women. By 2005, that number had nearly doubled, to 450. "Today female sportswriters are all over the place. No one gives it a second thought,"[10] says Vince Doria, who, as vice president and director of news at ESPN, made diversifying staff a priority.

ESPN was the first network to hire women as sports anchors and to make them part of reporting teams for high-profile events. Doria believes that in some cases women have an edge over men. He notes that men have been bombarded by sports clichés from an early age and often look for the conventional angle. Women might be more likely to offer a fresh view.

One thing that male sports writers could once offer their readers was an exclusive look at an all-male domain: the locker room. That came to end in 1990 with the work of Boston Herald reporter Lisa Olson.

Her saga began when the young reporter, covering the New England Patriots for the first time, asked defensive back Maurice Hurst to come to the media room for an interview.

"The player, however, insisted I come to him," wrote Olson, "saying he was icing his knee or ankle or whatever it was that was ailing him. I did, and, as we sat on the bench in front of his locker, the prank began." Other players began to approach Olson, flashing themselves at her while other players egged them on.

Some sports reporters, women's groups and others rushed to defend Olson, but she was attacked by fans of the team. Trash was thrown at her during Patriots games and one day she came home to find "Leave Boston or die" written in red spray paint on her living room walls.

Things got so bad that Olson requested a transfer and took one to the farthest place from Boston—Sydney, Australia. Eventually, she settled a civil harassment suit against the Patriots, reportedly for $250,000, and returned to the United States to work for New York's Daily News.[11]

The locker room, however, had been successfully integrated. Today, in many cases, reporters provide the names of players they would like to speak with, and the players report to an interview room.

Sports Writing Becomes Respectable

Gender diversity isn't the only major change to touch sports writing in the last generation or so. Thomas Boswell, Washington Post sports columnist, began his career with "little status, less respectability, and $90 a week."

Back then, Boswell notes, nobody called sports writing a profession. It was just a job: "Get the facts straight. Work hard when hard work is needed. Don't blow deadlines. Beyond this it was pretty loose. Nobody thought sports writing was a stepping stone toward a TV career, a six-figure talk radio gig or a big book contract. If you were in a rush, you were in the wrong racket."

Then sometime between the late '60s and the mid-70's, it all changed, thanks largely to the astronomical growth of sports on TV. The whole country watched the same games and then wanted to read and talk about them the next day. Many of the top athletes became entertainers and sports commentators.

So, as Boswell continues, "We became respectable. These days, the Post sports department is bigger than an airport. More and more sports writers resemble dentists or stockbrokers. They tend to have brains, ambition, organization, dedication, degrees from good colleges, straightforward writing styles, and upright private lives."[12]

Sports departments have become so respectable, in fact, that Boswell says he sometimes doesn't feel at home there any more. It's easy to see why: "The ballpark is the place you go to play hooky. When you get there, you scream, yell insults at grown millionaires, knock people aside chasing foul balls and eat nachos until your stomach is so full that you have to switch to ice cream sandwiches."

As a professional reporter, Boswell is committed to serving up journalism's daily slice-of-life. But he is under no illusions about the artistic grandeur of his work. Boswell promises his reader that he will never scrub the sport behind the ears or make it appear more upstanding or respectable. "Newspaper work can be a sort of writer's diary, a raw notebook to himself: 'This Is How It Seems Today.'"

With the advent of television and Internet journalism, however, print people have had to become dramatists, not just journalists; they must be storytellers. Now their major task is to explain what happened and why and what these athletes are really like.

Boswell, an English major at Amherst in his college days, treats his readers as intimates, not as ignoramuses. There is no talking down or dummying-up here—this is one sports writer who challenges his readers to be intelligent. He can also take certain liberties with his audience because he, too, is a fan. Writer and reader are, in this case, comrades-in-arms.

Where There's a Will, There's a Way

Another of sport's great modern masters is George Will, a Pulitzer Prize–winning political columnist for Newsweek. Will is also a great baseball fan and the owner of a small slice of the Baltimore Orioles. Despite the powerful pull of politics, Will says he would rather think about sports:

> Like the fellow in the Bible who tried to reason with the deaf adder and did not get to first base, Mrs. Will has been telling me that at 42 I should grow up. I see no merit in her suggestion, but have agreed to think about something other than baseball during the wasteland that stretches like the Sahara between the World Series and spring training.[13]

In just two sentences, Will reveals how much he expects of his reader. "I assume," we might imagine him thinking, "that you are familiar with the Bible, have a solid grounding in geography, and have probably read T.S. Eliot." His prose is heavily enriched with allusion and cross-reference. It is prose which does not pander to the modern reader too lazy to ground himself in the standard texts, but prose, nonetheless, which is marvelously rewarding.

Will's prose style demonstrates a remarkable connectedness; he makes sure that everything relates to everything else. Perhaps this is a function of the environment in which Will writes: he has a biweekly magazine column, as well as a syndicated column in over 460 newspapers nationwide, not to mention his frequent work as a commentator for ABC television.

Unlike the political arena, baseball represents a world where truth and justice prevail as Will notes: "Sport is one of America's remaining meritocracies, a realm where quality rises and excellence wins."

At times Will elevates the diction of his sports writing by alluding to heroes of the past. This is reminiscent of the grandiloquent Grantland Rice style of sports writing. There are also echoes of famous poems throughout Will's baseball essays, echoes that comically elevate baseball events to epic proportions.

> "Do not go gently into this season, Cub fans," counsels Will, "rage, rage against the blasting of our hopes. Had I world enough, and time, this slowness, Cubs, would be no crime. But I am halfway through my allotted three-score-and-ten and you, sirs, are overdue."

These echoes of Dylan Thomas, Andrew Marvell, and Abraham Lincoln provide a humorous counterpoint to the long-suffering fan's blasted hopes, and there is, too, a slight rhythmic echo of "Casey at the Bat," baseball's monument to shattered pride in Will's "you, sirs, are overdue."

Will brings to his sports writing the style of a literary master, but he never forgets the down-home appeal of the game, with its hot dogs, rally caps, and bat boys.

> "The World Series occurs four times as frequently as the Iowa caucuses," he reminds us. "What a wonderful country America is."

McPhee and Reilly

We shouldn't leave the topic of great modern sports writers without mentioning two more, John McPhee and Rick Reilly. McPhee is widely considered one of the pioneers of creative nonfiction. Along with Tom Wolfe and Hunter Thompson, he helped kick-start New Journalism, which, in the 1960s, revolutionized nonfiction by incorporating techniques from novels. McPhee's detailed description of characters, insatiable appetite for details, and masterful style make his writing lively, readable and personal.

McPhee has written on a marvelous variety of topics, but his sports writing has tended to focus on hiking, canoeing and fishing. His fascination with the great Princeton basketball star, Bill Bradley (a future presidential candidate), led to McPhee's book, "A Sense of Where You Are."

For that book, McPhee took Bradley first to a local high school gym to study his shot-making ability. Much to McPhee's surprise, Bradley missed shot after shot. Finally, in frustration, Bradley informed McPhee that the rim was half an inch too low. McPhee found a ladder and a tape measure to check Bradley's assertion. Sure enough, he was right.

McPhee's attention to detail means that sometimes the story away from the action is the story. Here is his description of Tiger Woods, for example, being distracted by a nearby train:

> I am inside the ropes and close beside a back-nine tee, watching Tiger Woods

---

Don't Forget to Leave the Light On

The battle has just begun for a sports writer when the game ends, but beware—if you're still composing those beautiful sentences long after everyone else has left the stadium, you might get stuck.

Nearly every sports writer who has ever covered a high school game has found the chains locked around the doors at some point—often around 11:30 at night and with no one in sight. Usually, it just means a slightly embarrassing phone call to a principal or athletic director.

But it can get worse. For the Lincoln Journal Star's Conde Sergeant, it meant calling in the entire utility company. Sergeant was in a small town to cover a conference playoff football game. "The press box was a little crow's nest on the opponent's side of the field, accessible only by a big aluminum ladder. The timer was in with us, and in the closing moments the home team was challenging and trying to preserve the clock. The fans weren't real happy because the clock didn't always stop fast enough for them. When the game ended, as they were filing out, one young fellow took the ladder. We saw him dump it in a ditch about two blocks away."

Stranded and on deadline, Sergeant was at his wit's end. Finally, the light company sent a cherry-picker truck to get him down, just in time to file his story.

---

making arcs in the air as he prepares his next shot in the U.S. Open. A couple of yards toward the back of the tee box, Woods stands motionless, feet together, his gaze leveled on the fairway, his posture as perpendicular as military attention. He steps forward and addresses the ball. About to hit he hears the long whistle of a locomotive,

on a track quite nearby. Approaching a
grade crossing, the train completes its
trombone chords: long, long, short,
long. Woods backs off, waits. Now he
re-addresses the ball. But another
grade crossing is close to the first one.
The engineer, at his console, again
depresses his mushroom plunger.
Woods again backs off, idly swings his
club, resumes his pre-shot routine.
Now, reorganized, he is over the ball,
but once again the engineer depresses
the plunger. Backing off, Woods looks
up at the sky.[14]

We never find out how well Tiger hit that drive, but we do have
an insight into the man's patience, deliberation, and intense competitiveness.

Rick Reilly, a former senior writer for Sports Illustrated, has
been voted National Sportswriter of the Year eight times (at last
count!). He was the author of the weekly "Life of Reilly" column
that ran on the last page of SI, the first regular opinion column in
the magazine's history.

Reilly's first book was "Missing Links," a comic golf romance
hailed by the New York Times as "three laughs per page." He has
also written books on the NBA, bad-boy Oklahoma linebacker
Brian Bosworth, and hockey superstar Wayne Gretzky, in addition
to co-authoring a screenplay for the movie "Leatherheads," a com-
edy about the 1927 Duluth Eskimos.

Like George Plimpton, Reilly has also had his share of participatory journalism. He has flown upside down in an F-14, driven a
stock car, competed for a spot in the WNBA, done three innings of
play-by-play for the Colorado Rockies, and staggered through 108
holes of golf in a single day.

What gives Reilly his enduring appeal, however, is his ability to
celebrate everyday heroes. In the following story, "Worth the Wait,"

he uses a litany of questions to ponder why fans are so excited by the slowest runner in cross-country history:

> Why do they come? Why do they hang around to watch a guy at the back of the pack? Why do they want to see a kid finish the 3.1 miles in 51 minutes when the winner did it in 16?
>
> Why do they cry? Why do they nearly break their wrists applauding a junior who falls flat on his face almost every race? Why do they hug a teenager who could be beaten by any other kid running backward? Why?
>
> Because Ben Comen never quits.

The answer, as the reader soon discovers, is that Ben has cerebral palsy. The disease doesn't affect his mind but it seizes his muscles and contorts his body, giving him the balance, as Reilly puts it, "of a Times Square drunk." Yet he competes, week after week. Why, Reilly asks?

> "Because I feel like I've been put here to set an example," says Ben, age 16. "Anybody can find something they can do—and do it well. I like to show people that you can either stop trying or you can pick yourself up and keep going. It's just more fun to keep going."[15]

The 1,440-Minute Cycle

Fast forward to the modern era. We are rapidly heading toward 24/7 newspapers, those driven by Web deadlines. The old idea of an 11 p.m. deadline each night for the morning edition will disappear; instead, as one sports writer put it, "your life will be a deadline." Reporters may find themselves working shifts instead of beats.

As the news industry becomes more attentive to online readers, journalists are being asked to produce news for print, broadcast and online delivery. Reporters now routinely carry video cameras and laptops with them on assignment. They are rushing to adapt to a world where "old news" can mean anything posted more than ten minutes ago.

Imagine this scenario. The college paper's sports editor does a live blog from Saturday's football game. As the teams run out onto the field, he notices that three key players for the home team are wearing T-shirts and jeans instead of their uniforms. He notes this information on his blog, realizing that they won't be playing today, and sends it as a text message to interested fans in the stands.

A few minutes later, the sports editor walks the sidelines and overhears what the coaches and players are saying to each other. He blogs this, too. Soon he's receiving messages from fans who want to know his opinion of a particular play or strategy.

And that's not all. The growing use of news blogs, text messaging and other technology means that anyone can be a reporter. Many news sites now invite people to participate in the news reporting process. Users can give instant feedback on stories, send story ideas and tips via e-mail, or upload personal photos and video clips for use on the air.

But the average person with a video recorder and a computer won't replace the trained reporter. "I'm not a fan of blogs because blogs step over the one thing that great journalism has to give us. And that is editing,"[16] said Bob Levey, former Washington Post columnist.

Rob Curley, vice president of Washingtonpost.Newsweek Interactive, reminds young reporters that "the most important part of newspaper is *news*, not paper."[17] Sports writers must remember that the old rules of journalism still apply to the new media. You are not protected from libel or defamation simply because you're posting in cyberspace.

Upon Further Review

1. One of George Plimpton's least complicated stunts was trying to mouth-catch a grape dropped from the top of the Trump Tower. Think of five teams you could join or activities you could try as a way of developing an insider, participatory sports story.
2. How has Title IX changed the way a sports department covers the news? Should coverage be perfectly balanced between men's and women's sports?
3. Discuss five offbeat sports stories you could cover on your campus. Consider, for example, profiles of trainers, statisticians, groundskeepers, volunteer coaches or injured players.

Notes

1. The lacrosse story appeared in Bark, Larkspur, California's high school paper, on May 13, 2005.

2. Some of the information about George Plimpton comes from an obituary called "The Natural" written by Terry McDonell, which appeared in Sports Illustrated on Oct. 6, 2003.

3. "Paper Lion" by George Plimpton (Harper & Row: New York, 1966), pp. 233–34.

4. Brown's comment appeared in an Associated Press story, "Team had one last reunion with Paper Lion," on Sept. 27, 2003.

5. The Grantland Rice couplet appears in a review of "Sportswriter: The Life and Times of Grantland Rice," by Charles Fountain, published in the American Journalism Review in April 1994.

6. Broun's description of Babe Ruth can be found in "Ruth comes into his own with two homers," which ran in the New York World on Oct. 12, 1923.

7. The stories appeared in the New York Times and the Des Moines Register on October 14, 1960. This description is presented in Bill Bryson's book, "The Life and Times of the Thunderbolt Kid" (New York: Broadway Books, 2006).

8. Heinz is quoted in Bryson's book, "The Life and Times of the Thunderbolt Kid."

9. Many of the malapropisms now attributed to Yogi Berra were stories originally told by Joe Garagiola, Berra's childhood friend. Many of these can be found at wikiquote: en.wikiquote.org/wiki/Yogi_Berra.

10. Doria's comments and a discussion of the battle for equality can be found in "Offensive Interference," by Sherry Ricchiaridi in the American Journalism Review, Dec./Jan. 2005.

11. Olson's saga is recounted in Ricchiardi's article, "Offensive Interference."

12. Boswell's description of the sports writing profession can be found in his introduction to "The Best American Sports Writing 1994," edited by Thomas Boswell (Boston, Houghton Mifflin: 1994).

13. Will's comments come from his book "Bunts" (New York: Scribner, 1998).

14. McPhee's description of Tiger Woods can be found in "Rip Van Golfer," his article in the New Yorker, Aug. 6, 2007.

15. Reilly's article about Ben Comen, "Worth the Wait," appears in Sports Illustrated, Oct. 20, 2003.

16. Bob Levey's columns can be found at the Washington Post's Web site, www.washingpost.com/wp-dyn/metro/columns/leveybob/.

17. Rob Curley, a self-described "Internet nerd in love with the evolution of traditional media," presents his views at www.robcurley.com.

AP Sports Guidelines
and Style

SPORTS GUIDELINES AND STYLE

Sports is entertainment. It is big business. It is news that extends beyond games, winners and losers.

It is also statistics — agate.

Writing about sports requires a broad understanding of law and economics and psychology and sociology and mores.

As the appetite grows, so too does the need for writing with style and consistency.

The constant is the need to write with clarity and accuracy.

Good sports writing depends on the same writing and reporting tools as any other story.

A stylebook, a sports section of a stylebook, is an aid in reaching that goal.

A note on BC filing of sports items:

The 24-hour BC cycle requires the following procedures to differentiate between (a) AMs games stories (and the optionals that move as leads to them), and (b) game stories designed as new wrapups for PMs:

'AMs' stories should be "BC-Reds-Padres" for the game story and "BC-Reds-Padres, 1st Ld-Writethru," etc., for optionals.

Game "PMs" stories should use the word "Folo" in digest lines and the slug ("BC-Reds-Padres Folo"). When a story carries "Folo" in its slug, it is, by definition, for PMs use. Therefore, it doesn't need "Eds: PMs."

"Folo" is used on PMs versions of game stories only.

On events like major golf and tennis tournaments, when there's a story for PMs papers that will develop with morning action, do it as follows:

Slug: [BC-GLF—US Open, Bjt]
Headline: [Mickelson holds slim lead after first round]
Eds. note: [Eds: PMs. Changes byline. Will be updated with early action in second round, about 8:30 a.m. EDT.]
Byline: [By TIM DAHLBERG]
Bytitle: [AP Sports Writer]
PEBBLE BEACH, Calif. (AP) _

or:
Slug: [BC-TEN—Wimbledon, Bjt]
Headline: [Agassi, Sampras advance; Hingis defeated]
Eds. note: [Eds: PMs. Changes byline. Will be updated with morning matches, about 7 a.m. EDT.]
Byline: [By STEPHEN WILSON]
Bytitle: [AP Sports Writer]
WIMBLEDON, England (AP) _

Sports Story-type Identifiers:

ARC — Archery
ATH — Athletics (Track & Field)
BAD — Badminton
BBA — Baseball-American League
BBC — Baseball-College
BBM — Baseball-Minor Leagues
BBN — Baseball-National League
BBO — Baseball-Other
BBH — Baseball-High School
BBI — Baseball-International
BBW — Baseball-Women's
BBY — Baseball-Youth
BIA — Biathlon
BKC — Basketball-College
BKH — Basketball-High School
BKL — Basketball-Women's Pro (WNBA)
BKN — Basketball-NBA
BKO — Basketball-Other
BKW — Basketball-Women's College
BOB — Bobsled
BOX — Boxing
BVL — Beach Volleyball
CAN — Canoeing
CAR — Auto Racing
CRI — Cricket
CUR — Curling
CYC — Cycling
DIV — Diving
EQU — Equestrian
FEN — Fencing
FIG — Figure Skating
FHK — Field Hockey
FBC — (American) Football-College
FBH — (American) Football-High School
FBN — (American) Football-NFL
FBO — (American) Football-Other
GLF — Golf
GYM — Gymnastics

HNB — Handball
HKC — (Ice) Hockey-College
HKN — (Ice) Hockey-NHL
HKO — (Ice) Hockey-Other
JUD — Judo
LUG — Luge
PEN — Modern Pentathlon
MOT — Motorcycling
OLY — Olympics (with a specific sport code added where applicable)
RAC — (Horse) Racing
ROW — Rowing
RGL — Rugby League
RGU — Rugby Union
SAI — Sailing
SHO — Shooting
SKE — Skeleton
SKI — Skiing
SPD — Speed Skating
SBD — Snowboarding
SOC — Soccer
SOF — Softball
SQA — Squash
SUM — Sumo Wrestling
SWM — Swimming
TAE — Tae Kwon Do
TEN — Tennis
TRI — Triathlon
TTN — Table Tennis
VOL — Volleyball
WPO — Water Polo
WEI — Weightlifting
WRE — Wrestling

SPORTS GUIDELINES AND STYLE

A

abbreviations It is not necessary to spell out the most common abbreviations on first reference: AFC, IRL, NASCAR, NBA, NCAA, NFC, NFL, NHL.

-added Follow this form in sports stories: *The $500,000-added sweepstakes.*

air ball

All-America, All-American The Associated Press recognizes only one All-America football and basketball team each year. In football, only Walter Camp's selections through 1924, and the AP selections after that, are recognized. Do not call anyone not listed on either the Camp or AP roster an *All-America* selection.

Similarly do not call anyone who was not an AP selection an *All-America basketball player.* The first All-America basketball team was chosen in 1948.

Use *All-American* when referring specifically to an individual: *All-American Michael Jordan,* or *He is an All-American.*

Use *All-America* when referring to the team: *All-America team,* or *All-America selection.*

archery Scoring is usually in points. Use a basic summary. Example:

(After 3 of 4 Distances)
1. Darrell Pace, Cincinnati, 914 points.
2. Richard McKinney, Muncie, Ind. 880.
3. etc.

AstroTurf A trademark for a type of artificial grass.

athlete's foot, athlete's heart

athletic club Abbreviate as *AC* with the name of a club, but only in sports summaries: *Illinois AC.* See **volleyball** for an example of such a summary.

athletic director Use the singular *athletic* unless otherwise in a formal title.

athletic teams Capitalize teams, associations and recognized nicknames: *Red Sox, the Big Ten, the A's, the Colts.*

auto racing Follow the forms below for all major auto races:

LINEUP
BC-CAR–IRL-GP of St Petersburg Lineup
IRL-Grand Prix of St. Petersburgh Lineup=
By The Associated Press=
After Saturday qualifying; race Sunday=
On the Streets of St. Petersburg, Fla.=
Lap length: 1.8 miles=
(Car number in parentheses)=
1. (11) Tony Kanaan, Dallara-Honda, 103.627 mph.
2. (8) Will Power, Dallara-Honda, 103.499
3. (02) Justin Wilson, Dallara-Honda, 103.444

RESULTS
BC-CAR–IRL-St Petersburg Results
IndyCar-Honda Grand Prix of St. Petersburgh Results=

By The Associated Press=
Sunday=
At streets of St. Petersburg=
St. Petersburg, Fla.=
Lap length: 1.8 miles=
(Start position in parentheses)=
1. (9) Graham Rahal, Dallara-Honda, 83 laps, 74.251 mph
2. (4) Helio Castroneves, Dallara-Honda, 83.
3. (1) Tony Kanaan, Dallara-Honda, 83.

For cars not finishing the race, include reason:
23. (5) Ryan Briscoe, Dallara-Honda, 56, contact.
24. (25) Bruno Junqueira, Dallara-Honda, 44, mechanical.
25. (12) Marco Andretti, Dallara-Honda, 41, mechanical.
26. (26) Marty Roth, Dallara-Honda, 0, DNS.

After the final driver, add:
Race Statistics=
Time of Race: 2:00:43.5562.
Margin of Victory: 3.5192 seconds.
Caution Flags: 6 caution flags for 29 laps.
Lead Changes: 7 among 8 drivers.
Lap Leaders: Kanaan 1-15, Wilson 16-33, Briscoe 34-44, Bernoldi 45-47, Viso 48-59, Meira 60, Hunter-Reay 61-64, Rahal 65-83.
Point Standings: 1, H.Castroneves, 72. 2, S.Dixon, 62. 3, T.Kanaan, 59. 4, G.Rahal, 53. 5, M.Andretti, 53. 6, D.Wheldon, 53. 7, D.Patrick, 48. 8, E.Viso, 45. 9, O.Servia, 44. 10, E.Bernoldi, 42.

B

backboard, backcourt, backfield, backhand, backspin, backstop, backstretch, backstroke
Some are exceptions to Webster's New World, made for consistency in handling sports stories.

badminton Games are won by the first player to score 21 points, unless it is necessary to continue until one player has a two-point spread. Most matches go to the first winner of two games.
Use a match summary.

ball carrier

ballclub, ballgame, ballpark, ballplayer

baseball The spellings for some frequently used words and phrases, some of which are exceptions to Webster's New World College Dictionary:

backstop	outfielder
ballclub	passed ball
ballpark	pinch hit (v.)
ballplayer	pinch-hit (n., adj.)
baseline	pinch hitter (n.)
bullpen	pitchout
center field	play off (v.)
center-field (adj.)	playoff (n., adj.
center fielder	put out (v.) putout (n.
designated hitter	RBI (s.), RBIs (pl.)
doubleheader	right field
double play	right-field (adj.)
fair ball	rundown (n.)
fastball	sacrifice
first baseman	sacrifice fly
foul line	sacrifice hit
foul tip	shoestring catch
ground-rule double	shortstop
home plate	shut out (v.)
home run	shutout (n., adj.)
left-hander	slugger
left field	squeeze play
left-field (adj.)	strike
line drive	strike zone
line up (v.)	Texas leaguer
lineup (n.)	triple play
major league(s) (n.)	twinight doubleheader
major league (adj.)	wild pitch
major leaguer (n.)[1]	

NUMBERS: Some sample uses of numbers: *first inning, seventh-inning stretch, 10th inning; first base, second base, third base; first home run, 10th home run; first place, last place; one RBI, 10 RBIs. The pitcher's record is now 6-5. The final score was 1-0.*

LEAGUES: Use *American League, National League, American League West, National League East,* or *AL West* and *AL East,* etc. On second reference: *the league, the pennant in the West, the league's West Division,* etc.
Note: No hyphen in *major league, minor league, big league* (n. or adj.)

BOX SCORES: A sample follows.

The visiting team always is listed on the left, the home team on the right.

Only one position, the first he played in the game, is listed for any player.

BC-BBN–BOX-Atl-SD

BRAVES 8, PADRES 3

ATLANTA	ab	r	h	bi	SAN DIEGO	ab	r	h	bi
Ogllen ss	5	1	1	1	QVeras 2b	4	1	0	0
Lckhrt 2b	5	2	2	0	SFinley cf	4	0	1	0
ChJnes 3b	4	2	2	1	Gwynn rf	4	1	1	1
Glrrga 1b	2	1	1	4	Cminiti 3b	3	0	1	0
Klesko lf	4	0	1	1	Leyritz 1b	3	1	2	2
Rocker p	0	0	0	0	Joyner 1b	1	0	1	0
Perez p	0	0	0	0	CHrndz c	4	0	1	0
Seanez p	0	0	0	0	RRivra lf	3	0	1	0
Lgtnbr p	0	0	0	0	MaSwy ph	1	0	0	0
JLopez c	4	1	1	1	Gomez ss	3	0	0	0
AJones cf	4	1	2	0	Miceli p	0	0	0	0
Tucker rf	2	0	1	0	Bhrngr p	0	0	0	0
GerWm rf	2	0	1	0	Lngstn p	0	0	0	0
Neagle p	2	0	0	0	GMyrs ph	0	0	0	0
DeMrtz p	0	0	0	0	JHmtn p	2	0	0	0
Clbrnn ph	1	0	0	0	RayMys p	0	0	0	0
DBtsta lf	1	0	0	0	Sheets ss	1	0	0	0
VnWal ph	1	0	0	0					
Totals	**36**	**8**	**12**	**8**		**34**	**3**	**8**	**3**

Atlanta	000 101 600 - 8
San Diego	000 200 000 - 2

DP_Atlanta 1, San Diego 2. LOB_Atlanta 4, San Diego 7. 2B_ChJones (1), Gwynn (1), RRivera (2). 3B_Lockhart (1). HR_Galarraga (1), JLopez (1), Leyritz (1).

	IP	H	R	ER	BB	SO
Atlanta						
Neagle	5 2-3	7	3	3	1	7
DeMrtz W, 1-0	1-3	0	0	0	0	0
Rocker	1 1-3	0	0	0	0	3
Perez	0	1	0	0	1	0
Seanez	2-3	0	0	0	0	0
Lightenberg	1	0	0	0	1	2
San Diego						
JHamilton L, 0-1	6	7	4	4	2	5
RaMyers	2-3	2	3	3	1	0
Miceli	1-3	1	1	1	0	1
Boehringer	1	2	0	0	0	0
Langston	1	0	0	0	0	0

Perez pitched to 2 batters in the 8th, JHamilton pitched to 2 batters in the 7th.

Umpires_Home, Bonin; First, Davis; Second, Rippley; Third, Tata; Left, Poncino; Right, Hallion.

T_2:58. A_65,042 (59,772).

Example of an expanded box score:

BC-BBA–EXP-BOX-Ana-Tex

Rangers 3, Angels 2

Anaheim	AB	R	H	BI	BB	SO	Avg.
Erstad cf	4	0	3	2	0	0	.750
Gil ss	3	0	0	0	0	0	.000
a-OPalmeiro ph	1	0	0	0	0	0	.000
Nieves ss	0	0	0	0	0	0	.000
Salmon rf	4	0	1	0	0	1	.250
Glaus 3b	4	0	1	0	0	1	.250
GAnderson lf	3	0	1	0	1	0	.333
GHill dh	4	0	0	0	0	1	.000
BMolina c	4	1	1	0	0	1	.250
Spiezio 1b	3	1	1	0	0	1	.333
Eckstein 2b	3	0	1	0	0	0	.333
Totals	**33**	**2**	**9**	**2**	**1**	**5**	

Texas	AB	R	H	BI	BB	SO	Avg.
Greer lf	3	0	0	1	0	1	.143
Velarde 2b	4	0	1	0	0	1	.250
ARodriguez ss	4	0	1	0	0	3	.375
RPalmeiro 1b	2	0	0	0	2	0	.167
IRodriguez c	4	1	2	0	0	0	.250
Galarraga dh	3	1	1	1	0	0	.167
Caminiti 3b	2	0	1	0	1	0	.500
Curtis lf	2	1	1	0	0	0	.500
Mateo rf	3	0	1	0	0	1	.429
^Totals	**27**	**3**	**8**	**2**	**3**	**6**	

Anaheim	001 000 010_2 9 2
Texas	020 000 10x_3 8 0

a-grounded into double play for Gil in the 8th.

LOB_Anaheim 5, Texas 5. 2B_Erstad 2 (2), Giaus (1), BMolina (1), Spiezio (1), Velarde (1), IRodriguez (1), Galarraga (1). RBIs_Erstad 2 (2), Greer (1), Galarraga (1). SB_ARodriguez (1). SF_Greer. GIDP_OPalmeiro, GHill 2, IRodriguez, Curtis, Mateo.

Runners left in scoring position_Anaheim 4 (Salmon, Glaus, BMolina 2); Texas 3 (Greer, RPalmeiro, Caminiti). Runners moved up_Gil 2, Eckstein.

DP_Anaheim 3 (Gil, Eckstein and Spiezio), (Gil, Eckstein and Spiezio), (Eckstein, Gil and Spiezio); Texas 3 (ARodriguez, Velarde and RPalmeiro), (Velarde, ARodriguez and RPalmeiro), (Caminiti, IRodriguez and RPalmeiro).

	IP	H	R	ER	BB	SO	NP	ERA
Anaheim								
Schoeneweis L, 0-1	7	8	3	3	3	5	108	3.86
Weber	1	0	0	0	0	1	13	0.00
Texas								
Rogers W, 1-0	7 1-3	7	2	2	0	5	96	2.45
JRZimmermn H, 4	2-3	0	0	0	0	2		0.00
Crabtree S, 1	1	2	0	0	1	0	12	0.00

Inherited runners-scored_JRZimmermn 2-0.

IBB_off Crabtree (GAnderson) 1. HBP_by Schoeneweis (Curtis).

Umpires_Home, Rippley; First, Winters; Second, Barrett, Ted; Third, Marquez.

T_2:31. A_49,512 (49,115).

LINESCORE: When a bare linescore summary is required, use this form:

Philadelphia	010 200 000 - 3 4 1
San Diego	000 200 000 - 2 9 1

K. Gross, Tekulve (8) and Virgil; Dravecky, Lefferts (3) and Kennedy. W - KGross, 4-6. LDravecky, 4-3. Sv - Tekulve (3). HRs - Philadelphia, Virgil 2 (8).

LEAGUE STANDINGS:
The form:

All Times EDT
NATIONAL LEAGUE

	EAST			
	W	L	Pct.	GB
Pittsburgh	92	69	.571	-
Philadelphia	85	75	.531	61/2
etc.				

	WEST			
	W	L	Pct.	GB
Cincinnati	108	54	.667	-
Los Angeles	88	74	.543	20
etc.				

(Night games not included)
Monday's Results
Chicago 7, St. Louis 5
Atlanta at New York, rain.
Tuesday's Games
Cincinnati (Gullett 14-2 and Nolan 4-4) at New York (Seaver 12-3 and Matlack 6-1) 2, 6 p.m.
Wednesday's Games
Cincinnati at New York
Chicago at St.Louis, night
Only games scheduled.

In subheads for results and future games, spell out day of the week as: *Tuesday's Games*, instead of *Today's Games*.

basic summary This format for summarizing sports events lists winners in the order of their finish. The figure showing the place finish is followed by an athlete's full name, his affiliation or hometown, and his time, distance, points or whatever performance factor is applicable to the sport.

If a contest involves several types of events, the paragraph begins with the name of the event.

A typical example:

60-yard dash — 1, Steve Williams, Florida TC, 6.0. 2, Hasley Crawford, Philadelphia Pioneer, 6.1. 3, Mike McFarland, Chicago TC, 6.2. 4, etc.

100 — 1, Steve Williams, Florida TC, 10.1. 2, etc.

Additional examples are provided in the entries for many of the sports that are reported in this format.

Most basic summaries are a single paragraph per event, as shown. In some competitions with large fields, however, the basic summary is supplied under a dateline with each winner listed in a single paragraph. See the **auto racing** and **bowling** entries for examples.

For international events in which U.S. or Canadian competitors are not among the leaders, add them in a separate paragraph as follows:

Also: 14, Dick Green, New York, 6.8. 17, George Bensen, Canada, 6.9. 19, etc.

In events where points, rather than time or distance, are recorded as performances, mention the word points on the first usage only:

1. Jim Benson, Springfield, N.J., 150 points. 2. Jerry Green, Canada, 149. 3. etc.

basketball The spellings of some frequently used words and phrases:

backboard	half-court pass
backcourt	halftime
backcourtman	hook shot
baseline	jump ball
fast break	jump shot
field goal	layup
foul line	man-to-man
foul shot	midcourt
free throw	pivotman
free-throw line	play off (v.)
frontcourt	playoff (n., adj.)
full-court press	up-tempo
goaltending	zone

NUMBERS: Some sample uses of numbers: *in the first quarter, a second-quarter lead, nine field goals, a 3-pointer, 10 field goals, the 6-foot-5 forward, the 6-10 center. He is 6 feet 10 inches tall.*

322 — SPORTS GUIDELINES

LEAGUE: *National Basketball Association* or *NBA*.

For subdivisions: *the Atlantic Division of the Eastern Conference, the Pacific Division of the Western Conference*, etc. On second reference: *the NBA East, the division, the conference*, etc.

BOX SCORE: A sample follows. The visiting team always is listed first.

In listing the players, begin with the five starters — two forwards, center, two guards — and follow with all substitutes who played.

Figures after each player's last name denote field goals, free throws, free throws attempted and total points.

Example:

BC-BKN—Lakers-Hawks, Box

Lakers-Hawks, Box

L.A. Lakers (108)

Jones 0-2 3-3 3, Odom 8-15 12-20 28, Mihm 0-1 0-0 0, Atkins 8-20 6-8 25, C. Butler 3-7 0-0 6, Cook 5-9 0-0 13, Walton 0-1 0-0 0, Brown 8-16 9-11 27, Grant 0-0 0-0 0, Vujacic 1-2 0-0 2, Medvedenko 1-3 2-2 4, Totals 34-76 32-44 108.

ATLANTA (114)

Childress 8-10 3-3 19, Walker 10-15 6-10 26, Ekezie 2-5 1-1 5, Anderson 2-7 1-2 5, Diaw 4-9 0-0 8, Drobnjak 1-2 0-0 2, D.Smith 4-6 3-4 11, Delk 7-20 8-9 25, Ivey 3-7 0-1 6, Collier 3-7. Totals 44-88 23-31 114.

L.A. Lakers 15 30 24 39_108

Atlanta 31 31 17 35_114

3-Point Goals – L.A. Lakers 8-23 (Cook 3-5, Atkins 3-10, Brown 2-3, Walton 0-1, Odom 0-1, Vujacic 0-1, Jones 0-2), Atlanta 3-8 (Delk 3-8). Fouled Out – None. Rebounds –L.A. Lakers 48 (Cook 10), Atlanta 58 (Childress 11). Assists_L.A. Lakers 12 (Atkins 5), Atlanta 23 (Delk 8). Total Fouls_L.A. Lakers 29, Atlanta 33. Technical_L.A. Lakers Defensive Three Second. A_15,633. (19,445).

STANDINGS: The format for professional standings:

Eastern Conference

Atlantic Division

	W	L	Pct.	GB
Boston	43	22	.662	—
Philadelphia	40	30	.571	5 1/2

etc.

In college boxes, the score by periods is omitted because the games are divided only into halves.

BC-BKC–Connecticut-Syracuse, Box

No. 19 CONNECTICUT 74, No. 8 SYRACUSE 66

CONNECTICUT (15-5)

Villanueva 9-13 3-7 21, Boone 2-4 3-5 7, Brown 0-2 5-6 5, Williams 3-11 1-2 9, Gay 6-13 4-4 18, Armstrong 2-2 2-2 6, Kellogg 0-0 0-0 0, Anderson 1-4 2-3 4, Nelson 1-1 2-3 4. Totals 24-50 22-32 74.

SYRACUSE (21-3)

Warrick 6-13 4-7 16, Pace 7-9 0-0 14, Forth 0-1 0-0 0, McNamara 4-18 0-0 9, McCroskey 2-5 0-0 4, Watkins 2-2 0-0 4, Edelin 3-8 1-2 7, Roberts 4-10 4-5 12. Totals 28-66 9-14 66.

Halftime_Connecticut 37-36. 3-Point Goals_Connecticut 4-14 (Gay 2-5, Williams 2-5, Brown 0-2, Anderson 0-2), Syracuse 1-9 (McNamara 1-9). Fouled Out_Roberts. Rebounds_Connecticut 36 (Villanueva 10), Syracuse 34 (Warrick 7). Assists_Connecticut 14 (Williams 6), Syracuse 17 (Edelin, McNamara 6). Total Fouls_Connecticut 15, Syracuse 24. A_27,651.

The format for college conference standings:

	Conference			All Games		
	W	L	Pct.	W	L	Pct.
Missouri	12	2	.857	24	4	.857

betting odds Use figures and a hyphen: *The odds were 5-4, he won despite 3-2 odds against him.*

The word *to* seldom is necessary, but when it appears it should be hyphenated in all constructions: *3-to-2 odds, odds of 3-to-2, the odds were 3-to-2.*

bettor A person who bets.

billiards Scoring is in points. Use a match summary. Example:

Minnesota Fats, St. Paul, Minn., def. Pool Hall Duke, 150-141.

bobsledding, luge Scoring is in minutes, seconds and tenths of a second. Extend to hundredths if available.

Identify events as *two-man, four-man, men's luge, women's luge.*

Use a basic summary. Example:

Two-man — 1, Jim Smith and Dick Jones, Alaska Sledders, 4:20.77.2, Tom Winner and Joe Finisher, Mountaineers, 4:31.14.3, etc.

bowl games Capitalize

them: *Cotton Bowl, Orange Bowl, Rose Bowl*, etc.

bowling Scoring systems use both total points and won-lost records.

Use the basic summary format in paragraph form. Note that a comma is used in giving pinfalls of more than 999.

Examples:

ST. LOUIS (AP) — Second-round leaders and their total pinfalls in the $100,000 Professional Bowlers Association tournament:

1. Bill Spigner, Hamden, Conn., 2,820.
2. Gary Dickinson, Fort Worth, Texas, 2,759.
3. etc.

ALAMEDA, Calif. (AP) — The 24 match play finalists with their won-lost records and total pinfall Thursday night after tour rounds — 26 games — of the $65,000 Alameda Open bowling tournament:

1. Jay Robinson, Los Angeles, 5-3, 5,937.
2. Butch Soper, Huntington Beach, Calif., 3-5, 5,932.
3. etc.

boxing The three major sanctioning bodies for professional boxing are the World Boxing Association, the World Boxing Council and the International Boxing Federation.

Weight classes and titles by organization:

105 pounds — Mini Flyweight, WBF, IBF; Strawweight, WBC

108 pounds — Light Flyweight, WBA, WBC; Junior Flyweight, IBF

112 pounds — Flyweight, WBA, WBC, IBF

115 pounds — Super Flyweight, WBA, WBC; Junior Bantamweight, IBF

118 pounds — Bantamweight, WBA, WBC, IBF

122 pounds — Super Bantamweight, WBA, WBC, Junior Featherweight, IBF

126 pounds — Featherweight, WBA, WBC, IBF

130 pounds — Super Featherweight, WBA, WBC; Junior Lightweight, IBF

135 pounds — Lightweight, WBA, WBC, IBF

140 pounds — Super Lightweight, WBA, WBC; Junior Welterweight, IBF

147 pounds — Welterweight, WBA, WBC, IBF

154 pounds — Super Welterweight, WBA, WBC; Junior Middleweight, IBF

160 pounds — Middleweight, WBA, WBC, IBF

168 pounds — Super Middleweight, WBA, WBC, IBF

175 pounds — Light Heavyweight, WBA, WBC, IBF

190 pounds — Cruiserweight, WBA, WBC, IBF

More than 190 pounds — Heavyweight, WBA, WBC, IBF

Some other terms:

kidney punch A punch to an opponent's kidney when the puncher has only one hand free. An illegal punch. If the puncher has both hands free, a punch to the opponent's kidney is legal.

knock out (v.) **knockout** (n. and adj.) A fighter is knocked out if he takes a 10-count.

If a match ends early because one fighter is unable to continue, say that the winner stopped the loser. In most boxing jurisdictions there is no such thing as a technical knockout.

outpointed Not *outdecisioned.*

rabbit punch A punch behind an opponent's neck. It is illegal.

SUMMARIES: Use a match summary.

Some examples, with the fighters weights after their names and the number of rounds at the end.

Randy Jackson, 152, New York, outpointed Chuck James, 154, Philadelphia, 10.

Muhammad Ali, 220, Chicago, knocked out Pierre Coopman, 202, Belgium, 5.

George Foreman, 217, Hayward, Calif., stopped Joe Frazier, 214, Philadelphia, 2.

TALE OF THE TAPE:
An example:

SAN JUAN, Puerto Rico (AP) — The tale of the tape for the Jean Pierre Coopman-Muhammad Ali world heavyweight championship fight Friday night:

	Coopman	Ali
Age	29	34
Weight	202	220
Height	6-0	6-3
Reach	75	80
Chest Normal	43	44
Chest Expanded	45 1/2	46
Biceps	15	15
Forearm	13	13 1/2
Waist	34 1/2	34
Thigh	25 1/2	26
Calf	15	17
Neck	17	17 1/2
Wrist	7 1/2	8
Fist	12 1/2	13
Ankle	9	9 1/2

SCORING BY ROUNDS:
An example:

NEW YORK (AP) — Scorecards for the Muhammad Ali-Joe Frazier heavyweight title fight Friday night:

Scoring by rounds:

Referee Tom Smith

AAA FFF AAA AFA FFF — A8-7

Judge Bill Swift

AAA FFF FFF AFA FFF — F10-5

Judge Ralph Cohen

AAA FFF FFF FFF AFF — F11-4

Scoring by points system:

Referee Tom Smith

A 10 10 10 10 10 10 10 10 10 10 9 9 9 9 10

F 10 9 9 9 9 9 9 10 10 9 10 10 10 10 10

Total — Ali 146, Frazier 143.

Judge Ralph Cohen

A 10 9 10 10 10 10 10 10 10 10 9 9 9 9 9

F 9 10 10 9 9 9 9 10 10 9 10 10 10 10 10

Total — Ali 145, Frazier 143.

box office (n.) box-office (adj.)

bullfight, bullfighter, bullfighting

bullpen One word, for the place where pitchers warm up.

C

Canada goose Not Canadian goose.

canoeing Scoring is in minutes, seconds and tenths of a second. Extend to hundredths if available.

Use a basic summary. Example:

Canoeing, Men

Kayak Singles, 500 meters

Heat 1 — Rudiger Helm, Germany, 1:56.06. 2. Zoltan Sztanity, Hungary, 1:57.12. 3. etc.

Also: 6. Henry Krawczyk, New York, 2 04.64.

First Repechage — 1, Ladislay Soucek, Czech Republic, 1:53.20. 2. Hans Eich, Germany, 1:54.23. 3. etc.

coach Lowercase as a job description, not a formal title. Capitalize only when substituted for a name as a term of address.

collective nouns Nouns that denote a unit take singular verbs and pronouns: *class, committee, crowd, family, group, herd, jury, orchestra, team.*

However, team names such as *the Jazz, the Magic, the Avalanche,* take plural verbs.

colt A male horse 4 years and under.

conferences A listing of major college basketball conferences is on the following page. (Football affiliations, where different, are in parentheses.)

cross-country Note hyphen, which is an exception to the practices of U.S. and international governing bodies for the sport.

Scoring for this track event is in minutes, seconds and tenths of a second. Extended to hundredths if available.

National AAU Championship

Cross-Country

Frank Shorter, Miami, 5:25.67; 2. Tom Coster, Los Angeles, 5:30.72; 3. etc.

Adapt the basic summary to

Major College Basketball Conferences
(Football affiliations, where different, are in parentheses.)

AMERICA EAST CONFERENCE — Albany, NY (Northeast); Binghamton (no program); Boston University (no program); Hartford (no program); Maine (Colonial); Maryland-Baltimore County (no program); New Hampshire (Colonial); Stony Brook (Ohio Valley); Vermont (no program).

ATLANTIC 10 CONFERENCE — Charlotte (no program); Dayton (Pioneer); Duquesne (Northeast); Fordham (Patriot); George Washington (no program); La Salle (MAAC); Massachusetts (Colonial); Rhode Island (Colonial); Richmond (Colonial); St. Bonaventure (no program); Saint Joseph's (no program); Saint Louis (no program); Temple (Mid-American); Xavier (no program).

ATLANTIC COAST CONFERENCE — Boston College; Clemson; Duke; Florida State; Georgia Tech; Maryland; Miami; North Carolina; N.C. State; Virginia; Virginia Tech; Wake Forest.

ATLANTIC SUN CONFERENCE — Belmont (no program); Campbell (Pioneer); East Tennessee State (no program); Florida Gulf Coast (no program); Gardner-Webb (Big South); Jacksonville (Pioneer); Kennesaw State (no program); Lipscomb (no program); Mercer (no program); North Florida (no program); South Carolina Upstate (no program); Stetson (no program).

BIG 12 CONFERENCE — Baylor; Colorado; Iowa State; Kansas; Kansas State; Missouri; Nebraska; Oklahoma; Oklahoma State; Texas; Texas A&M; Texas Tech.

BIG EAST CONFERENCE — Cincinnati; Connecticut; DePaul (no program); Georgetown (Patriot); Louisville; Marquette (no program); Notre Dame (FBS Independent); Pittsburgh; Providence (no program); Rutgers; St. John's (no program); Seton Hall (no program); South Florida; Syracuse; Villanova (Colonial); West Virginia.

BIG SKY CONFERENCE — Eastern Washington; Idaho State; Montana; Montana State; Northern Arizona; Northern Colorado; Portland State; Sacramento State; Weber State.

BIG SOUTH CONFERENCE — Charleston Southern; Coastal Carolina; High Point (no program); Liberty; North Carolina Asheville (no program); Radford (no program); VMI; Winthrop (no program).

BIG TEN CONFERENCE — Illinois; Indiana; Iowa; Michigan; Michigan State; Minnesota; Northwestern; Ohio State; Penn State; Purdue; Wisconsin.

BIG WEST CONFERENCE — Cal Poly (Great West); Cal State Fullerton (no program); CS Northridge (no program); Long Beach State (no program); Pacific (no program); UC Davis (Great West); UC Irvine (no program); UC Riverside (no program); UC Santa Barbara (no program).

COLONIAL ATHLETIC ASSOCIATION — Delaware; Drexel (no program); George Mason (no program); Georgia State (no program); Hofstra; James Madison; North Carolina Wilmington (no program); Northeastern; Old Dominion (no program); Towson; Virginia Commonwealth (no program); William & Mary (no program).

CONFERENCE USA — Alabama-Birmingham; Central Florida; East Carolina; Houston; Marshall; Memphis; Rice; SMU; Southern Mississippi; UTEP; Tulane; Tulsa.

HORIZON LEAGUE — Butler (Pioneer); Cleveland State (no program); Detroit (no program); Illinois-Chicago (no program); Loyola of Chicago (no program); Valparaiso (Pioneer); Wisconsin-Green Bay (no program); Wisconsin-Milwaukee (no program); Wright State (no program); Youngstown State (Gateway).

IVY LEAGUE — Brown; Columbia; Cornell; Dartmouth; Harvard; Pennsylvania; Princeton; Yale.

METRO ATLANTIC ATHLETIC CONFERENCE — Canisius (no program); Fairfield (no program); Iona (FCS Independent); Loyola, Md. (no program); Manhattan (no program); Marist (FCS Independent); Niagara (no program); Rider (no program); St. Peter's (no program); Siena (no program).

MID-AMERICAN CONFERENCE — East: Akron; Bowling Green; Buffalo; Kent State; Miami (Ohio); Ohio. West: Ball State; Central Michigan; Eastern Michigan; Northern Illinois; Toledo; Western Michigan.

MID-EASTERN ATHLETIC CONFERENCE — Bethune-Cookman; Coppin State; Delaware State; Florida A&M; Hampton; Howard; Maryland-Eastern Shore; Morgan State; Norfolk State; North Carolina A&T; South Carolina State.

MISSOURI VALLEY CONFERENCE — Bradley (no program); Creighton (no program); Drake (no program); Evansville (no program); Illinois State (Gateway); Indiana State (Gateway); Missouri State (Gateway); Northern Iowa (Gateway); Southern Illinois (Gateway); Wichita State (no program).

MOUNTAIN WEST CONFERENCE — Air Force; BYU; Colorado State; UNLV; New Mexico; San Diego State; TCU; Utah; Wyoming.

NORTHEAST CONFERENCE — Central Connecticut State; Fairleigh Dickinson (no program); Long Island University (no program); Monmouth, N.J.; Mount St. Mary's, Md. (no program); Quinnipiac (no program); Robert Morris; Sacred Heart; St. Francis, NY (no program); St. Francis, Pa.; Wagner.

OHIO VALLEY CONFERENCE — Austin Peay; Eastern Illinois; Eastern Kentucky; Jacksonville State; Morehead State (Pioneer); Murray State; Southeast Missouri State; Tennessee-Martin; Tennessee State; Tennessee Tech.

PACIFIC-10 CONFERENCE — Arizona; Arizona State; California; Oregon; Oregon State; Southern California; Stanford; UCLA; Washington; Washington State.

PATRIOT LEAGUE — American (no program); Army (FBS Independent); Bucknell; Colgate; Holy Cross; Lafayette; Lehigh; Navy (FBS Independent).

SOUTHEASTERN CONFERENCE — East: Florida; Georgia; Kentucky; South Carolina; Tennessee; Vanderbilt. West: Alabama; Arkansas; Auburn; Mississippi; Mississippi State; LSU.

SOUTHERN CONFERENCE — North: Appalachian State; Chattanooga; Elon; North Carolina Greensboro; Western Carolina. South: College of Charleston; Davidson; Furman; Georgia Southern; Samford; The Citadel; Wofford.

SOUTHLAND CONFERENCE — East: Central Arkansas; Lamar (no program); McNeese State; Nicholls State; Northwestern State; Southeastern Louisiana. West: Sam Houston State; Stephen F. Austin; Texas-Arlington (no program); Texas-San Antonio (no program); Texas A&M-Corpus Christi (no program); Texas State.

SOUTHWESTERN ATHLETIC CONFERENCE — Alabama A&M; Alabama State; Alcorn State; Arkansas-Pine Bluff; Grambling State; Jackson State; Mississippi Valley State; Prairie View A&M; Southern University; Texas Southern.

SUMMIT LEAGUE — Centenary (no program); Indiana-Purdue-Fort Wayne (no program); Indiana-Purdue-Indianapolis (no program); Missouri-Kansas City (no program); North Dakota State (Great West); Oakland, Mich. (no program); Oral Roberts (no program); South Dakota State (Great West); Southern Utah (Great West); Western Illinois (Gateway).

SUN BELT CONFERENCE — East: Florida Atlantic; Florida International; Middle Tennessee; South Alabama (no program); Troy; Western Kentucky. West: Arkansas-Little Rock (no program); Arkansas State; Denver (no program); Louisiana-Lafayette; Louisiana-Monroe; New Orleans (no program); North Texas.

WEST COAST CONFERENCE — Gonzaga (no program); Loyola Marymount (no program); Pepperdine (no program); Portland (no program); Saint Mary's, Calif. (no program); San Diego (no program); San Francisco (no program); Santa Clara (no program).

WESTERN ATHLETIC CONFERENCE — Boise State; Fresno State; Hawaii; Idaho; Louisiana Tech; Nevada; New Mexico State; San Jose State; Utah State.

INDEPENDENTS — Chicago State (no program); Longwood (no program); NJIT (no program); North Carolina Central (FCS Independent); Presbyterian (FCS Independent); Savannah State (FCS Independent); Texas-Pan American (no program); Utah Valley State (no program); Winston-Salem (Mid-Eastern).

paragraph form under a dateline for a field of more than 10 competitors.

See **auto racing** and **bowling** for examples.

cycling Use the basic summary format.

D

decathlon Summaries include time or distance performance, points earned in that event and the cumulative total of points earned in previous events.

Contestants are listed in the order of their overall point totals. First name and hometown (or nation) are included only on the first and last events on the first day of competition; on the last day, first names are included only in the first event and in the summary denoting final placings.

Use the basic summary format. Include all entrants in summaries of each of the 10 events.

An example for individual events:

Decathlon
(Group A)
100 — 1. Fred Dixon, Los Angeles, 10.8 seconds, 854 points. 2. Bruce Jenner, San Jose State, 11:09, 783. 3. etc.
Long jump — 1. Dixon, 24-7 (7.34m), 889, 1,743. 2. Jenner, 23-6 (7.17m), 855, 1,638. 3. etc.
Decathlon final — 1. Bruce Jenner, San Jose State, 8,524 points. 2. Fred Dixon, Los Angeles, 8,277. 3. etc.

discus The disc thrown in track and field events.

diving Use a basic summary.

E

ERA Acceptable in all references to baseball's *earned run average.*

F

fencing Identify epee, foil and saber classes as: *men's individual foil, women's team foil,* etc.

Use match summary for early rounds of major events, for lesser dual meets and for tournaments.

Use basic summary for final results of major championships.

For major events, where competitors meet in a round-robin and are divided into pools, use this form:

Epee, first round (four qualify for semi-finals) Pool 1 — Joe Smith, Springfield, Mass., 4-1. Enrique Lopez, Chile, 3-2. etc.

figure skating See **skating, figure** for guidelines on the summary form.

filly A female horse under the age of 5.

football The spellings of some frequently used words and phrases:

ball carrier	lineman
ballclub	line of scrimmage
blitz (n., v.)	out of bounds (adv.)
end line	out-of-bounds (adj.)
end zone	pitchout (n.)
fair catch	place kick
field goal	place-kicker
fourth-and-1 (adj.)	play off (v.)
fullback	playoff (n., adj.)
goal line	quarterback
goal-line stand	runback (n.)
halfback	running back
halftime	split end
handoff	tailback
kick off (v.)	tight end
kickoff (adj.)	touchback
left guard	touchdown
linebacker	wide receiver

NUMBERS: Use figures for yardage: *The 5-yard line, the 10-yard line, a 5-yard pass play, he plunged in from the 2, he ran 6 yards, a 7-yard gain; a fourth-and-2 play.*

Some other uses of numbers: *The final score was 21-14. The team won its fourth game in 10 starts. The team record is 4-5-1.*

LEAGUE: *National Football League,* or *NFL.*

STATISTICS: All football games, whether using the one- or two-point conversion, use the same summary style.

The visiting team always is listed first.

Field goals are measured from the point where the ball was kicked — not the line of scrimmage. The goal posts are 10 yards behind the goal lines. Include that distance.

Abbreviate team names to four letters or fewer on the scoring and statistical lines as illustrated.

The passing line shows, in order: completions-attempts-interceptions.

A sample agate package:

BC-FBN–Jets-Giants Stats

N.Y. Jets	7	10	7	0_24
N.Y. Giants	0	7	14	14_35

First Quarter
NYJ_Rhodes 11 fumble return (Nugent kick), 8:36.

Second Quarter
NYG_Ward 8 run (Tynes kick), 10:54.
NYJ_B.Smith 16 pass from Pennington (Nugent kick), :33.
NYJ_FG Nugent 47, :00.

Third Quarter
NYG_Jacobs 19 run (Tynes kick), 11:17.
NYJ_L.Washington 98 kickoff return (Nugent kick), 11:03.
NYG_Shockey 13 pass from Manning (Tynes kick), :33.

Fourth Quarter
NYG_Burress 53 pass from Manning (Tynes kick), 7:52.
NYG_Ross 43 interception return (Tynes kick), 3:15.
A_78,809

	NYJ	NYG
First downs	16	21
Total Net Yards	277	374
Rushes-yards	22-55	39-188
Passing	222	186
Punt Returns	2-20	2-16
Kickoff Returns	5-200	3-62
Interceptions Ret.	1-1	3-68
Comp-Att-Int	21-36-3	13-25-1
Sacked-Yards Lost	1-7	0-0
Punts	4-45.3	5-46.8
Fumbles-Lost	0-0	1-1
Penalties-Yards	6-40	3-37
Time of Possession	26:15	33:45

INDIVIDUAL STATISTICS

RUSHING_N.Y. Jets, T.Jones 13-36, L.Washington 9-13, Pennington 2-6, B.Smith 1-0. N.Y. Giants, Jacobs 20-100, Ward 13-56, Manning 4-17, Droughns 2-15.

PASSING_N.Y. Jets, Pennington 21-36-3-229. N.Y. Giants, Manning 13-25-1-186.

RECEIVING_N.Y. Jets, Coles 8-89, Cotchery 4-31, Baker 3-52, B.Smith 3-44, T.Jones 2-14, L.Washington 1-(minus 1). N.Y. Giants, Burress 5-124, Ward 3-8, Shockey 2-33, Moss 1-10, Matthews 1-6, Hedgecock 1-5.

MISSED FIELD GOAL_N.Y. Jets, Nugent 42 (WL).

The rushing and receiving paragraph for individual leaders shows attempts and yardage gained. The passing paragraph shows completions, attempts, interceptions and total yards gained.

STANDINGS: The form for **professional standings:**

American Conference
East

	W	L	T	Pct.	PF	PA
Baltimore	10	4	0	.714	395	269
New England	9	5	0	.643	387	275
Etc.						

The form for college **conference standings:**

Atlantic Coast Conference
Atlantic Division

	Conference			All games		
	W	L	PF	PA	W	L	PF	PA
Wake Forest	6	2	175	145	11	2	289	191
Boston College	5	3	189	133	9	3	313	180
Etc.						

In college conference standings, limit team names to nine letters or fewer. Abbreviate as necessary.

fractions Put a full space between the whole number and the fraction.

G

game plan

gelding A castrated male horse.

golf Some frequently used terms and some definitions:

birdie, birdies One stroke under par.

bogey, bogeys One stroke over par. The past tense is *bogeyed.*

caddie

eagle Two strokes under par.

fairway

hole-in-one

Masters, Masters Tournament No possessive. Use *the Masters* on second reference.

tee, tee off

NUMBERS: Some sample uses of numbers:

Use figures for handicaps: *He has a 3 handicap; a 3-handicap golfer, a handicap of 3 strokes; a 3-stroke handicap.*

Use figures for par listings: *He had a par 5 to finish 2-up for the round, a par-4 hole; a 7-under-par 64, the par-3 seventh hole.*

Use figures for club ratings: *a 5-iron, a 7-iron shot, a 4-wood.*

Miscellaneous: *the first hole, a nine-hole course, the 10th hole, the back nine, the final 18, the third round. He won 3 and 2.*

ASSOCIATIONS: *Professional Golfers' Association of America* (note the apostrophe) or *PGA.* Headquarters is in Palm Beach Gardens, Fla. Members teach golf at golf shops and teaching facilities across the country.

The *PGA Tour* is a separate organization made up of competing professional golfers. Use *tour* (lowercase) on second reference.

The PGA conducts the PGA Championship, the Senior PGA Championship, and the Ryder Cup as well as other golf championships not associated with the PGA Tour.

SUMMARIES — Stroke (Medal) Play: List scores in ascending order. Ties are listed in the order

in which they were played. Use a dash before the final figure, hyphens between others.

On the first day, use the player's score for the first nine holes, a hyphen, the player's score for the second nine holes, a dash and the player's total for the day:

First round:

Lorena Ochoa   35-34 — 69

Se Ri Pak   36-33 — 69

Etc.

On subsequent days, give the player's scores for each day, then the total for all rounds completed:

Second round:

Tiger Woods   65-71 — 136

Damien McGrane 68-69 — 137

Etc.

Final round, professional tournaments, including prize money:

Final Round:

(FedExCup points in parentheses)

J.B. Holmes (4,500), $1,080,000 68-65-66-70 — 269

Phil Mickelson (2,700), $648,000 68-68-67-67 — 270

Use hometowns only on national championship amateur tournaments. For tournaments including both amateurs and professionals, indicate amateurs with an "a-" before the name:

a-Stacey Lewis, The Woodlands, Texas 70-69 — 139

The form for cards:

Par out	444 343 544-35
Watson out	454 333 435-34
Nicklaus out	434 243 544-33
Par in	434 443 454-35 — 70
Watson in	434 342 443-31 — 65
Nicklaus in	433 443 453-33 — 66

SUMMARIES — Match Play: In the first example that follows, the and 2 means that the 17th and 18th hole were skipped because Rose had a three-hole lead with two to play. In the second, the match went 18 holes. In the third, a 19th and 20th hole were played because the golfers were tied after 18.

Justin Rose def. Charles Howell III, 3 and 2.

Paul Casey def. Shaun Micheel, 2 up.

Nick O'Hern def. Tiger Woods, 20 holes.

Grey Cup The Canadian Football League's championship game.

Gulfstream Park The racetrack.

gymnastics Scoring is by points. Identify events by name: Men: *floor exercise, vault, pommel horse, still rings, horizontal bar* (or *high bar), parallel bars.* Women: *floor exercise, vault, balance beam, uneven bars.*
Use a basic summary. Example:

Parallel Bars _ 1. Joe Smith, Houston, 9.675 points. 2. Ed Jones, Albany, N.Y., 9.54. 3. Andy Brown, Los Angeles, 9.4, etc.

H

halfback

handball Games are won by the first player to score 21 points or, in the case of a tie breaker, 11 points. Most matches go to the first winner of two games.
Use a match summary. Example:

Bob Richards, Yale, def. Paul Johnson, Dartmouth, 21-18, 21-19.

Tom Brenna, Massachusetts, def. Bill Stevens, Michigan, 21-19, 17-21, 21-20.

handicaps Use figures, hyphenating adjectival forms before a noun: *He has a 3 handicap, he is a 3-handicap golfer, a handicap of 3 strokes, a 3-stroke handicap.*

hit and run (v.) **hit-and-run** (n. and adj.) *The coach told him to hit and run. He scored on a hit-and-run.*

hockey The spellings of some frequently used words:

blue line	play off (v.)
crease	playoff (n., adj.)
face off (v.)	power play
faceoff (n., adj.)	power-play goal
goalie	red line
goal line	short-handed
goal post	slap shot
goaltender	two-on-one break
penalty box	

The term *hat trick* is jargon for scoring three goals in a game. Use it sparingly.

LEAGUE: *National Hockey League* or *NHL.*
For NHL subdivisions: *the Central Division of the Western Conference, the division, the conference,* etc.

SUMMARIES: The visiting team always is listed first in the score by periods.
Note that each goal is numbered according to its sequence in the game.
The figure after the name of a scoring player shows his total goals for the season.
Names in parentheses are players credited with an assist on a goal.
The final figure in the listing of each goal is the number of minutes elapsed in the period when the goal was scored.

BC-HKN–Senators-Flyers Sums, 1st Ld-Writethru
Eds: UPDATES with third period penalties.
Senators-Flyers, Sums

Ottawa	1 1 1_3
Philadelphia	3 1 1_5

First Period_1, Ottawa, Neil 8 (Simpson, Havlat), 4:07. 2, Philadelphia, Lapointe 4 (Somik, Slaney), 10:41. 3, Philadelphia, Recchi 25 (LeClair, Handzus), 11:11. 4, Philadelphia, Markov 6 (Handzus, LeClair), 16:10. Penalty_Amonte, Phi (ob.-holding), 16:10.

Second Period_5, Philadelphia, Johnsson 9 (Zhamnov, Slaney), 5:22 (pp). 6, Ottawa, Chara 15 (Spezza, Schaefer), 14:32 (pp). Penalties_Fisher, Ott (tripping), 3:57; Simpson, Ott (holding), 6:06; Somik, Phi (slashing), 13:08; Fisher, Ott (high-sticking), 17:07.

Third Period_7, Philadelphia, Zhamnov 10 (Gagne, Amonte), 6:54. 8, Ottawa, Bondra 23 (Alfredsson, Schaefer), 19:47 (pp). Penalties_Alfredsson, Ott (rough) 9:03; Zhamnov, Phi (roughing), 9:03; Smolinski, Ott (roughing), 12:18; Sharp, Phi (roughing), 12:18; Simpson, Ott (slashing), 14:21; Philadelphia bench, served by Sharp (too many men), 15:57; Van Allen, Ott, major-double game misconduct (fighting),

18:15; Ray, Ott, major (fighting), 18:15; Lalime, Ott, minor-major-game misconduct (leaving the crease, fighting), 18:15; Simpson, Ott, major-game misconduct (fighting), 18:15 Brashear, Phi, double minor-double major-misconduct-game misconduct; (instigator, roughing, fighting), 18:15; Radivojevic, Phi, major-double game misconduct (fighting), 18:15; Esche, Phi, minor-major-double game misconduct (leaving the crease, fighting), 18:15; Markov, Phi, major-game misconduct (fighting), 18:15; Chara, Ott, minor-major-misconduct-game misconduct (instigator, fighting), 18:18; Neil, Ott, major (fighting), 18:18; Somik, Phi, major (fighting) 18:18; Timander, Phi, major (fighting), 18:18.

Shots on goal_Ottawa 7-9-10_26. Philadelphia 13-11-6_30.

Power-play Opportunities_Ottawa 2 of 6; Philadelphia 1 of 4.

Goalies_Ottawa, Lalime 22-19-7 (30 shots-25 saves), Prusek (18:15 third, 0-0). Philadelphia, Esche 18-7-5 (22-20), Burke (18:15 third, 4-3).

A_19,539 (19,519). T_2:39.

Referees_Marc Joannette, Dan Marouelli. Linesmen_ Jonny Murray, Tim Nowak.

STANDINGS: The form:

Eastern Conference

Atlantic Division

	W	L	OT	Pts.	GF	GA
Philadelphia	47	10	14	108	314	184
NY Islanders	45	17	9	99	310	192
Etc.						

home-field (adj.), home field (n.)

horse races Capitalize their formal names: *Kentucky Derby, Preakness, Belmont Stakes*, etc.

horse racing Some frequently used terms and their definitions:

broodmare A female horse used for breeding.

bug boy An apprentice jockey, so-called because of the asterisk beside the individual's name in a program. It means that the jockey's mount gets a weight allowance.

colt A male thoroughbred horse 4 years old and under, or a standardbred 3 years of age.

entry Two or more horses owned by same owner running as a single betting interest. In some states two or more horses trained by same person but having different owners also are coupled in betting.

filly A female horse under the age of 5.

furlong One-eighth of a mile. Race distances are given in furlongs up through seven furlongs (spell out the number), after that in miles, as in *one-mile, 1/1-16 miles.*

gelding A castrated male horse.

graded stakes A thoroughbred race that derives its name from the stake, or entry fee, that owners must pay. There are three levels, assigned by the American Graded Stakes Committee. *Grade 1* is the highest level, the most prestigious, based partly on purse but also on such considerations as previous winners and race history. The other levels are *Grade 2* and *Grade 3*. Do not use Roman numerals. *Grade 2*, not *Grade II.*

half-mile pole The pole on a racetrack that marks one-half mile from the finish. All distances are measured from the finish line, meaning that when a horse reaches the quarter pole, he is one-quarter mile from the finish.

horse A male horse over 4 years old.

long shot (two words)

mare A female horse 5 years and older.

mutuel field Not *mutual field.* Two or more horses, long shots, that have different owners and trainers. They are coupled as a single betting interest to give the field not more than 12 wagering interests. There cannot be more than 12 betting interests in a race. The bettor wins if either horse finishes in the money.

stallion A male horse used for breeding.

horses' names Capitalize.

See **animals** in main section.

I

IC4A See **Intercollegiate Association of Amateur Athletes of America.**

indoor (adj.) **indoors** (adv.) *He plays indoor tennis. He went indoors.*

Intercollegiate Association of Amateur Athletes of America In general, spell out on first reference.

A phrase such as *IC4A tournament* may be used on first reference, however, to avoid a cumbersome lead. If this is done, provide the full name later in the story.

J

judo Use the basic summary format by weight divisions for major tournaments; use the match summary for dual and lesser meets.

K

Kentucky Derby *The Derby* on second reference. An exception to normal second-reference practice. Plural is *Derbys* — an exception to Webster's New World College Dictionary.

See **capitalization** in main section.

L

lacrosse Scoring in goals, worth one point each.

The playing field is 110 yards long. The goals are 80 yards apart, with 15 yards of playing area behind each goal.

A match consists of four 15-minute periods. Overtimes of varying lengths may be played to break a tie.

Adapt the summary format in **hockey.**

Ladies Professional Golf Association No apostrophe after *Ladies.* Use *LPGA Tour* in all references.

left hand (n.) **left-handed** (adj.) **left-hander** (n.)

M

marathon Use the formats illustrated in the **cross-country** and **track and field** entries.

mare A female horse 5 years and older.

match summary This format for summarizing sports events applies to individual contests such as tennis, match play golf, etc.

Give a competitor's name, followed either by a hometown or by a college or club affiliation. For competitors from outside the United States, a country name alone is sufficient in summaries sent for domestic use.

Rafael Nadal, Spain, def. Jarkko Nieminen, Finland, 7-5, 6-3, 6-1.

Serena Williams, United States, def. Nicole Vaidisova, Czech Republic, 6-3, 6-4.

metric system See main section.

minicamp

motor sports (two words unless different in the official name of an event)

motorboat racing Scoring may be posted in miles per hour, points or laps, depending on the competition.

In general, use the basic summary format. For some major events, adapt the basic summary to paragraph form under a dateline. See **auto racing** for an example.

motorcycle racing Follow the formats shown under **auto racing**.

N

NASCAR Acceptable in all references for National Association for Stock Car Auto Racing.

NCAA Acceptable in all references for National Collegiate Athletic Association.

numerals See the main section on general use and entries on **betting odds, handicaps** and **scores**.

O

odds See **betting odds**.

offseason (no hyphen)

Olympics Capitalize all references to the international athletic contests: *the Olympics, the Winter Olympics, the Olympic Games, an Olympic-size pool.*

Lowercase *the games* in second reference.

P

pingpong A synonym for *table tennis.*

The trademark name is *Ping-Pong.*

play off (v.) **playoff, play-offs** (n. and adj.)

postseason, preseason No hyphen.

R

racket Not *racquet*, for the light bat used in tennis and badminton.

racquetball Amateur games are played to 15 points in a best-of-three match. Professional matches are played to 11 points, unless it is necessary to continue until one player has a two-point spread. Most matches go to the winner of three of five games.

Use a match summary.

record Avoid the redundant *new record.*

right hand (n.) **right-handed** (adj.) **right-hander** (n.)

rodeo Use the basic summary format by classes, listing points.

rowing Scoring is in minutes, seconds and tenths of a second. Extend to hundredths if available.

Use a basic summary. An example, for a major event where qualifying heats are required:

Single Sculls Heats (first two in each heat qualify for Monday's quarterfinals, losers go to repechage Friday): Heat 1 — 1, Peter Smith, Australia, 4:24.7. 2. Etc. Heat 2 — 1, John Jones, Canada, 4:26.3. 72, Etc.

runner-up, runners-up

S

scores Use figures exclusively, placing a hyphen between the totals of the winning and losing teams: *The Reds defeated the Red Sox 4-3, the Giants scored a 12-6 football victory over the Cardinals, the golfer had a 5 on the first hole but finished with a 2-under-par score.*
Use a comma in this format: *Boston 6, Baltimore 5.*
See individual listings for each sport for further details.

short-handed

skating, figure Use a basic summary. Examples:
Junior Women
Short Program
1. Mirai Nagasu, Arcadia, Calif., 54.26 points.
2. Caroline Zhang, Irvine, Calif., 53.87.
3. Blake Rosenthal, Newton Square, Pa., 51.67.
Ice Dance
Compulsory Dance
1. Tanith Belbin, Bloomfield Hills, Mich., and Ben Agosto, Chicago, 38.23.
2. Morgan Matthews, Fairfax, Va., and Maxim Zovozin, Ashburn, Va., 31.17.
3. Tessa Virtue and Scott Moir, Canada, 30.79.

skiing Identify events as: *men's downhill, women's slalom,* cross-country (note hyphen), etc. In ski jumping, note style where two jumps and points are posted.
Use a basic summary. Example:
90-meter special jumping — 1, Karl Schnabel, Austria, 320 and 318 feet, 234.8 points. 2, Toni Innauer, Austria, 377-299, 232.9. 3, Etc. Also; 27, Bob Smith, Hanover, N.H., 312-280, 201. 29, Etc.

ski, skis, skier, skied, skiing Also: *ski jump, ski jumping.*

soccer The spellings of some frequently used words and phrases:
AFC (Asian Football Confederation)
Bundesliga (German League first division)
CAF (Confederation Africaine de Football; refer to as the governing body of African soccer rather than spelling out French acronym)
Champions League
coach (also known as *manager* on British teams and *technical director* on some Latin American teams)
CONCACAF (Confederation of North and Central American and Caribbean Football — use full name somewhere in story)
Conference National (fifth-highest division of English soccer)
Conference North, Conference South (sixth-highest division of English soccer)
CONMEBOL (Confederacion Sudamerica de Futbol; refer to as South America's governing body rather than spelling out Spanish acronym)
Copa America South American national team championship. Use the Spanish name, not *America Cup.*
Copa Libertadores South American club championship. Use the Spanish name, not *Liberators Cup.*
defender (rather than defenseman)
Eredivisie (Netherlands first division)
FA Cup acceptable on first reference for The Football Association Cup.
FIFA (Federation International de Football Association, FIFA acceptable as first reference, refer to as the international soccer foot-

ball governing body rather than spelling out French acronym)

forward or **striker**

friendly (use *exhibition game* on U.S. wires)

goalkeeper (*goalie* is acceptable but goaltender is not)

La Liga (Spanish first division)

League Championship (second-highest division of English soccer)

League Cup The number two cup competition in England (Do not refer to as *Carling Cup*)

League One (third-highest division of English soccer)

League Two (fourth-highest division of English soccer)

Ligue 1 (French first division)

midfielder

MLS (Major League Soccer, MLS acceptable on first reference)

OFC (Oceania Football Confederation)

offside

penalty area (sometimes penalty box — do not refer to solely as box on U.S. wires)

Premier League (top league in England; also the name of the top league in Scotland. Note, too, that England, Scotland, Wales and Northern Ireland have separate national teams. Do not refer to *Premiership* or *Barclay's Premier League*)

Serie A (Italian League first division)

sideline (*touchline* for international wires)

UEFA (Union of European Football Associations)

World Cup (Not *World Cup Finals*)

In summaries and key lines for international wires, the home team is listed first; on U.S. wires, the visiting team is listed first.

SUMMARY:

At Saint-Denis, France

Italy 0 2 — 2

France 2 0 — 2

(France won 4-3 on penalty kicks)

First half — 1, France, Zidane 4 (Djorkaeff), 12th minute. 2, France, Deschamps (penalty kick), 45th minute.

Second half — 3, Italy, own goal, 88th minute. 4, Italy, R. Baggio 6 (D. Baggio), 90th minute.

First overtime — None.

Second overtime — None.

Penalty kicks — France 4 (Zidane G, Lizarazu NG, Trezeguet G, Henry G, Blanc G); Italy 3 (Baggio G, Albertini NG, Costacurta G, Vieri G, Di Biagio NG).

Yellow Cards — Italy, Del Piero, 26th minute; Bergomi, 28th; Rostacurta, 113th. France, Guivarc'h, 53rd minute; Deschamps, 63rd.

Referee — Dallas (Scotland). Linesmen — Grigorescu (Romania),

Warren (England).

A—77,000

Lineups

Italy — Gianluca Pagliuca; Giuseppe Bergomi, Fabio Cannavaro, Alessandro Costacurta, Paolo Maldini; Francesco Moriero, Dino Baggio (Demetrio Albertini, 52nd), Luigi Di Biagio, Gianluca Pessotto (Angelo Di Livio, 90th); Christian Vieri, Alessandro Del Piero (Roberto Baggio, 67th).

France — Fabien Barthez; Lilian Thuram, Laurent Blanc, Marcel Desailly, Bixente Lizarazu; Didier Deschamps, Emmanuel Petit, Zinedine Zidane, Christian Karembeu (Thierry Henry, 65th); Stephane Guivarc'h (David Trezeguet, 65th), Youri Djorkaeff.

Lineup order is goalkeepers, defenders, midfielders, forwards.

Separate the different positions with semicolons and the players within a position with commas.

STANDINGS: The form:

Scores and standings move in separate files.

Schedule on world wires has times GMT instead of EST or EDT.

Schedule lists home teams first.

Sunday, Jan. 31

Bari vs. Lazio of Rome, 0130

Cagliari vs. Juventus of Turin, 0130

Fiorentina vs. Vicenza, 0130

Standings for international leagues have a different style: *GP* (games played), *W* (wins), *D* (draws), *L* (losses), *GF* (goals for), *GA* (goals against) and *Pts* (points). Standings for Major League Soccer follow the same style as National Football League: *W* (wins), *L* (losses), *T* (ties), *Pts* (points), *GF* (goals for) and *GA* (goals against).

Spanish Soccer At A Glance

By The Associated Press

La Liga

Team	GP	W	D	L	GF	GA	Pts
Real Madrid	25	8	2	5	54	21	56
Barcelona	25	16	6	3	49	17	54
Villarreal	25	14	4	7	43	35	46

Major League Soccer

By The Associated Press

EASTERN CONFERENCE

	W	L	T	Pts	GF	GA
D.C. United	16	7	7	55	56	34
New England	14	8	8	50	51	43
New York	12	11	7	43	47	45

speedskating Scoring is in minutes, seconds and tenths of a second. Extend to hundredths if available.

Use a basic summary.

sports editor Capitalize as a formal title before a name. See **titles** in main section.

sports sponsorship If the sponsor's name is part of the event name, such as Buick Open, use the name in the title. If there is a previously established name commonly accepted for the event — *Orange Bowl, Sugar Bowl* — use that name even if there currently is a corporate sponsor. *Orange Bowl,* not *FedEx Orange Bowl.* However, mention the sponsor somewhere in the story or in a self-contained paragraph after a 3-em dash at the bottom of the story.

sports writer Two words. An exception to Webster's New World College Dictionary.

stadium, stadiums Capitalize only when part of a proper name: *Yankee Stadium.*

swimming Scoring is in minutes, if appropriate, seconds and tenths of a second. Extend to hundredths if available.

Most events are measured in metric units.

Identify events as *men's 4x100 relay, women's 100 backstroke,* etc.

See **track and field** for the style on relay teams and events where a record is broken

Use a basic summary. Examples, where qualifying heats are required:

100 Butterfly

Final

1, Michael Phelps, United States, 50.77. 2, Ian Crocker, United States, 50.82. 3, Albert Subirats, Venezuela, 51.82.

T

table tennis See **pingpong**.

tennis The scoring units are points, games, sets and matches.

A player wins a point if his opponent fails to return the ball, hits it into the net or hits it out of bounds. A player also wins a point if his opponent is serving and fails to put the ball into play after two attempts (*double faults,* in tennis terms).

A player must win four points to win a game. In tennis scoring, both players begin at *love,* or zero, and advance to 15, 30, 40 and game. (The numbers *15, 30* and *40* have no point value as such — they are simply tennis terminology for *1 point, 2 points* and *3 points.*) The server's score always is called out first. If a game is tied at 40-all, or *deuce,* play continues until one player has a two-point margin.

A set is won if a player wins

six games before his opponent has won five. If a set becomes tied at five games apiece, it goes to the first player to win seven games. If two players who were tied at five games apiece also tie at six games apiece, they may play a tiebreaker — a game that goes to the first player to win seven points. A player must win a tiebreaker by at least two points. In some cases, the rules call for a player to win by two games without a tiebreaker.

A match may be either a best-of-three contest that goes to the first player or team to win two sets, or a best-of-five contest that goes to the first player or team to win three sets.

Set scores would be reported this way: *Chris Evert Lloyd defeated Sue Barker 6-0, 3-6, 6-4.* Indicate tiebreakers in parentheses after the set score, using only the lower number: *7-6, (9)*

SUMMARIES: Winners always are listed first in agate summaries. An example:

Singles
Fourth Round
Roger Federer (1), Switzerland, def. Tomas Berdych (13), Czech Republic, 6-4, 7-6 (7), 6-3.
Doubles
Second Round
Eric Butorac, United States, and Kevin Ullyett, Zimbabwe, def. Juan Pablo Brzezicki and Agustin Calleri, Argentina, walkover.
Mixed Doubles
Second Round
Yan Zi, China, and Mark Knowles, Bahamas, def. Vladimira Uhlirova, Czech Republic, and Simon Aspelin, Sweden, 6-7 (4), 6-1, 10-5 tiebreak.

track and field Scoring is

in distance or time, depending on the event.

Most events are measured in metric units. For those meets that include feet, make sure the measurement is clearly stated, as in *men's 100-meter dash, women's 880-yard run,* etc.

For time events, spell out *minutes* and *seconds* on first reference, as in *3 minutes, 26.1 seconds.* Subsequent times in stories and all times in agate require a colon and decimal point: *3:34.4.* For a marathon, it would be *2 hours, 11 minutes, 5.01 seconds* on first reference then the form *2:12:4.06* for later listings.

Do not use a colon before times given only in seconds and tenths of a second. Use progressions such as *6.0 seconds, 9.4, 10.1,* etc. Extend times to hundredths, if available: *9.45.*

In running events, the first event should be spelled out, as in *men's 100-meter.* Later references can be condensed to phrases such as *the 200, the 400,* etc.

For hurdle and relay events, the progression can be: *100-meter hurdles, 400 hurdles,* etc.

For field events — those that do not involve running — use these forms: *26 1/2 for 26 feet, one-half inch; 25-10 1/2 for 25 feet, 10 1/2 inches,* etc.

In general, use a basic summary. For the style when a record is broken, note the mile event in the example below. For the style in listing relay teams, note 4x400 meter relay.

60-yard dash — 1, Steve Williams, Florida TC, 6.0 2, Hasley Crawford, Philadelphia Pioneer, 6.2 3, Mike McFarland, Chicago TC. 6.2 3. Etc.
100 — 1, Steve Williams, Florida TC 10.1. 2. Etc.
Mile — 1, Filbert Bayi, Tanzania, 3:55.1, meet record, old record 3:59, Jim Beatty, Los Angeles TC. Feb. 27, 1963; 2. Paul Cummings, Beverly Hills TC. 3:56.1; 3, Etc.
Women's 880 — 1, Johanna Forman, Falmouth TC. 2:07.9. 2. Etc.
4x400 relay — 1, St. John's, (Jon Kennedy, Doug Johnson, Gary Gordon, Ordner Emanuel), 3:21.9. 2. Brown, 3:23.5. 3. Fordham, 3:24.1. 4. Etc.
Team scoring — Chicago TC 32. Philadelphia Pioneer 29, Etc.

Where qualifying heats are required:

Men's 100-meter heats (first two in each heat qualify for Friday's semifinals): Heat 1 — 1, Steve Williams, Florida TC. 10.1. 2. Etc.

V

volleyball International and USA Volleyball sets are won by the first team to score 25 points in the first four sets. If the match is tied in sets after the first four sets, a deciding fifth set will be played to 15 points. In all five sets, teams must win by two points without a cap on points.

U.S. college games are won by the first team to score 30 points in the first four sets. If the match is tied in games after the first four games, a deciding fifth game will be played to 15 points. In all five sets, teams must win by two points without a cap on points.

Use a match summary. Example:

College:
State University def. State Tech 30-22, 31-33, 30-28, 24-30, 15-12.

International:
U.S.-Women def. Korea 21-25, 25-16, 29-27, 16-25, 15-12.

volley, volleys

W

water polo Scoring is by goals. List team scores. Example:
World Water Polo Championship
First Round
United States 7, Canada 1
Britain 5, France 3
Etc.

water skiing Scoring is in points. Use a basic summary. Example:
World Water Skiing Championships
Men
Overall — 1, George Jones, Canada, 1,987 points. 2, Phil Brown, Britain, 1,756. 3, Etc.
Slalom — 1, George Jones, Canada, 73 buoys (two rounds). 2, Etc.

weightlifting Identify events by weight classes. Use a basic summary. Example:
Flyweight (114.5 lbs.) — 1, Zygmont Smalcerz, Poland, 337.5 kg. 2, Lajos Szuecs, Hungary, 330 kg. 3, Etc.

wild-card (adj.), **wild card** (n.)

World Series Or *the Series* on second reference. A rare exception to the general principles under **capitalization**.

wrestling Identify events by weight division.

Y

yachting Use a basic summary, identifying events by classes.

yard Equal to 3 feet. The metric equivalent is approximately 0.91 meter. To convert to meters, multiply by 0.91 (5 yards x 0.91 = 4.55 meters). See **foot; meter;** and **distances.**

yard lines Use figures to indicate the dividing lines on a football field and distance traveled: *40-yard line, he plunged in from the 2, he ran 6 yards, a 7-yard gain.*

yearling An animal 1 year old or in its second year. The birthdays of all horses arbitrarily are set at Jan. 1. On that date, any foal born in the preceding year is considered 1 year old.

Society of Professional
Journalists' Code of Ethics

Preamble

Members of the Society of Professional Journalists believe that public enlightenment is the forerunner of justice and the foundation of democracy. The duty of the journalist is to further those ends by seeking truth and providing a fair and comprehensive account of events and issues. Conscientious journalists from all media and specialties strive to serve the public with thoroughness and honesty. Professional integrity is the cornerstone of a journalist's credibility. Members of the Society share a dedication to ethical behavior and adopt this code to declare the Society's principles and standards of practice.

Seek Truth and Report It

Journalists should be honest, fair and courageous in gathering, reporting and interpreting information.

Journalists should:

- Test the accuracy of information from all sources and exercise care to avoid inadvertent error. Deliberate distortion is never permissible.

- Diligently seek out subjects of news stories to give them the opportunity to respond to allegations of wrongdoing.
- Identify sources whenever feasible. The public is entitled to as much information as possible on sources' reliability.
- Always question sources' motives before promising anonymity. Clarify conditions attached to any promise made in exchange for information. Keep promises.
- Make certain that headlines, news teases and promotional material, photos, video, audio, graphics, sound bites and quotations do not misrepresent. They should not oversimplify or highlight incidents out of context.
- Never distort the content of news photos or video. Image enhancement for technical clarity is always permissible. Label montages and photo illustrations.
- Avoid misleading re-enactments or staged news events. If re-enactment is necessary to tell a story, label it.
- Avoid undercover or other surreptitious methods of gathering information except when traditional open methods will not yield information vital to the public. Use of such methods should be explained as part of the story.
- Never plagiarize.
- Tell the story of the diversity and magnitude of the human experience boldly, even when it is unpopular to do so.
- Examine their own cultural values and avoid imposing those values on others.
- Avoid stereotyping by race, gender, age, religion, ethnicity, geography, sexual orientation, disability, physical appearance or social status.
- Support the open exchange of views, even views they find repugnant.
- Give voice to the voiceless; official and unofficial sources of information can be equally valid.
- Distinguish between advocacy and news reporting. Analysis and commentary should be labeled and not misrepresent fact or context.

- Distinguish news from advertising and shun hybrids that blur the lines between the two.
- Recognize a special obligation to ensure that the public's business is conducted in the open and that government records are open to inspection.

Minimize Harm

Ethical journalists treat sources, subjects and colleagues as human beings deserving of respect.

Journalists should:

- Show compassion for those who may be affected adversely by news coverage. Use special sensitivity when dealing with children and inexperienced sources or subjects.
- Be sensitive when seeking or using interviews or photographs of those affected by tragedy or grief:
- Recognize that gathering and reporting information may cause harm or discomfort. Pursuit of the news is not a license for arrogance.
- Recognize that private people have a greater right to control information about themselves than do public officials and others who seek power, influence or attention. Only an overriding public need can justify intrusion into anyone's privacy.
- Show good taste. Avoid pandering to lurid curiosity.
- Be cautious about identifying juvenile suspects or victims of sex crimes.
- Be judicious about naming criminal suspects before the formal filing of charges.
- Balance a criminal suspect's fair trial rights with the public's right to be informed.

Act Independently

Journalists should be free of obligation to any interest other than the public's right to know.

Journalists should:

- Avoid conflicts of interest, real or perceived.
- Remain free of associations and activities that may compromise integrity or damage credibility.
- Refuse gifts, favors, fees, free travel and special treatment, and shun secondary employment, political involvement, public office and service in community organizations if they compromise journalistic integrity.
- Disclose unavoidable conflicts.
- Be vigilant and courageous about holding those with power accountable.
- Deny favored treatment to advertisers and special interests and resist their pressure to influence news coverage.
- Be wary of sources offering information for favors or money; avoid bidding for news.

Be Accountable

Journalists are accountable to their readers, listeners, viewers and each other.

Journalists should:

- Clarify and explain news coverage and invite dialogue with the public over journalistic conduct.
- Encourage the public to voice grievances against the news media.
- Admit mistakes and correct them promptly.
- Expose unethical practices of journalists and the news media.
- Abide by the same high standards to which they hold others.

The SPJ Code of Ethics is voluntarily embraced by thousands of writers, editors and other news professionals.

The present version of the code was adopted by the 1996 SPJ National Convention, after months of study and debate among the Society's members.

Glossary of News and Sports Terms

Actuality	Recorded voice or natural (nat) sound from a news event inserted in a broadcast story; includes quotes from coaches and players, sounds of band, crowd cheering.
Advance	A story about an upcoming game that compares teams and players, discusses team records and gives lineups.
Allusion	A reference to a well-known person, place or event, often literary or historical, in relation to a current person or topic. Grantland Rice used an allusion to the Four Horsemen, known in dramatic lore as Famine, Pestilence, Destruction and Death, to describe four linemen who played for Notre Dame in 1924.
Anonymous source	Unnamed sources, known only to reporters and their supervisors, who become primary sources, usually in a breaking news story.
Associated Press	Largest wire service in United States; delivers global news to member media continuously.

Associated Press Stylebook	Style guide published by the Associated Press; regarded as the standard for print and online writing.
Attribution	Crediting a quotation or information to a source.
Attributive verb	Verb connecting quotation or paraphrase with source; *said* is the preferred attributive verb.
Backgrounder	A document or story that contains information about the sport, team, coaches, events and issues that could potentially be covered in future stories.
Batting average	The classic measure of batting proficiency. Ted Williams once had a batting average above .400. Calculated as base hits divided by at-bats, not counting walks, hit by pitchers or sacrifices.
B-copy	Body paragraphs, usually background material, written before an event ends if it will end too close to deadline to allow time for writing the entire story.
Beat reporter	A reporter who covers the same team or the same sport on a regular basis.
Behind-the-scenes sources	People who provide pertinent information or ideas for stories but aren't necessarily used as primary or secondary sources in the actual story.
Biography	A person's life story; in this context, highlighted specifically by key sports accomplishments.
Blog	Formed from the words *Web* and *log*, a *blog* is an online journal maintained by a person or entity to engage a community in conversation; often themed, blogs invite Web users' participation; allows bloggers to add entries 24/7.
Blurb	A summary sentence, sometimes the nut graf of the story, inserted between the headline and the text on online news story; gives reader more information in less time.

Boilerplate	Final paragraph of news release, provides basic information about the organization or program sponsoring the news release; same paragraph included on all releases from that sponsor; historically, type set and saved for repeated use.
Box score	A statistical tabulation of a game giving the names and positions of the players and a record of their individual performances; first appeared in a newspaper in 1913.
B-roll	Video or visuals without audio; generic footage of place or event; used to give setting, background visuals for story.
Byline	Name of reporter, usually at top of print story and beginning and end of broadcast story on location.
Caption	Words describing the action and identifying the people in a photo; also called *cutline*; usually written by photographer.
Circular story structure	Story organization in which the end circles back to make a connection with the lead; usually used in feature stories, profiles.
Cliché	Old saying, overused phrase; avoid in all stories.
Closed-ended questions	Questions that limit sources in how they're able to respond.
Code of ethics	Written statement of expectations or conduct in the pursuit of a profession or within a workplace; see Society of Professional Journalists' Code of Ethics in appendix B.
Column	Regular opinion feature by one author; identified by column head.
Column head	Indicates material is an opinion column or review containing personal commentary; column head includes tagline (column name), byline and mug shot of columnist.

Commercial use   Use of copyrighted material in a way that will make a profit for a person or business; is illegal without written permission; applies to team logos or mascots depicted in advertising paid for by someone other than the owner of the trademark or copyright.

Copyright   Legal protection of the right to ownership of an original work produced in a tangible form (writing, photos, art, etc.); protects works from use by others without permission.

Cutline   Traditional term for words describing the action and identifying the people in a photo; usually written by photographer; also called *caption*.

Dateline   Appears at beginning of a story or news release; indicates where story originated if it is not written locally; historically, dateline included the date the story was written.

Delayed lead   Story lead in which the focus is not known for several paragraphs; also called indirect lead.

Diction   Your choice of words, either high or low, formal or informal, such as "The thing that really gets me about that guy" versus "What most disturbs me about Professor Snooze."

Direct lead   Story lead that tells most of the 5 Ws and an H in the first one or two paragraphs.

Direct quotation   An exact, word-for-word account of what a person said, enclosed in quotation marks and attributed to the source.

Download   The transfer of data, through a file, from one computer to another.

Down style   Headline with only the first word and proper nouns capitalized; also called sentence style.

Embargo	On a news release or wire story, request by source that media not publish the story until a specified date.
End mark	Symbol indicating the end of a page or story in hard or electronic copy; standard end marks include — ### —, — 30 —, — end —, — more —.
Euphemism	A word used in place of another to make the topic sound less harsh; dressing up plain language; AP styie is to use literal, factually correct words, not euphemisms.
Fact sheet	A list of facts; similar to a news release in that it is a way to communicate information quickly and easily to the media.
Fair comment	Legal protection for journalists who offer opinion or commentary on the performance of anyone in the public eye; comments must be based on correct, factual information and not be intentionally malicious.
Feature	Story that focuses on people, places, issues or the human interest side of story; less timely, can run anytime and be equally newsworthy; if feature has a news hook, should run within a few days of news event.
Flash interview	An unusually quick and informal interview when a reporter and athlete or coach speak just outside the locker room or off the field.
Follow-up question	Question asked to clarify or expand on an original question.
Gamer	Sports story covering a game or competition.
Gender-biased language	Language which favors one gender over another; avoid use of language that assumes all sports fans are 20-something males or that a female reporter

	is less capable of covering sports than her male counterparts
Gutter	Narrow strip of white space between columns of text; especially center of double truck.
Hard copy	Story in print; script for news or sportscaster.
Headline	Summarizes the story; is written by copy editors; appears in larger type above the story it describes.
Homer	Reporter who shows bias for his or her hometown team.
Idiom, Sports	A collection of terms and phrases used and understood by people who are familiar with the literal as well as the idiomatic meanings of words, e.g., *sacked* as a verb means to put things, usually groceries, into a sack, but in football *sacked* means that the quarterback was tackled behind the line before he could pass the ball.
Inverted pyramid	Most common structure for news stories; information is organized in most important to least important order.
-isms	Short for words that end in *-ism*, such as ageism, racism, sexism; a practice likely to offend large segments of audience.
Kicker	Unexpected ending; may be an anecdote, quote or amazing fact used as a conclusion; used in circular structures, features, broadcasts. Also a jump-start beginning, an action-packed sentence or lively anecdote before the lead. Also a word or small heading above the main headline.
Lead	Beginning of news story, introduces topic; may be the first sentence or several paragraphs; also called an intro.
Leading question	Questions that try to lead the source to respond in a certain manner.

Libel	A false written statement that damages a person's character and causes that person to be ridiculed or shunned, or jeopardizes his or her occupational credibility.
Line score	A summary of a game's score displayed in the form of a horizontal table; for example, in baseball as an inning-by-inning record of the runs scored followed by the total of each team's runs, hits and errors.
Link	A connection between pages within a Web site and other pages or sites; a shortcut to reach supplementary material.
Live coverage	Broadcast coverage of an event in progress, such as a game, awards ceremony or halftime show.
Local angle	Focus of a news story on a local person, place or issue within a larger story to increase story appeal to local audience.
Material sources	Physical items such as record books, media guides or other stories that can provide information for a reporter.
Media credentials	These "passes" are assigned to individual reporters or news organizations and provide access to games, news conferences, practices or other game-related activities.
Minutia	Precise details or small, trifling matters, depending on your point of view.
Model T	MSNBC's name for an organization pattern of online news stories; 5 Ws form the horizontal top of the T, chunks of information in descending order of importance form the trunk.
Mug shot	Head and shoulders photo; close-up photo of a person's face, usually run 1 to 2 inches with a story or column; may be of writer, source or subject of story.

Multimedia	In general, multimedia includes a combination of text, audio, still images, animation, video and interactivity content forms.
Nat sound	Natural sound of an environment such as a game; used as sound bites to capture flavor, ambience of event.
News conference	A formal interview setting designed for sources to share information simultaneously with members of the media and, usually, for the media to ask questions. In sports, the source may be an athlete, official or coach speaking to an audience of mostly sports reporters. Also see *press conference*.
News release	Publicity tool; information sent to media with the intention of attracting media interest that will result in a story about a topic or source.
Nut graf	Paragraph or point in a story where the reader or listener knows exactly what the story is about; may be first paragraph or it may occur several paragraphs into the story.
Open-ended questions	Questions that ask an opinion or interpretation from a source.
Paraphrase	A summary of what a source said, attributed to that source, without changing the meaning; does not require quotation marks.
Participatory journalism	When a reporter becomes a participant in the story he or she is covering; in another sense, this also happens when citizens contribute their own blogs, photos or videos to a mainstream journalism outlet.
Podcasting	One way of broadcasting via the Internet; audio and/or video packaged together in a "pod," made available in RSS format to users of iPods and devices with similar retrieval software.

Post	To upload information, story to Web site.
Post-game analysis	An attempt to break down the various successes and failures of a team during a recent game.
Press box	A group of seats at an athletic event that usually provide a good view of the entire field, reserved and equipped for members of the press.
Press conference	Prefer more inclusive term: *news conference.*
Press row	A row of seats at an athletic event that are reserved for the press, usually at courtside.
Primary sources	Sources with information or opinions vital to the outcome of a story.
Private person	In law, a person unintentionally exposed to public view who suffers mental distress as a result of the publicity; protected from invasion of privacy.
Privilege	A defense against libel; journalists' right to report what government officials say and do in the conduct of their official duties without fear of being sued for libel.
Pronouncer	Phonetic spelling inserted (in pah-REN-tha-sees) with unfamiliar names and words in a broadcast script.
Public figure	Person who voluntarily seeks a role of prominence in society or who gains persuasive power and influence through that role, or who intentionally inserts him- or herself into public controversies; includes professional athletes, coaches.
Quotation	Citation and attribution of the exact words of a source.
Quote sheet	A written transcription of direct quotations from a source or sources, usually from news conferences.

Recap	A brief summary that repeats (recapitulates) the main points of a longer explanation.
Scoop	Reporting a news story before competing media outlets do.
Scorekeeper	Someone who keeps score during a game and is responsible for compiling the official results.
Secondary headline	Headline, sentence or phrases inserted between the main headline and the story; works with headline to add information and entice reader into the story; also called subhead or deck.
Secondary sources	Sources that aren't essential to the outcome of a story, but add information that makes a story more complete.
Sentence style	Headline with only the first word and proper nouns capitalized; also called down style.
Shooting percentage	A measure of a basketball player's accuracy determined by dividing the number of attempts by the number of field goals made.
Sidebars	Short, related stories run in conjunction with a larger news story.
Slander	Spoken defamation of character; recorded words are considered libel, as are scripted words read during a broadcast, because they are in a tangible form.
Slug	Short label that identifies a story in process.
Sound bite	Prerecorded excerpt inserted in video programming.
Source	People or reference material from which information is gathered for news stories.
Sports feature	Story about a person or issue related to sports; a player profile, a seasonal story about training camp or bowl selections, an informative, time-

less story on, for example, sports medicine or nutrition.

Sports information director Title given to person(s) responsible for managing communications between teams and media; job includes such things as preparing news releases, arranging news conferences and interviews, publishing a media guide, and providing statistics and data to media during games; generally known as an SID.

Sports record book Similar to an almanac, this compilation of top sports performances over time can be a valuable resource for writers; entries often include career leaders, longest plays, single bests and individual and team records; the book is typically updated at the end of each sport's season.

Statistics The collection, classification, analysis and interpretation of numerical facts that help sports writers analyze a game.

Streaming Sending compressed audio and/or video in a continuous stream over the Internet to be viewed as it arrives; programming from radio or television distributed via the Internet; moving visual images delivered online.

Title IX Now known as the Patsy Mink Equal Opportunity in Education Act (1972), this law essentially banned discrimination on the basis of sex; although the law itself doesn't mention sports, its passage lead to varsity athletic teams for women at the high school and collegiate levels.

Trademark Name and/or logo registered by an entity such as a college or a business; users must have permission, and sometimes pay a fee, to reproduce a trademark in any context.

Verification Rechecking information for accuracy and validity.

Wire services Membership organizations that gather news from around the world and distribute it to local members; the way most local media outlets receive national and international news.

Work made-for-hire Work created for an employer, such as stories a reporter writes for a newspaper or Web site; the property of the employer, not the creator.

Wrap A broadcast story that begins and ends with the reporter's voice "wrapped around" one or more actualities; also called a package.

Index

Page numbers in italic indicate an illustration.

Aaron, Hank, 66, 126
accuracy, 10, 128; archival material
    and, 35; legal issues and, 189
action verbs, 115; for headlines, 182
actuality, 114
adjectives, 128; sports reporters
    using, 24
advance(s), 11; basic information for
    all, 15; characteristics/content of,
    144; formula of, 14; improving,
    14–15; preparation for, 12–14
advance front page printing, 180–82
ageism, 126–28
Aikman, Troy, 119
Ali, Muhammed, 206
"alleged," 190
alternative sports, 10–11
Andrews, Phil, 108
Angell, Roger, 23–24
anonymity, behind-the-scenes sources
    and, 35
anonymous sources: avoiding, 38;
    backlash from, 40; defining, 37;
    risks of, 38–41; verifying, 41–42
AP. *See* Associated Press

APSE. *See* Associated Press Sports
    Editors
AP Sportswriting (Wilstein), 130
AP stylebook. *See* Associated Press
    stylebook
archival material, 35
Armacost, Michael, 207
Armstrong, Lance, 139
Associated Press (AP): news release
    conforming to guidelines of, 91;
    professionalism of, 171–72
Associated Press Sports Editors
    (APSE), 197
Associated Press stylebook (AP style-
    book), 73; creation of, 171; dates
    in, 172; sports section of, 174;
    standardization with, 171–72
athletes: age and expectations with,
    51; beat reporters' relationships
    with, 50–52; quote sheet of,
    77–78; statistics' importance to,
    213
attachments, 97
attribution: quotations/paraphrases
    and, 68–69; style/placing,
    69–72; verbs to avoid in, 69
attributive verbs, 116–17
awards, 33

Babcock, Mike, 5, 58, 165
Barfkr echt, Lee, 2–3, 16–17
Barkow, Al, 134, 152
Barnum, P. T., 90
baseball: box scores, 208–9; softball compared with, 13–14; statistics and, 201–2, 210–11
basketball scorebook, 204
beat reporter(s): athletes' relationships with, 50–52; behind-the-scenes sources and, 35–36; as bloggers, 37; coaches relationships with, 49–50; defining, 30; goals of, 31; interview guidelines of, 45; as interview subjects, 62–63; message boards and, 42–44; nightmare of, 45–48; off-season and, 31; responsibilities of, 30–31; sources contacted by, 44–49; sources cultivated by, 31–32. See also source(s)
Beck, Howard, 46
Beckham, David, 115
behind-the-scenes sources: anonymity and, 35; beat reporters using, 35–36; story tips from, 37
Berra, Yogi, 224
Berringer, Brook, 36
biographies, 86
bloggers: beat reporters as, 37; credential requests and, 9; credentials and, 9–10; human interest and, 142–43
blogging, 9; opinions in, 108
blogs: credential requests impacted by, 88; fans and, 8–9; functions of, 166; learning, 8; sports journalism compared to, 233. See also citizen journalists
blurbs, 185–86
Bonds, Barry, 126
Boswell, Thomas, 226–27
Bosworth, Brian, 231

Bowyer, Clint, 143
box scores: baseball, 206, 208–9
Bradley, Bill, 229–30
Brady, Tom, 187
Brennan, Colt, 181
Brett, George, 68
broadcast journalists: journalistic style of, 112; statistics and, 212; stylebooks for, 174
broadcast writers, 112
B-roll, 92
Broun, Heywood, 221
Brown, Nick, 47
Brown, Roger, 219
Brown, Troy, 109
Brueggemann, Gert-Peter, 143
Bryant, Kobe, 136
Bryson, Bill, 222
Bryson, William, 222–23
Bunner, Tamara, 155

Callahan, Bill, 3–4
call-in shows, 196
captions: checklist for, 188; history of, 186; information in, 187–88; length for, 188; photographs needing, 186–87; purpose of, 189; "rule of five" for, 187
Caray, Harry, 224
championships, 53
Chatelain, Dirk, 152–53
cheering, 17
Cherwa, John, 11
Chestnut, Joey, 135
circular story structure, 160–63, 162
citizen journalists, 42–44. See also blogs
City Editor (Walker), 115
Clay, Cassius, 206
clichés: example speech with, 121–22; identifying, 122–23; in interviews, 53–54; jargon and, 19;

journalistic style, eliminating, 121; opinions as, 123; quotations and, 66–67
closed-ended questions, 59
coaches: access denied by, 45; beat reporters' relationships with, 49–50; chasing, 2; quote sheets of, 75–79
Cobb, Tyrus, 220–21
code of ethics, 196–98
collective nouns, 118–19
columns: form of, 166–67; functions of, 166; labeling, 165–66; personality in, 163; popularity of, 163, 165; readers identifying with, 165
Comen, Ben, 232
commercial use, copyright materials and, 194, 196
conflict, 135–36
consequence or impact, 140–41
copyright: commercial use and, 194, 196; protections provided by, 193; violation determinations for, 193–94
corrections, 191
credential requests: bloggers and, 9; blogs/message boards impacting, 88; SIDs and, 88
Crowley, Jim, 147, 147–48
Cruise, Tom, 212
Curley, Rob, 233
cutlines. See captions

Dalton, Cindy, 40–41
Damon, Grant, 217
delayed leads: anecdote setting up, 152–54; benefits of, 151; direct leads compared to, 155; forms of, 151–52
Derowitsch, Mark, 14
direct leads: appeal of, 150; complaints with, 151; delayed leads compared to, 155

direct quotations, 66–67
Dolan, James, 47
Doria, Vince, 225
Dryden, Charles, 115

editorials: form of, 166–67; functions of, 166; labeling, 165–66; personality in, 163; popularity of, 163, 165; readers identifying with, 165
Egan, Jeanne, 155
electronic interviews, 64–65
electronic news releases, 91–92; attachments and, 97; tips for writing, 96–97
Elias Sports Bureau, 202
Eliot, T. S., 228
Elliott, Tag, 110
e-mail news releases: attachments and, 97; length and, 96; style and, 96–97; subject lines in, 94–95
emotions, 19–20
Enberg, Dick, 19
error-free stories, 128–30
Erskine, Carl, 224
ethics, 196–98
euphemisms: journalistic style and, 124; sports reporters using, 123–24
exaggerations, 24
Eyetrack studies, 175

facts: gathering, 108–9; lead, identifying, 149; opinions compared to, 107–8
fair comment, 192
fair use, 195
fans: blogs by obsessive, 8–9; box scores and, 208; complexity of, 106; headlines, expectations of, 174–75; internet confusing journalists with, 9–10; inverted pyramid and, 158–59; statistics and, 212

Favre, Brett, 127
feature stories: characteristics of,
    141; circular story structure for,
    160–63, 162
Federer, Roger, 115
"5 Ws and an H," 148–49
flash interview, 22
follow-up questions, 61
follow-up stories, 164
the Four Horsemen, 147, 147–48
Frazier, Herman, 181
Frazier, Tommie, 36, 209
free admission, 1
front page printing, advance, 180–82

Gail, Cassidy, 111
gamer. See recap
game stories, 156
game summary. See recap
Gerstner, Joanne, 10
Gibson, Bob, 24
Gillette, Gary, 212
Gisondi, Joe, 14
Golovin, Tatiana, 143
grammar, 106
grammar check, 117–18, 129
Green, Kelley, 13
Gretzky, Wayne, 231
Grice-Mullins, Ryan, 181
Gyimah, David Dunkley, 9–10

Hahn, Alan, 46–48
Hambleton, Ken, 2–3, 5, 8, 20, 36,
    74, 209
Hannemann, Mufi, 181
Harbin, Ted, 102–3
Harrison, E. J., 133, 152
Harrower, Tim, 163
Harvick, Kevin, 143
headlines: action verbs for, 182; as
    ads, 175; blurbs and, 185–86;
    checklist for, 185; fans expecta-
    tions for, 174–75; internet and

importance of, 175; links and,
    186; names and, 177; "Perfect!",
    180, 180–82; punctuation in,
    183–85; secondary, 183–84; space
    for, 179; styles for, 179; syntax
    for, 184–85; tips for writing,
    177–78
Heinz, Bill, 223
Hemingway, Ernest, 219; style of,
    221–22
Higa, Jay, 181–82
Hobson, Toby, 111
Hooker, Destinee, 110
hours, of sports reporters, 1–2
human interest, 142–43. See also fea-
    ture stories

Iba, Moe, 177
impact or consequence, 140–41
impromptu questions, 56
Imus, Don, 126, 128
incue, 114
information: in captions, 187–88;
    verifying, 108–9
information directors. See sports
    information directors
inspiration, 7
internet: blurbs and, 185–86;
    date/day on, 173; fans confused
    with journalists in, 9–10; fresh
    content demands of, 3; headlines'
    importance on, 175; interviews
    over, 65; inverted pyramid and,
    160; learning, 8; legal issues
    involving, 196; SIDs, impact of,
    83
interpreters, 74
interview(s): beat reporters' guide-
    lines for, 45; beat reporters receiv-
    ing, 62–63; championships and,
    53; clichés in, 53–54; colleges
    and, 57; electronic, 64–65; flash,
    22; ground rules for, 44–45;

impromptu questions in, 56; internet and, 65; interpreters and, 74; nonverbal signs in, 61; note taking in, 55–56; observations in, 61; one-on-one, 62; with players, *84*; postgame, 62; preparation for, 12, 54–56; research benefits for, 54–55; settings, 62–65; skills for, 54; small group, 62; tape recorder etiquette for, 55; transcribing, 74–75. *See also* news conferences; questions
inverted pyramid, *159*; effectiveness of, 160; fans and, 158–59; internet and, 160; lead for, 158; process of, 157–58; story structure of, 157
Isola, Frank, 46–48

Jackowski, Bill, 223
Jackson, Phil, *176*
Jackson, Reggie, 173
Jade, Katie, 111
James, Bill, 210–11
jargon: on air, 114; clichés and, 19; on page, 125; sports and, 18–19
Jones, Calvin, 209
Jones, June, 181
Jones, Pacman, 179
Jordan, Michael, *176*
journalistic style: action verbs in, 115–16; attributive verbs in, 116–17; of broadcast journalists, 112; clichés eliminated in, 121; collective nouns in, 118–19; elements of, 106–7; error-free stories in, 128–30; euphemisms in, 124; modifiers in, 119; redundant phrases avoided in, 124, 126; sexism/racism/ageism and, 126–28; short paragraphs in, 110–12; short sentences/S-V-O sentences in, 109–10; short words/precise meanings for, 114–15; spell check/

grammar check used in, 117–18, 129; of sports reporters, 106; weasel words in, 120
journalists, xi; internet confusing fans with, 9–10; legal issues, fair comment protecting, 192; legal issues, privilege protecting, 191–92
Joyner-Kersey, Jackie, 139
"the joy of six," *176*

Kansas State High School Activities Association (KSHSAA), 6
Katahara, Alvin, 181–82
Keller, Sam, 71
Kempton, Murray, 206
Knight, Bobby, 56, 66
Kobayashi, Takeru, 135
Koblin, John, 45–48
Kodama, Lester, 181–82
Kolodzy, Janet, 160
Kroenke, Stan, 85
Krzyzewski, Mike, 68, 73, 75–77
KSHSAA. *See* Kansas State High School Activities Association

lacrosse, 217
Lage, Larry, 128
Landis, Floyd, 136
Lardner, Ring, 115
Larsen, Don, 146
Layden, Elmer, *147*, 147–48
lead(s), 141; avoiding, 154–55; facts identified for, 149; "5 Ws and an H" for, 148–49; for inverted pyramid, 158; job of, 148; nut graf and, 154; questions as, 154; quotations as, 154–55; responsibilities of, 145; sports news values determining, 145–46; timeliness examples with, 137–38, 149–50; tone set in, 146; toss compared to, 146; types of, 150; writing, 146–50. *See also* delayed leads; direct leads

lead-in, 114
leading questions, 60
Leatherheads, 231
legal issues: accuracy and, 189; call-
    in shows and, 196; corrections
    and, 191; fair comment protecting
    journalists from, 192; fair use
    and, 195; internet and, 195; open
    records and, 192–93; privilege
    protecting journalists from,
    191–92; sports reporters and,
    189; sunshine laws and, 192. *See
    also* copyright; libel charges; pri-
    vate persons; public figures
legwork, 29
Leith, Will, 9
Leriger, Lee, 153
Levey, Bob, 233
Lewis, Michael, 11
libel charges: defense against, 190;
    defining, 189; private persons
    and, 191; public figures and, 191
Lincoln, Abraham, 229
links: headlines and, 186; in news
    releases, 92
Liston, Sonny, 206
local stylebooks, 172
locker room, women in, 225–26
Lunder, Leon, 207

Mairin, Trista, 111
Mangino, Mark, 42
Mantle, Mickey, 67
Marinelli, Rod, 128
Maroney, Laurence, 173
Marvell, Andrew, 229
material sources, 34–35
math, statistics and, 211
May, Isaiah, 122
Maynard, Kyle, 21
Mazeroski, Bill, 222–23
McBride, Charlie, 209

McCarthy, Mike, 127
McDonald, Will, 8–9
McPhee, John, 7, 229–31
media: news releases and
    advisory/alert for, 100, *101*;
    SIDs accommodating, 94
media guides: biographies in, 86; key
    information in, 85–87; media
    information in, 87; opponent sec-
    tion in, 86; record book in, 86–87;
    season in review in, 86; uses of, 85
media kit, 100
media relations personnel, 81–82
message boards: beat reporters and,
    42–44; credential requests
    impacted by, 88
Miles, Les, 41
Miller, Don, *147*, 147–48
Missing Links (Reilly), 231
mobile journalists, 8
Model T, 160, *161*
modifiers, 119
Moen, Daryl, 19
Moore, Archie, 219
Mouton, Ryan, 181
mult box, 93

Nadal, Rafael, 115
names: headlines and, 177; in style-
    books, 173
news conferences, *83*; SIDs organiz-
    ing, 92–93; source in control of,
    63; tips for dealing with, 64
news releases: AP guidelines for, 91;
    audience considerations for,
    90–91; format needs for, 94; goal
    of, 88–89; information in, 89;
    links in, 92; media advisory/alert
    in, 100, *101–2*; non-traditional,
    102–3; rewriting, 90; role of, 88;
    sports reporters verifying, 89–90;
    subject lines' importance of,

94–95; writing, 91. *See also* electronic news releases; e-mail news
releases; print news releases
news teleconferences, 65
news tip, 36
nicknames, 173
"no comment" responses, 33
non-traditional news releases, 102–3
nonverbal signs, in interviews, 61
Norworth, Jack, 224
note taking: importance of, 16; in
interviews, 55–56; verifying, 108–9
nouns, collective, 118–19
"numbers to note," 211
nut graf, 154

objectivity, 17–18
observations, in interviews, 61
Oden, Robert, Jr., 207
O'Dwyer, Jack, 92
off-season, 31
Olson, Eric, 149
Olson, Lisa, 225
one-on-one interviews, 62
open-ended questions, 59–60
opening statements, 63
open meetings laws, 192–93
open records, 192–93
opinions: in blogging, 108; as clichés,
123; facts compared to, 107–8; in
quotations, 107
Osborne, Tom, 40, 209
OTS. *See* over the shoulder
outcue, 114
over the shoulder (OTS), 114
overwriting, 83–84

Palmatier, Robert, 19
paragraphs, short, 110–12
paraphrases: attribution for, 68–69;
quotations compared to, 67–68
Parker, Bill, 174–75

participatory journalism: Damon
and, 217; of Plimpton, 218; of
Reilly, 232
Paulus, Greg, 77–78
Pavan, Sarah, 137–38
Pederson, Steve, 38–41
Penna, Toney, 133, 152
"Perfect!", *180*, 180–82
perspective, 24
photographs, captions and, 186–87
Pistorius, Oscar, 142–43
Plati, David, 57, 82–85, 88
players. *See* athletes
Plimpton, George, 25; participatory
journalism of, 218
politics, 227–28
post-game analysis, 11; opportunities
provided by, 23–24; perspective
in, 24; sentence structure in, 25
post-game interviews, 62
Povich, Shirley, 146
Poynter Institute, 175
preparation: for advance, 12–14; for
interviews, 12, 54–56; for sports
reporters, 2–5
press box etiquette, 17
press conference, *10*
primary sources, 32–33
print news releases: templates and,
95; tips for writing, 97–100
private persons: defining, 190; libel
charges from, 191
privilege, 191–92
profanity, 73
profiles, 160–63, *162*
prominence, 138–39
pronouncers, 112
proofreading: importance of, 128;
strategies for, 129–30
proximity, 139–40
public figures: defining, 190; libel
charge from, 191

Pulitzer, Joseph, 128
punctuation: in headlines, 183–85;
  quotations and, 69–72

questions: closed-ended, 59; evaluat-
  ing, 58; follow-up, 61; leading,
  60; as leads, 154; open-ended,
  59–60; statements compared to,
  58–59
quotations: attribution for, 68–69;
  benefits of using, 65–66; cleaning,
  73–74; clichés and, 66–67; direct,
  66–67; as leads, 154–55; omitting
  words in, 73; opinions in, 107;
  paraphrases compared to, 67–68;
  profanity in, 73; punctuation and,
  69–72; for recap, 16–17; statistics
  and, 67; statistics compared to,
  205; as weasel words, 120
quote sheets: of athletes, 77–78; of
  coaches, 75–79; considerations for,
  75; creating, 74; example, 75–79

racism, 126–28
Ray, Harold, 19
recap, 11; descriptions for, 20–22; for
  professional events, 22–23; quotations for, 16–17
records, 126; sources for, 33
redundant phrases, 124, 126
Reilly, Rick, 21, 229, 231; participatory journalism of, 231–32
reporters. See beat reporter(s); sports
  reporter(s)
research: biographies and, 86; interviews, benefits of, 54–55; pre-
  game, 11
Rice, Grantland, 115, 146–48, 220,
  228
Richardson, Charles, 32–33
Roberts, Selena, 15, 22
Robertson, Linda, 20
Robinson, Sugar Ray, 219

Rockne, Knute, 148
Rodeo Media Relations, 102–3
Rodriguez, Rich, 41–42
Romano, Ray, 8
Rose, Malik, 47
Rosenthal, Brian, 1
routine, 4–5
"rule of five," 187
Runyon, Damon, 115
Ruth, Babe, 221

schedule, 4
Schoux, George, 133, 152
scorekeeper, 203
scripts: format style of, 112, 114; pronouncers in, 112; television, *113*
secondary headlines, 183–84
secondary sources, 34
Seitel, Fraser P., 95
A Sense of Where You Are (McP-
  hee), 229
senses, appealing to, 20–21
sentence structure: in post-game
  analysis, 25; short, 109–10
Sergeant, Conde, 230
sexism, 126–28, 225–26
SFX. *See* sound effects
short paragraphs, 110–12
short sentences, 109–10
SIDs. *See* sports information directors
Sipple, Steve, 12
slander, 190
small group interviews, 62
Snead, Sam, 133, 152
Snodgrass, Fred, 24
Society of Professional Journalists'
  Code of Ethics, 261–64
softball, 13–14
Solich, Frank, 38–41
Solotaroff, Paul, 21
SOT. *See* sound on tape
sound bite, 114
sound effects (SFX), 114

sound on tape (SOT), 114
source(s): for awards/records, 33;
    beat reporters contacting, 44–49;
    beat reporters cultivating, 31–32;
    citizen journalists as, 42–44; mate-
    rial, 34–35; news conference con-
    trolled by, 63; primary, 32–33;
    secondary, 34. *See also* anony-
    mous sources; behind-the-scenes
    sources
spell check, 117–18, 129
Spiller, Bill, 134, 152, 154
sports: AP stylebook section for, 174;
    differences of, 13–14; jargon in,
    18–19; life lessons learned from,
    206–7; politics compared to,
    227–28; Will on importance of,
    227–28. *See also* alternative sports
sports idiom, 105
sports information directors (SIDs),
    81; credential requests and,
    87–88; internet impacting, 83;
    media accommodation by, 94;
    negative statistics and, 84–85;
    news conferences organized by,
    92–93; responsibilities of, 82–83;
    role of, 82; writing for, 83–85
sports journalism: blogs compared to
    professional, 233; expanding
    requirements of, 10; issues/chal-
    lenges facing, xii; modern changes
    in, 81, 232–34; respect for,
    226–27; rules of, 105; rush of, xi;
    sexism/racism/ageism and,
    126–28; women changing face
    ofin, 224–26
sports media relations director, 82
sports news values, 134; commonal-
    ties in, 135; conflict, 135–36; con-
    sequence or impact, 140–41;
    human interest, 142–43; leads
    determined by, 145–46; promi-
    nence, 138–39; proximity,
    139–40; timeliness, 136–37;
    unusual stories, 143
sports record books, 213
sports reporter(s): adjectives used by,
    24; cheering and, 17; code of
    ethics and, 196–98; creativity and,
    5–6; euphemisms used by,
    123–24; expectations of, xi; free
    admission for, 1; grammar rules
    for, 106; hours of, 1–2; inspiration
    and, 7; journalistic style of, 106;
    legal issues and, 189; legwork of,
    29; media relations personnel's
    obligations compared to, 81–82;
    as mobile journalists, 8; modern
    requirements of, xiv; news releases
    verified by, 89–90; objectivity and,
    17–18; preparation for, 2–5;
    responsibilities of, 16; routine for,
    3–4; senses appealed to by, 20–21;
    statistics personally kept by, 203;
    statistics philosophies of, 203,
    205–6; as storytellers, 134;
    women as, 15
sports section: accomplishments in, 7;
    popular rise of, 221
Sports Team Analysis and Tracking
    Systems (STATS), 202
staff columnist, 165
statements, 58–59
statistics: athletes and value of, 213;
    baseball and, 201–2, 210–11; bas-
    ketball scorebook for, 204; broad-
    cast journalists and, 212; fans
    and, 212; foreign country issues
    with, 209; for interpreting games,
    210–11; math for, 211; "numbers
    to note" providing useful, 211;
    obsession and, 202–3; quotations
    and, 67; quotations compared to,
    205; role of, 202; SIDs and nega-
    tive, 84–85; sports reporters keep-
    ing personal, 203; sports

reporters' philosophies with, 203,
205–6. *See also* box scores
STATS. *See* Sports Team Analysis and
Tracking Systems
STATS Baseball Scoreboard, 213
steroids, 10
Stieffel, Kristen, 94
still frame, 114
still store, 114
story structure: circular, 160–63,
162; inverted pyramid for, 157;
Model T, 160, *161*
Stovall, James Glen, 175
structure. *See* story structure
Stuhldreher, Harry, *147*, 147–48
Stumpe, Deann, 95
stylebooks: for broadcast journalists,
174; dates and, 172–73;
names/nicknames in, 173. *See also*
Associated Press stylebook; local
stylebooks
subject lines, 94–95
subject-verb-object sentences (S-V-O
sentences), 109–10
sunshine laws, 192
Supranowitz, Jonathan, 47–48
S-V-O sentences, 109
Sweeney, Mike, 172, 177

tag, 114
"Take Me Out to the Ball Game," 224
tape recorders, 55
Terry, Ralph, 223
Thomas, Dylan, 229
Thomas, Isaiah, 45
Thompson, Hunter, 229
Thorman, Chris, 9
Tidwell, James, 196
timeliness: lead examples with differ-
ences in, 137–38, 149–50; sports
news values, relevance of, 136–37
Title IX, 224
toss, 146

trademarks, 194
Twain, Mark, 173

unnamed sources. *See* anonymous
sources
unusual stories, 143

values. *See* sports news values
verbs: action, 115; attribution, avoiding, 69; attributive, 116–17; headlines using action, 182
video, 8
vloggers, 9–10
voice sound over videotape (VOSAT),
114
Von Tilzer, Albert, 224
VOSAT. *See* voice sound over
videotape

Wagner, Honus, 213
Walker, Jerry, 92
Walker, Stanley, 114–15, 123
Warren, Earl, 7
Watkins, Barry, 47–48
weasel words, 120
Weaver, Earl, 66
Wie, Michelle, 139
Wilbon, Michael, 14
Will, George, 201, 213; on sports'
importance, 227–28; style of,
228–29
Williams, Roy, 78–79
Williams, Serena, 15
Wilstein, Steve, 117, 130
Wolfe, Tom, 229
women: in locker room, 225–26;
sports journalism impact of,
224–26; as sports reporters, 15.
See also sexism
Wood, Abby, 155
Woods, Tiger, 139, 230–31

Zminda, Don, 213

About the Authors

Kathryn T. Stofer is a professor of communication arts at Hastings College and co-author of the secondary text "Journalism Matters" (with James Schaffer and Randall McCutcheon). She is active in developing college and high school journalism curricula and has frequently lectured on censorship and student freedom of expression.

James R. Schaffer is a professor of journalism at Nebraska Wesleyan University. The winner of several teaching awards, he has also worked as an advertising director, writing and designing print and television advertising. He is co-author of nine books including "Journalism Matters" (see above), "Increase Your Score in 3 Minutes a Day: SAT Essay"; "Increase Your Score in 3 Minutes a Day: SAT Critical Reading"; "Speech: Communication Matters" and "Communication Applications."

Brian A. Rosenthal is a sports writer at the Lincoln Journal Star, covering University of Nebraska football and men's basketball, and has won journalism/sports writing awards from the Nebraska Press Association and the Nebraska Associated Press. He maintains a sports blog and makes guest appearances on area television and radio shows. He is an adjunct professor at Hastings College, teaching sports writing and reporting, and contributed a chapter on interviewing and using quotations to the textbook "Journalism Matters" (see above).